ZSA ZSA GABOR

Books by Gerold Frank

(in collaboration)

OUT IN THE BOONDOCKS

U.S.S. SEAWOLF

I'LL CRY TOMORROW

TOO MUCH, TOO SOON

BELOVED INFIDEL

ZSA ZSA GABOR

Zsa Zsa Gabor

MY STORY

WRITTEN FOR ME BY GEROLD FRANK

CLEVELAND AND NEW YORK

THE WORLD PUBLISHING COMPANY

PUBLISHED BY The World Publishing Company
2231 West 110th Street, Cleveland 2, Ohio

Published simultaneously in Canada by
Nelson, Foster & Scott Ltd.

Library of Congress Catalog Card Number: 60–11458

FIRST EDITION

A condensation of this book has appeared
in *McCall's* magazine.

To be loved is a strength; to love, a weakness.

—FRENCH PROVERB

LIST OF ILLUSTRATIONS

*(The following photographs will be found
in sequence after page 158.)*

16. Zsa Zsa, Errol Flynn, and George Sanders at Cannes, 1953. (Photo by J. Feneyrol.)

17. George Sanders and Zsa Zsa, after their divorce.

18. Francesca Hilton in Paris, 1953.

19. Zsa Zsa in her first film, *Lovely to Look At.*

20. Zsa Zsa with Jean Pierre Aumont in rehearsals for *Lili,* 1952.

21. Francie posing as Zsa Zsa posing as Jane Avril.

22. Zsa Zsa as Jane Avril in *Moulin Rouge,* 1953.

23. Francie, Bundy Solt, and Zsa Zsa in Rome.

24. Zsa Zsa and Francie after costume birthday party, 1958.

25. Conrad Hilton takes Zsa Zsa and Francie to lunch at the Beverly Hilton, 1960. (Photo by Don Ornitz—Globe.)

26. Alfred Hitchcock and Zsa Zsa at the Coconut Grove, Los Angeles, 1958. (Photo by Walter Zurlinden.)

27. Porfirio Rubirosa in Hollywood. (Sunday Pictorial Photograph.)

28. Rubi at Le Mans, France, June 1953. (Photo by Michel Bodin.)

29. Bill Cavanaugh, Zsa Zsa, Baron Elie Rothschild, and Rubi at Maxim's, Deauville.

30. Mr. and Mrs. Edmund de Szigethy (Jolie Gabor) at Zsa Zsa's party for Ramfis Trujillo. (Globe Photos.)

31. Kim Novak, Ramfis Trujillo, Zsa Zsa, Rubi, and Rubi's wife, Odile, at Zsa Zsa's Bel Air home.

32. Zsa Zsa and the Aga Khan in Cannes.

33. Cy Howard, Bill Cavanaugh, Gloria Graham, Derek Goodman, and Zsa Zsa at Deauville.

34. Ingrid Smadja, Zsa Zsa, Rubi, Pierre Smadja, and Mrs. Jean Roi at Longchamps.

35. Francesca Hilton photographing the Gabor family—Zsa Zsa, Vilmos, Magda, Jolie, and Eva, Vienna 1958. (Photo by Paris Match.)

I FINISH writing my fourth letter of the morning. The noonday sun shines warmly through the window of my suite in the Plaza Hotel, here in New York. My California house is being decorated for the summer; Francesca, my twelve-year-old daughter, is in summer camp; in a few hours I shall fly to Rome to start my seventeenth film. I am proud of that: after all, I began my career only eight years ago, and I look on what I've done since then with both wonder and satisfaction.

I stamp the letter and place it with the others and ring for the bellboy to take them down to mail. What will go through his mind, I think, as he glances at the addresses? One, to the Duke of Marlborough, in Palm Beach, to regret that I can't dine with him when he arrives in New York two days from now; another, to Prince Parenti, in Capri, to say I will be delighted to attend his party next week; the third, to ex-King Farouk, in Monte Carlo, to thank him belatedly for his birthday greeting; and the fourth, to Sir Percy Loren, in London, who has been my father confessor for more than twenty years. Will the bellboy think, "That Zsa Zsa!—"? Does he believe what he reads about me—this silly, frivolous, gold-digging Lorelei from some Hungarian version of *Gentlemen Prefer Blondes*? . . . Does he believe all that has been written—and whispered—about the Gabors? Will he think the letters real? Does he think I am real?

To do a book about one's life means to relive and to remember. This hotel is the appropriate place to begin it, for so

11

many dramatic scenes in my life were played out on the stage of the Plaza. Here I first came when I arrived in the summer of 1941 as Mrs. Burhan Belge of Ankara, Turkey; here, later, I lived proudly as Mrs. Conrad Hilton. Here I wept myself to sleep more than once as Mrs. George Sanders; and here I first met Porfirio Rubirosa . . . The ghosts of the past haunt this place, while I watch as from a great distance and ask myself, did all this happen? Or was it all—the adventures, the men I have known, the career I have made, the Zsa Zsa I have created—was it all a fantasy of Sari Gabor of Budapest, who saw herself as the heroine of every book she read, and the princess of every fairy tale, the courtesan *sans pareille* who made the Kings of France forget their Pompadours and Du Barrys, and who was never certain, and is not certain today, what is really true and what is enchanting make-believe?

The telephone breaks into my thoughts. It is Mother, calling to say goodbye. We are very close. Hardly a day passes that I am not on the telephone with her, no matter where I find myself—London, Paris, Hollywood. *"Isten veled!"* she says— that marvelous Hungarian goodbye, which means God take care of you, all be well with you. I hang up, thinking all I do is done to impress her. Yet no success I achieve really impresses her. So, too, with my sisters Magda and Eva. Nothing we can do will bring complete praise from Mother. Rather, how can one of us excel the other at whatever we put our hand, and how can each of us excel any other woman in the world. I think back to a day in our childhood when she took the three of us—Eva, five, me, seven, Magda, nine—to the circus. We sat spellbound as an Indian fakir swallowed fire; than, in an awed silence, flames spurting from his mouth, he slowly, incredibly, climbed a ladder of razor-sharp swords on his naked feet. And in the silence Mother turned to us and demanded, "Now, when will *you* be able to do that?" For her nothing was impossible. If anyone could do it, we could do it. It would never be enough to be the most glamorous, the most elegant, the most beautiful, pursued by the most desirable men. For any other woman than her three daughters, this would be enough. But for Eva, Zsa Zsa, and Magda: *When would we be able to swallow fire and walk on swords?*

And, looking back on my life till now, in my way, I suppose, I have done so . . .

Book 1

1

I BEGAN as a tomboy.

I never liked girls then; and today few women are my friends. It was a man I wanted to be, men that I admired, and a man's world in which I wanted to live. My father likes to tell me that when I was six months old, if a woman bent over my crib, I cried; if a man, I cooed. But this is probably exaggeration, a trait not foreign to the Gabor family—one, really, which belongs to the Hungarian character, to a people both medieval and highly civilized, who speak a language no one understands beyond their borders, and who live in a secret grandeur of their own.

Whatever the case, I was born at 8:08 P.M. of a wintry February evening in the bedroom of our fifth-floor apartment at No. 31 Muzeum Korut (Circle) in Budapest, Hungary. Impatient as I have been all my life, I was even impatient to begin it. I insisted on arriving two weeks ahead of schedule. My mother, at the moment, was helping herself to her favorite dessert of apricot *palacsinta* and cream. As she tells it, when Father realized that I would not wait, he leaped from the table, drove wildly to our doctor's apartment a mile away, burst in on him while he was at dinner with *his* family, picked him up without a word, carried him into the carriage with the napkin still around his neck, and only then told him Gabor's first son was on the way.

"Impossible," sputtered the doctor. "It's too early. Take me back, you madman!" But it was possible, for when our carriage came to a halt in front of No. 31, I had arrived and was already screaming furiously, our German shepherd dog, Lady, was barking excitedly at the door, Emmy, Mother's maid, was tying a bright pink bow in Mother's hair, my two-year-old sister, Magda, was wailing in the nursery, and Cuki, our nanny, was praying in German to be saved from this wild Hungarian family. "Well," said the doctor, as he examined me and found me whole, "this one waits for no man."

I wish he had been right.

Sometimes, looking back on my childhood, I think of it as a Hungarian version of the Broadway play, *Life With Father*. Ours was an emotional household with crisis after crisis. At the table there were always guests: the piano teacher, the fencing instructor, the seamstress, whose fees included lunch and a talent to pretend they saw and heard nothing. For when Father and Mother engaged in their sudden, violent quarrels, the very chandeliers shook: vases were hurled, mirrors shattered, maids fled weeping, and we children, bursting into tears at the commotion, were herded into our nursery to wait until the storm had passed. The storm began and ended with Father.

He was a handsome man, powerfully built, blond, blue-eyed, ruddy-faced, with a bristly red mustache—a suspicious, stubborn man whose temper was ungovernable. There was no longer an Emperor Franz Josef, on the Austro-Hungarian throne, but Father was Franz Josef in his own house. He ruled unchallenged. Somewhere hidden in him raged a medieval baron to whom women were slaves, beautiful, helpless creatures to be won, protected, and guarded from their own frailty. He distrusted us and was convinced that any woman would easily succumb to any man with a bold eye—like himself—and he was ready to believe the worst. Especially of Mother.

He was eighteen years older than she, and passionately in love. When they were married she was seventeen, a strikingly beautiful girl with blonde hair falling to her shoulders, an exquisitely fair complexion, huge dark eyes, a skin of incredibly velvety texture, and a zest for living that nothing could

18

extinguish. Almost the first fact of life we children learned was our father's insane jealousy. He was jealous not only if she looked at another man—and Mother was a flirtatious girl in a city where one breathes romantic intrigue—but he also resented her attention even to her sisters and her friends: he wanted her only for himself. And while Mother admired and feared him, she did not deeply love him. She married him because marriage was a steppingstone to the stage. She saw herself as another Bernhardt or Duse—or, at least a Sari Fedak, then Hungary's greatest actress.

When, so another of our family stories goes, Father threatened to throw himself into the Danube if she did not marry him, she said, "All right, Vilmos, I'll marry you if you let me go on the stage. But I marry you for only six months. Then I want a divorce."

Father agreed. But at the end of six months Mother was pregnant. "Very well," said Father. "Give me a son and you have your freedom." Perhaps he knew how unlikely this was. Save for my Uncle Seby, Mother's younger brother, no male had been produced for three generations. Mother was one of four sisters, her mother was one of four sisters.

So the marriage stood when the first baby—Magda—arrived. A month later Mother presented herself before Father at breakfast. She was fully dressed, a packed suitcase was at her side, and behind her stood a tearful Cuki, hat on head, carrying little redheaded Magda. "Vilmos, I go. I cannot wait any longer for my career."

Father said nothing. He rose, took the sleeping Magda from Cuki, walked to the open window, and held the baby far out, at arm's length, five flights above the street. "Go—and I drop her. I wanted a son and you gave me no son." Mother—I only quote the story—stayed. There certainly would be a second child; it would be a boy; Father would take the boy, Mother the girl, and a sensible separation would be arranged.

It was then that I was born. Father looked at me, bald and squalling until I was blue in the face, and said heavily,

19

"In any other household anything so ugly surely would have been a boy."

"All right, so make a boy out of her," Mother said unhappily, and in a kind of stubborn protest at fate named me Sari, after her stage idol, Sari Fedak. Since all Hungary called the actress Zsa Zsa—her little daughter couldn't pronounce the name Sari—I became Zsa Zsa, too.

When Eva arrived two years later, Mother recalls emerging from the ether to hear Father's voice booming through the corridor. It seems that as he rushed into the hospital to learn if at last he was the father of a son, a nurse stopped him, "Oh, Mr. Gabor, congratulations! It's a beautiful baby girl!"

For a moment he turned white; then he roared, "Woman, get out of my way! How is my wife?"

That we were not boys we were never allowed to forget. At any household disaster—a dinner burned, ink spilled on the rugs, a window broken—Cuki would turn to us and groan, "Well, what can you expect with only girls in the house!" If Mother and Father had a violent quarrel, Mother would wander into our nursery, beautiful but tear-stained, to lament, "I can't live with your father. It's because you're girls that I suffer so!" And at the theater, she would turn to us after a moving moment on the stage, "Ah, I would be up there now if only you hadn't been girls. I gave up my career for you."

We loved and adored her and never forgave ourselves for depriving her of her rightful fame. When she took the three of us walking, we fought for the privilege of clutching her hand. "But darlings, I have only two hands and there are three of you," she would say. "You must take turns." And so we did—and so we do even today. When we walk with Mother, I will walk beside her, chatting with her, with Magda and Eva behind. Then, in a moment, Magda will be at her side, chatting with her, and I will drop back to walk with Eva. Then Eva takes her turn. We were—and are—our Mother's children.

But if Mother had no career, she showed her originality and theatrical temperament in many ways. She was a one-woman

20

Hungarian freedom movement. She was one of the first women in Budapest to bob her hair, and one of the first to drive her own car. She dressed us as she did herself, beautifully and strikingly: her taste in clothes was faultless. We were always dressed alike—the same dainty white shoes, the same exquisite organdy or silk or velvet frocks, even the same ribbons in our hair. When Father gave her, on their eighth wedding anniversary, a Mercedes car—a beautiful gray touring car upholstered in red leather—Mother took us riding. We drove down Andrassy Ut, Budapest's Fifth Avenue; Mother behind the wheel in a red sports outfit matching the upholstery, her bobbed hair tucked under a red straw sailor hat; Lady, our dog, on the seat beside her; while we perched elegantly in the back—three pretty little girls, identical as dolls in gray coats matching the car's exterior—brushed, polished, shining props to show her off. It was as though unable to fulfill her dream of the theater she would make everyday life a stage for herself, a spectacular in which she was the star.

She was determined that we would make our mark. We would be no ordinary girls. We must be taught every accomplishment befitting young ladies; then it would be up to us to make the world take notice. So we learned, whether we wanted to or not, piano, ballet, fencing, tennis, riding. We could not swim; at Lake Balaton, three hours from Budapest, where we had a summer home, she took us out in a rowboat and dropped each of us over the side. "Swim," she said. "If little puppies can do it, so can you." We floundered and sputtered and choked—but we swam. When she decided we must know how to ice-skate, she had to face the fact that she had not learned, either. "We will learn together," she said. One cold wintry day—we were perhaps four, six, and eight— she took us to a fashionable rink in Stadtwaldchen and had us fitted with skates. She helped us as we slipped and teetered forward to a railing, where we clung for dear life. "Now, you wait for me while I learn," she said. An instructor fitted Mother with skates, took her arm and off they went. We waited. She forgot completely about us. We waited, we shivered, time passed. We could not help it—when she came into sight again, we stood there frozen to the ice, each still clinging to the railing, weeping, "Mommy—Mommy."

"See, my little birds," she cried triumphantly as she balanced herself before us. "See how I skate!"

If we had tribulations with Mother, it was even worse for Father. He was doomed to be the only male in an establishment completely female even to our pets, Lady and Elizabeth, the canary. Because of the difference in age, he often seemed the only grown-up in the Gabor household, and he treated Mother—with good reason—like one of us. More than once Magda, Eva, and I were found rolling on the nursery floor in a battle royal. Mother would hurry in. "What's going on here, you silly little geese! Stop it! Stop it, I say!"

But trying vainly to pull us apart, she would suddenly lose patience, and when Father, muttering under his breath, would stalk in to find out what was happening, he would discover the four of us rolling on the floor, tearing each other's hair and screaming at the top of our voices. "Children!" he would roar. And then despairing, "Great God, why does this happen to me!"

Always his jealousy over his young wife gave him no peace. If Mother held the telephone a moment too long, he cross-examined her. If she returned late from one of her innumerable luncheons, he bellowed, "You have a lover!" At one time he went so far as to order Miklos, our coachman, to harness up our horse, Simon, and surreptitiously follow Mother when she went shopping in the afternoon. This came to a sudden halt one day when Mother, standing before a furrier's salon on Vaczi Utcza, lost in admiration over an ermine wrap, felt a hot, wet breath on her neck. She wheeled around to find Simon nuzzling her shoulder. Miklos had driven too closely behind Mother, and the horse, recognizing his mistress, started up in a trot, pulled the carriage up over the curb despite Miklos' frantic tugging, and was now showing his affection, while a crowd chuckled. "Such humiliation!" Mother stormed when she came home. "You're out of your mind!"

"And any man who trusts a woman is out of his mind!"
Father roared back.

Sometimes in these arguments he tried to call Mother's bluff.
Once after a particularly wild quarrel—Father actually heaved
a bronze gondola (souvenir of an ardent reconciliation in
Venice) into the mirror—Mother said, for the hundredth time,
"Vilmos, I leave."

"All right!" he shouted at her. "Leave. Move out. Go. Talk
to your lawyer!"

Mother promptly moved to the Hotel Gellert, which she
adored because it had a swimming pool with artificial waves,
and came each day, weighted down with toys, to visit us. We
were too young to realize what had happened, but we sensed
disaster. When Mother was home the crystal chandeliers
blazed with light, the house was full of laughter and perfume,
and friends came over night after night. Now the apartment
was dark, Father was not home for lunch or dinner, and when
we caught a glimpse of him, he sat brooding and silent.

At the end of a week Father's lawyer talked to him. "If you
want her back, this is no way," he said. He gave him the
magic formula. "Don't allow her to see the children."

Next afternoon when Mother rang the bell, Cuki locked us
in the nursery before answering it. We pressed against our
door, holding our breath, listening. We heard Cuki: "I'm sorry
Madam, you are not permitted to come in." And Mother's
voice: "What do you mean, *not permitted?*—How dare you—
I want to see my children!" Then Cuki's voice, quavering yet
undaunted, because every German Fräulein through the years
considered Mother far too emancipated and always sided with
Father. "I'm sorry, Madam, it's Mr. Gabor's strict orders." We
heard the front door shut.

The bell again, loud and long. Then Mother's voice, on the
edge of tears. "I want to see my babies!" It was more than
we could bear. All three of us burst into sobs and began
pounding and kicking wildly on the nursery door. "Mommy
—Mommy—we want our mommy—"

Outside, Mother was sobbing loudly, but through her tears

we heard her choked voice, "Cuki, I'll have you fired! You know Mr. Gabor *always* does what I want!"

The front door swung shut again and then Cuki, her face perspired, her big bosom heaving, was on her knees comforting us. "My Magdika, my Zsazsika, my Evika . . . my poor motherless children! . . ."

How we wept!

It seemed the tears were still wet on our cheeks when Mother, suitcase, swimming suit, and all, was back, and the chandeliers once more blazed with light.

My childhood is a rich *mélange* of these emotional crises, dominated always by Mother and Father. Appearing and reappearing like extras in a play were Mother's three sisters: Aunt Jennie, hearty and explosive, who studied foreign languages from 5 to 6 A.M. every morning, bathed in snow everyday, and went on eight-hour hikes twice a week; Aunt Rosie, roly-poly, blonde, and laughing, who always brought us candies and jellies; and Aunt Dora, forbidding and proper as a judge—and all with their jovial husbands whose faces were bristly and smelled of tobacco when they bent down to kiss us. It was a big family and closely knit, held together by Mother's mother, my Grandmother Franceska Kende, a tiny, regal woman of such authority that no one dared use the familiar "thou" to her, who inspired such respect that even her four daughters—none of them easily subdued—rose automatically when she entered a room.

On Father's side there was only an older brother, Lajos, who rarely visited us. Father's mother had died when I was an infant, and he never spoke of his father. But Mother had a favorite story. She described her father-in-law as a tall, beautiful, black-mustached, black-bearded man who was even more melodramatic than his son. He was a man of grand gestures and his grandest was the manner in which he silenced his wife. He and Father's mother were in a violent quarrel. She grew hysterical. He thundered. "Shut up, woman!" When she would not, he walked majestically to the window of their

24

fourth-floor apartment, threw it open and stepped out. "He just opened the window and walked out," Mother said, marveling. She was deeply impressed and so was I. To end an argument with such a gesture! How noble! How Hungarian!

Our money came, on both sides, from the manufacture and sale of jewelry. Grandmother Franceska Kende owned one of the oldest jewelry *fabriques* in Hungary; she was among the first to produce handmade costume jewelry fashioned with the same painstaking labor associated only with antique gems of great value. Her shop, The Diamond House, at 54 Rokoczy Ut, in the heart of downtown Budapest, was equally well known, as was Father's thriving establishment, Vilmos Gabor's, at No. 6 Rakoczy Ut. Mother's only brother, young Sebastian—he came late in Grandmother's life—was the proprietor of Sebastian's, on Andrassy Ut. And Mother, as we girls were growing up, had two shops of her own: Jolie's, a fashionable costume jewelry salon at No. 4 Kigyo Utcza, off Budapest's Madison Avenue, and Crystello, a shop of fine crystal and porcelain, which she opened around the corner.

Father, like Mother, loved the beautiful and the luxurious, but while Mother delighted in the tiny and exquisite, he was a compulsive collector of whatever was, like himself, sturdy and massive. He had a passion for heavy bronzes: book ends, busts, full-length statues, and especially figures of wild animals, the wilder the better—roaring lions, snarling tigers, rhinoceroses rearing on their hind legs—these were everywhere about. Our apartment was immense, running the entire floor through, high-ceilinged and pillared, with huge red silk brocade chairs, heavy rosewood furniture, two enormous salons each with its piano—everything seemed bigger than life. Our dining table, when opened, seated twenty-four. What with my grandmother, my aunts and uncles and cousins, and the ever-present guests, the table remained open to its full size most of the time.

Until I was thirteen, and sent off to Madame Subilia's School for Young Ladies in Lausanne, Switzerland, my life centered around our apartment and the neighborhood of

Muzeum Korut. The street on which we lived was a wide, tree-lined avenue of shops and stately apartment buildings. Directly opposite us was an exquisite little park in which stood Hungary's National Museum. In the spring the street and the park were fragrant with the blossoms of the deep purple lilac and the white flower of the acacia tree. At night, after Mother and Father, dressed for Mother's endless round of parties, came to kiss us good night and after we three had talked ourselves into drowsiness, I would fall asleep to the faint strains of gypsy music from the open-air cafés below. My dreams sprang from the Victor Hugo stories Cuki read to us—of black-eyed, copper-faced gypsies who kidnaped babies from their cribs, cut their lips wide open to make them laugh forever in order to exhibit them in circuses. I would toss and turn and wake up terrified. It took all my strength not to cry out, "Cuki, Cuki!" But Eva and Magda slept peacefully in their white beds on either side of me and I could not let them know I was afraid.

I was afraid of many things but I kept them to myself. To show fear, to admit that I was hurt, to reveal my true feelings, to be *pitied*—this I could not bear, then or now.

No one knew how much I feared a painting in one salon. It was a striking portrait of a Cardinal, austere and icy in his crimson robes, and it was Father's pride because no matter where you moved in the room, the eyes followed you.

The painting haunted me when I practiced. Seated at the piano, it was impossible to avoid the Cardinal's eyes. I suffered as I played my études, struggling sometimes almost in panic to keep my eyes averted from that stern, accusing gaze. He made me feel guilty and I did not know why. Nor could I explain why, like someone drawn to danger, I would sometimes deliberately edge into the room, dart a fearful glance to see if he was still there, then rush under the piano to hide from him, hugging Lady, my dog, tightly to me.

I told no one of my fears, not even my sisters. Mother might dress us alike but I knew I was different. I *had* to be different. I still remember the chill in the pit of my stomach when I

26

overheard Aunt Rosie say to Mother, "Eva is getting so beautiful—the two girls look more alike every day." I hated Aunt Rosie at that moment. I wanted no one to be like me or me to be like anyone. The only tantrum I ever threw came when Mother had our hair bobbed. I didn't want my hair to look like my sisters'. I became hysterical. Not until Mother used her most terrible weapon—a threat to shave off all Lady's fur —did I agree. I couldn't bear—and still cannot—the thought of an animal hurt or humiliated.

The fact was that we three girls *were* different. Magda was the scholar: quiet, restrained, always reading books, rarely playing with dolls. My first vivid memory of her is at the Opera. Mother took us each Saturday afternoon, starched, gloved, and beribboned, with little bouquets of violets in our hands. We made a pretty picture at the overture. But by first intermission Eva and I were a sight. Our dresses were crumpled, our gloves were gone, our violets trampled underfoot. But Magda sat beside Mother as unruffled as when we came, even to the violets in her hand. Mother would look at us and sigh, "Why can't you be ladies like Magda?" We couldn't. We despaired of achieving her elegance. Green-eyed, with Titian hair, she carried herself with such poise that when she was ten the family had already nicknamed her "the Duchess." She took it as her due and looked down on Eva and me as noisy brats. "Those peasants!" she would say to Cuki. "How can I live with them!"

Eva, with fluffy blonde hair and Mother's big black eyes, was dainty, giggly, and single-minded. If Magda dreamed of being an ambassador's wife, or perhaps a great woman scientist like Madame Curie, Eva at ten was already stage-struck. Once every few days I found her in bed in midafternoon, the curtains drawn, her eyes closed, and her face and hands shining with Mother's expensive night cream. "Don't wake me up, whoever it is," she would murmur, without bothering to open her eyes. "This is my beauty day. I must rest."

I wanted to be beautiful, too, but I would never dress up in Mother's clothes or cream my hands and face. Cukie used to call me her "little freckled gypsy," and I was happiest at that time being my father's son—frightening Cuki at night with a sheet over my head, pretending I was a ghost, hiding little green tree frogs in her bed, or with a string pulling her pillow suddenly from under her head when she napped. I delighted in wearing the Tyrolean outfit Father brought home to make me look like a little boy—the gray leather Tyrolean pants, which Mother said was the only thing I could not tear, the little green Tyrolean hat, the little flowered suspenders, the white socks with green embroidery, even the dark green walking shoes.

Then, as sometimes happened, he took me with him, perhaps to a wrestling match. I would sit proudly with him, imitating him as he cheered, as he leaped to his feet to applaud, to shout, "Give it to him!" to goad on the men struggling on the mat. Once when one wrestler drew blood, Father turned to me and said, a little uncomfortably, "Let's go, darling. It's not right for a little girl to see this."

"Oh, no," I spoke up. "I want to stay. I like to watch it."

He beamed at me. "Just like a little soldier!" he said, delightedly. I glowed at the compliment.

I adored my mother, but it was Father I admired, and it was Father I wanted to please. He was unreasonable, he was jealous, he was violent, he was overwhelming—he was a *man.*

2

SOONER or later there had to come a day when I filled out my leather pants too well. I can't pinpoint the time I first became conscious of boys—as boys. The only place we were permitted to meet them was at the rink. There we skated, sometimes daringly arm in arm with a boy, while Cuki or Emmy kept watch from a second-floor café overlooking the ice. I liked to be with boys. They skated better than girls, they were quicker witted, they laughed instead of giggled, they dared anything—I felt at home with them.

About my tenth or eleventh year I began to realize that the older boys liked me. Each morning as I turned the corner leading to Notre Dame de Sion where the Sisters taught me the rudiments of French, English, history, and mathematics, a chorus of shouts would greet me. "Here she comes! Hello, pretty Zsa Zsa!" Boys were leaning out the windows of St. Stephen's Academy, across the street, waving frantically, "Zsa Zsa, look up here, Zsa Zsa! Look at me! Please, Zsa Zsa!"

Cuki, who escorted me daily back and forth, would grip my arm warningly. "Don't you dare look up," she would mutter fiercely under her breath. "Your father will skin you alive if he catches you flirting."

I was not flirting. At school they called me a flirt, and perhaps I was, but not consciously. I blushed when the boys shouted after me, but I adored them for doing it, and I couldn't help smiling back. I knew I was pretty, now. We were three pretty sisters: everyone said so. When the boys shouted, I imagined all sorts of delicious adventures happening to me,

29

although I was not quite sure of what they would be. Neither Mother nor Father had told me anything I should know. Magda was too regal to discuss such matters and Eva and I were convinced that a boy's kiss made you pregnant.

Father's attitude only confused me. Once boys had been the noblest of creatures: now they were a menace. We were never to be left unguarded with one. The fact is that Father was in a difficult mood at this time. When his unmarried cashier confessed tearfully one day that she was going to have a baby, he came home furious, not with the girl, but with us. "But, Vilmos, it isn't our fault," Mother protested, as he carried on. "No matter," he shouted, "all women are no good!" It did not help much that after seeing Marlene Dietrich in *The Garden of Allah*, I plucked my eyebrows to a fine, elegant line and, a little later, appeared at dinner with my nails painted jade green, to look like Cleopatra. "I won't have my daughters grow up to be bad women," Father shouted across the chicken paprika at Mother. "It's your fault because you're not raising them like normal girls but want them to be so damned glamorous!"

He still smarted over the Magda episode. Magda, returning from school in Switzerland, had no sooner walked into the apartment when Mother exclaimed, "My God, look at your eyelashes! They're red!"

"But Mother, they've always been red," poor Magda said. "I was born with red eyelashes."

"Yes, yes, I know. But red hair, red eyebrows, red eyelashes —I can't let your Father see you this way." She hurried Magda to a hairdresser who dyed her lashes black. Father never got over it.

Actually we girls were kept so busy we had little time to make any of Father's fears come true. For all her impulsiveness Mother was a highly organized woman. Even today, like ourselves, she knows the contents of every drawer, can put her hand on any letter, and prides herself on never making two telephone calls where one will do. She regimented our day to exhaustion. Breakfast, 7 A.M.; school, 8 to 1. Then, home for lunch where our piano teacher, Miss Rigot, already waited at the table. After lunch we literally played a game of musical chairs. While Magda studied with Miss Rigot at one piano, I practiced at the other, and Eva did her homework. An hour later I slipped beside Miss Rigot, Eva moved to my piano, and Magda proceeded to her homework. Then we were ready for dancing and fencing lessons, and on alternate days, riding or ice-skating. By the time dinner came at 8 P.M. we all but collapsed in our seats.

Only at night, in the pages of books, did I lead the wanton life Father feared. I became the heroine—wicked, helpless, outrageously kissing my master's hands—of books I dared let no one see. Some I read secretly at home; others were handed from girl to girl during my two-year stay in Switzerland. Night after night I pulled from under my pillow *The Dairy of a Young Cadet of the Hungarian Hussars* and read it avidly. Dashing, devil-may-care Count Pista gambled at cards all day, drank and made love all night. He seduced waitresses, salesgirls, even respectable married women, then celebrated his conquests in sumptuous *maisons de luxe.* I stayed up nights dreaming of Serge. Serge was a man of mystery with penetrating gray eyes the color of steel who served as chauffeur to Baron Hanvany, a rich Hungarian landowner. One day the Baron's lovely seventeen-year-old daughter returns from finishing school abroad; a glance from Serge's hypnotic gray eyes and she is lost; helpless, she goes to him in a hunting lodge and cannot stop making love. The Baron is about to have Serge flogged to the death when he reveals he is really Prince Serge Misnikov of Petrograd, miraculously escaped from the Bolsheviks. "I will marry your daughter," he says proudly . . .

I would fall asleep, thinking: oh, to be wicked and glamorous, beyond good or evil, a great woman with countless distinguished lovers . . .

There had been one episode with a boy—really a young man. We had moved to a lovely house on Stephanie Ut, a

31

street of embassies and private homes, and here my joy was our garden. Often before dinner I wandered downstairs to sit in the half dusk, breathing the perfume of the acacia trees, feeling secure and protected behind a high grilled iron fence. I came to be aware of a tall young man who hurried by always a few minutes before eight o'clock, when I went upstairs. He wore a dark hat and carried a brief case. Obviously he was a third or fourth secretary at one of the embassies hurrying to replace his superior at the dinner hour.

One night he slackened his step as he came by. "Good evening," he said in a pleasant voice, in a strangely accented Hungarian. I had deliberately stood near the fence but I was shy, I was frightened of Father appearing any moment. I have no idea what I said to the young man then or on the following evenings. He told me that his name was Philip, and he was attached to the Romanian Embassy. But I do remember after the third or fourth meeting I dared to put my fingers through the fence grating and he closed his hand, hot and dry, on them—and how my heart pounded! He was a mysterious figure, not clearly seen; this was forbidden, a secret assignation in the dark. . . . Long after he left, my fingers tingled where he had held them so warmly, so tightly. Then one evening he did not appear. I never saw him again.

From Madame Subilia's School for Young Ladies, I wrote my first letter home:

> . . . I'm the only Hungarian girl here, all the rest are English. And they're so silly about me. They think all Hungarians are gypsies and are amazed that I know how to use a knife and fork. Madame is very strict; we sing psalms before dinner and are in bed by 10 P.M. . . . Mamika, I want you to burn this letter as soon as you finish it so Father won't see it—but Mama, dear, I'd love to have a garter belt. All the English girls have them . . .

I was not a good student but I was a quick one. My mind was amazingly fast; I always seemed to know far more than I really knew because of a word here, a phrase there, and I was able to catch meanings instantly. Sometimes if my answers were outrageously wide of the mark, the girls would burst into laughter—I didn't mean them to be so. My French had a Hungarian accent no one had heard before; it brought giggles, too. When I tried English, inverting words Hungarian fashion, everyone seemed to find that hilarious. I adored the English girls, especially Phyllis, a tall, languid brunette whose mother was a Dame. She was so British! In contrast to the explosive temperament I knew at home, Phyllis' calm, her indifference to argument, her cool disdain seemed to me the height of all that was elegant. When one day, laughing at something I said or the way I said it, she put her arm around me and announced, "I'm taking this little barbarian under my wing," I became her slave. I ran errands for the English girls, and found myself locked in my room repeatedly to write in French, "I won't climb out of the window," or, "I won't raid the icebox," one hundred times each. When this failed, Miss McClain, a ruddy-faced, red-haired Scotswoman, was delegated to watch me. Her room faced mine across a court. Each time I was about to put my leg over the window sill, I looked up—there was her pink face watching me. She dressed all in pink, her room had pink wallpaper—I was inspired. I dashed off a long verse, half French, half German, the first and most flattering stanza reading:

> Rose est la chambre,
> Rose est la blouse,
> Rose ist Miss McClain,
> Vom kopf bis fuss.

The girls began chanting it and I was a hero. Madame Subilia called me before her to explain my disrespectful verse. Ultimately a letter went home—I disrupted classwork, I was disobedient, I was a trial. Mother replied with a soothing note, taking my sins on her shoulders. But the English girls liked me and I did not care.

I was beginning to show what my ex-husband George Sanders calls my "Colonial complex," a blind admiration for

33

everything British: men, women, clothes, customs. Actually I think there was more to it. These girls applauded me—they were my audience.

I came home for summer vacation my second year, walking on air. I had discovered a real talent: I could paint, and paint well. A canvas I had done of the Château de Chillon—about which Byron wrote his famous *The Prisoner of Chillon* —as seen from the Swiss shore, had been shown in the school exhibition. Miss McClain, no friend of mine, praised it warmly. I had a "real feeling" for painting.

I boarded the train for Budapest thinking myself quite sophisticated because I was reading Zola's *Nana,* lent to me by Phyllis. At Zurich half a dozen boys trooped aboard. They immediately began to fuss about me; all but one, and he kept his face in a book, as if I didn't exist. I thought, annoyed, I'll *make* him look at me. I flirted outrageously with the others. Soon I saw him put down his book, surreptitiously draw out a comb, and straighten his hair. During a silence he leaned forward to offer me a bar of Swiss chocolate. I smiled sweetly. "No, thank you." I was no longer interested in him or in any of the boys. I went back to *Nana.* It was always to be like that. The indifferent man, not the eager one, attracted me, but once he lost his indifference, he lost his hold over me.

When we pulled into Budapest, there was Mother waiting. She gathered me into her arms. Again I was enveloped in the lovely perfume I always associated with her. At Madame Subilia's, the teachers smelled antiseptically of soap. Once at home, I could not wait to unpack my paintings and line them against the wall. Mother stood back, her favorite pose, resting most of her weight on one foot like a soldier at ease, and surveyed them, especially my prize-winning canvas. "Lovely, lovely," she said. She looked around the salon at Father's heavy bronzes, its gold and gilt and mirrors, "I really don't know what we'll do with it," she said. Then, "Darling, hang it in Cuki's room. She'll adore it."

I began to unpack, wishing she had said, "It's a lovely

painting, darling. I'm going to hang it in my room." But if I was unhappy at that moment, I had no time to feel sorry for myself. We were all swept into the hustle and excitement of preparing for a party Grandmother was giving that night, and we three girls had to look our best.

When we arrived, Grandmother took me by the arm and led me to a dark man who stood rather stiffly, by himself. "Zsa Zsa," she said, "this is His Excellency, Monsieur Belge. He doesn't know many people here. He's a very important gentleman from Turkey and I want you to entertain him. And don't you be too saucy—"

My first impression was of a dour, almost sinister-looking man of medium height, with a wide pale forehead which only emphasized his dark eyes and the little pouches beginning to show under them. He must have been in his middle thirties, and he looked world-weary and bored.

I said, a little uncertain how to address an excellency, "May I bring you some Tokay wine, sir? I don't think you have it in Turkey."

He shook his head. "I drink very little," he said. He spoke perfect German. There was an awkward silence while I tried to think what else to say and he said nothing. Then, almost wanly, he asked, "Are you at school?" I told him where, thinking: he is a Turk, a real Turk. The Turks were a fierce, warlike people who once had conquered Hungary and ruled it like tyrants for a hundred and fifty years. In the old city we still had twisting little streets with unpronounceable Turkish names. I was intrigued and began to ask questions about the new Turkey we'd read about in our history books, and about their dictator, the great Kemal Ataturk, who forced the Turkish women to unveil themselves. M. Belge's face lit up a little. He answered my questions like a schoolmaster, and as I listened, he began to tease me. "A pretty girl like you—surely you're not interested in these matters. You are pretty—and you know it, don't you?"

I said, not altogether lying, "Oh, I find my sister Eva prettier than me."

35

He said, "If you were only a little older, I'd buy you from your father for three pounds of coffee and make you one of my harem. Do you know how the Turkish pashas used to choose their favorites?" he went on, still solemn. "They measured the circumference of the girl's head. Her waist had to be no larger than that."

"Really?" I asked, wide-eyed.

"Yes," he said. "But I shouldn't tell you such things. You're such a little girl you wouldn't understand—"

I bristled. What he was telling me was fascinating, but now he was making fun of me, and I resented it. I might be only fifteen, but I would be a woman soon . . .

He laughed. "I see what your grandmother meant. All right, Fräulein Gabor—" He inclined his head in a little bow. "When you grow up, I'll marry you. You have too much spirit to be a concubine."

At this point Grandmother came to his rescue. I wandered over to Magda, who was up on social matters. Yes, she knew all about M. Belge. He was the Director of Press of Turkey. *And I had been so saucy to him!* He had been on a government mission to Germany and broke his return trip with a twenty-four-hour stopover in Budapest, halfway between Berlin and Istanbul. He was staying at the Turkish Embassy and the Turkish Ambasador, a friend of Grandmother's, had brought him to the party.

That night before going to bed, I wound a ribbon around my head and cut it where the ends met. Then I measured my waist. There was an inch of ribbon to spare! I'd have no trouble passing M. Belge's test. I wondered idly, how would I like to be the wife of a Turkish diplomat? Or would it be more exciting to be his concubine, living in a harem behind latticed windows, feasting all day on bonbons and French novels, and waiting His Excellency's call?

I fell asleep trying to make up my mind.

It seemed only minutes later that Mother was shaking me. "Get up, Zsa Zsa!" She was tremendously excited. She had

36

been up all night, turning an idea over in her mind. My aunts hadn't been able to get over how pretty I had become. Aunt Rosie had said, "Why don't you enter her? Let's see what the little monkey can do."

"Enter me, Mother? Enter me in what?" I had no inkling what she was talking about.

While she helped me dress, Mother explained. The finals of the annual Miss Hungary contest were to be held at eleven that morning at the Hotel Royale. It was now 6 A.M. We must work fast. "Me?" I said, in alarm. I was petrified. But Mother took over. She slipped one of Magda's gowns on me. It was a lovely floor-length black taffeta with a rose print, but it hung on me like a nightgown. Cuki got down on her knees and began pinning it around. "Shoes," Mother muttered, almost to herself. "You need shoes." I had no high-heeled shoes. She telephoned the owner of a shop, and although it was Sunday, he opened it for us. We hurried down and I emerged with a pair of black satin pumps. "Your hair," said Mother. And a moment later Cuki was washing it with egg and lemon to make it a shade lighter.

From then on everything took place in a daze. I recall Father's furious, "It's white slavery! I won't have my daughter put on display!" Mother wasn't listening. She was too busy rouging my cheeks and giving me instructions while Cuki fitted Magda's dress to me. I recall the trip downtown and Mother shepherding me through a back entrance of the hotel, of finding myself in a line of nervous, tittering girls, a card pinned on my shoulder with the number 146 crayoned on it; I remember teetering on my unaccustomed high heels across a stage, while Mother stood in the wings smiling encouragement at me; I remember a small bright room and a woman with a purple sash across one shoulder saying, "Stand up, my dear," and "Now, turn around and walk away from me," and then, "May I see your hands?"

I recall clearly what I did then. I hid my hands behind my back. "Oh, no," I said in panic. I couldn't. I was still biting my nails and I dared not let her see.

Then Mother was hugging me ecstatically. "You've won—you're Miss Hungary! Darling, congratulations!" But I was not Miss Hungary. I was not sixteen and I had to be sixteen. The judges met in emergency session; there was nothing to do but name my runner-up Miss Hungary, and name me runner-up, or first Maid of Honor. I posed with the new Miss Hungary, a tall, dark-eyed girl, and with the second Maid of Honor. Next day there was my picture and interviews with me on the front pages. It was all unreal. "You should have won!" Mother said over and over again. Later on I heard all kinds of stories as to why I did not win, including the charge that some of the judges had been at Grandmother's party the night before. Mother was in tears: it was bad enough that I had lost my rightful title—everyone agreed I should have been Miss Hungary—but she had also been deprived of a trip to Cannes. Had I won, I would have been sent to France for the Miss Europe finals, and Mother would have come along as my chaperone. She was heartbroken for both of us.

Father, relieved that I wasn't to be sent to the wicked Riviera, made a grand gesture. "Jolie, don't take on so. I give you both a consolation prize. Take Zsa Zsa to Vienna for a week. If it will make you happy, go!"

"Vilmos!" Mother threw her arms around him.

How could Father have known what a Pandora's box he had opened?

3

THE waiter leaned over us confidentially. "Gnädige Frau, the gentleman over there"—he gestured discreetly—"wishes you to receive this." He gave Mother a folded note.

I watched as she read it. A slow blush rose in her cheeks. "Yes, yes, of course. Please have him come over." She turned to me, almost stammering with excitement. "It's Richard Tauber! He wants to put you on the stage!"

From the very beginning of this unbelievable adventure I never quite understood how it happened. Mother and I were sitting with two of Mother's friends at an open-air concert at Grinzing, outside Vienna. It was August, and we had all been given tall, thin tumblers of heady wine. I had been chatting away happily when the note came.

Now he was sitting at our table, Herr Kammersinger Tauber, the great operatic tenor, the matinee idol of Europe! A handsome hearty man who looked like a German officer, a monocle glittering in his right eye, his black hair brushed back to reveal a widow's peak, and a voice gentle and musical. His note had read, "Forgive me, Madame, but I am seeking a girl to play an American debutante in my new operetta. If it is your daughter with you, may I have a word?"

He had been intrigued, he explained, watching me. "How beautiful, how animated, how full of life!" I looked exactly as he pictured Violet, the sixteen-year-old soubrette of *The Singing Dream*, for which he had composed the music. The part called for her to sing and dance with the well-known comedian, Fritz Steiner. It was to open August 31—three weeks

39

away—in Der Theater an der Wien. Would she permit me to audition for him?

I listened, not quite comprehending. Everyone knew the name of Richard Tauber, of course, but I had no idea that this was the first operatic score he had written; that its opening would be an international event; that the Theater an der Wien was one of Europe's outstanding music institutions, the home of Franz Lehár's great operettas, where *The Merry Widow* had its world première.

Mother rose to the occasion. She was proud to present her daughter to him. And while I had no stage experience, I had studied music and dancing almost since infancy and my only dream was to be on the stage. How fortunate that he came when I was on holiday from school in Switzerland . . .

Herr Tauber was all smiles. He rose, bowed, and kissed Mother's hand, then held mine for a moment and looked into my eyes. I blushed. "Tomorrow, then, at eleven."

Next morning Herr Tauber, the producer, Hubert Marishka, owner of the Theater an der Wien, and Mother sat in the huge, darkened auditorium. With the courage of only those who don't know how bad they can be, I tried one of the three German songs I was to sing. We had spoken German even before Hungarian: I got through it. A dance instructor had coached me for ten minutes; in his arms I stumbled and giggled and somehow managed one of the routines. Perhaps I should have been more awe-struck by it all, but I took it almost as a lark. I couldn't believe Herr Tauber was really serious. But Mother, sitting out front, gave me courage.

"All right," Herr Tauber called out. "That's enough, Fräulein Gabor." He turned to Mother. A moment later she was backstage hugging me. "Zsa Zsa, he thinks you'll do but we must work, work, work. Three weeks of solid work!"

Mother threw herself into the job of transforming me into a musical comedy star. Within an hour she had hired dancing, singing, and dramatic instructors and had Father on the phone. He raged at her over the long-distance wire. "Zsa Zsa on the stage? Are you mad?"

"Not Zsa Zsa—Sari," said Mother. We've changed it back. It's more dignified."

"Sari or Zsa Zsa, I don't give a damn," Father exploded. "Wasn't that beauty contest enough? Now the stage? Jolie, she's just a schoolgirl!" And then, an anguished roar, "Why didn't I let *you* go on the stage!"

The next three weeks were a nightmare. Herr Steiner, my singing teacher, was a tyrannical little Prussian with a goatee who always carried a violin bow as though it were an officer's stick. When he was annoyed, he rapped me over the head with it. "You can't sing, you have to learn!" he shouted. He ordered me to lie flat on my back on the floor and piled five books on my stomach. "Now, sing from down there!" I did my best. He rapped me on the forehead, smartly. "The scales, again!"

When I managed to get back on my feet, my dancing master took over, then my dramatic coach. The more I studied the more bewildered I became. Hadn't Herr Tauber hired me because he liked how I appeared, talked, smiled? Now they were laboring to change me into somebody else, I became self-conscious of every step, every gesture, that had been natural to me. "That's not acting," sighed Madame Irene, my dramatic coach. She read the script again. "You are flirting with this handsome sailor on your father's yacht. Now, glance back and blink your eyelashes—the young coquette. Like this." I could not blink my eyelashes under instruction. "I can do it perfectly well myself if you don't tell me how!" I shouted at her. Herr Werner, the dancing master, said, "Shoulders facing me, extend your right hand—" Herr Steiner, wagging his violin bow warningly, "Hold it to the count of four—"

But it was Hubert Marishka at rehearsal who finally lost his temper. He turned on me. "Look, you can't sing, you can't dance, you can't act—at least keep that pretty face of yours to the audience!"

I ran home in tears. "I can't go through with it, I can't!"
Mother said, "You can. Go back. If other girls can do it,
you can do it."

On August 29, the day before full dress rehearsal, Marishka
called me into his office. "Look, Sari, it is no use. I know how
hard you have been working, but you simply aren't ready yet.
You need more time, more stage experience . . ."

When I informed Mother, she said, "Wait." On dress rehearsal night she took me to a beauty parlor, had my hair
bleached a shade lighter, carefully supervised my make-up,
put me in a white organza hat, a dazzling white organza
gown, and led me into Mr. Marishka's office.

"Look at this girl," she said. "Can you imagine her on that
stage tomorrow night? The audience will gasp when she
comes out!"

Marishka sighed. "Mrs. Gabor, she is Violet to a T, she is
beautiful—"

Mother went on. "I want you to do one thing. You must give
Sari another chance. Let her play the part in dress rehearsal
tonight. It is only fair. Herr Tauber put this entire idea into
her head. You can't break her heart now. Give her another
chance."

Marishka relented. I was given another chance. Whether I
was moved to superhuman effort or whether my appearance
was irresistible in full costume, I don't know, but after dress
rehearsal the part was mine again. I woke the next morning
to find an advertisement in all the newspapers:

DER SINGENDE TRAUM

Operetta in Three Acts
By Ernst Marishka and Herman Feiner
Music by Richard Tauber
WORLD PREMIÈRE

Below it, the cast, famous throughout Europe:

PLAYERS

Richard Tauber, Mary Losseff, Ellen Schwanneka,
Fritz Steiner, Sari Gabor, Felix Gruenfeldt . . .

42

Sari Gabor!
With Herr Kammersinger Richard Tauber!

Opening night was a triumph. Mother, Father, my aunts and cousins—all were there. Father growled but accepted it. "Imagine! My Zsa Zsa acting with Richard Tauber!" He took us all to dinner at the Hotel Sacher, where we waited for the morning papers. The reviews actually singled me out. In the Vienna *Neue Freie Presse*, the distinguished critic, Dr. Kurt Roger, wrote: "And extremely amusing was the charming Sari Gabor." In the *Wiener Zeitung*, Dr. Rudolf Bolzer: "Miss Sari Gabor, who played Violet, bears great promise for the future . . ."

I remembered Herr Dr. Schmidt, the conductor, a grouchy Hungarian whose only interest was classical music. When we left the theater that opening night, there were the crowds at the stage door to applaud Tauber and his leading lady, the beautiful Mary Losseff. And they recognized me! They applauded, they shouted, "Sari! Sari!" as if they had known me all their lives. Herr Dr. Schmidt muttered to himself. "Toscanini? No. Wagner? No. But this one with no voice— her they want!"

Herr Dr. Schmidt had reason to be even more upset later. For on the fourth or fifth night, at the operetta's crucial moment, I succeeded in reducing cast and audience to shambles. The high point of my performance came when I delivered an important letter to Tokito, the magician, telling him that his lovely songstress has fallen in love with another and is lost to him forever.

It was a tragic scene, made the more so because I, the messenger, had no idea what the letter contained. The curtain rose to show me strolling gaily down a garden path in Capri, with the Mediterranean shining green and lovely in the distance. I come upon Tokito sitting on a garden bench. I hasten up to him, sing a light hearted little song, "I Have a Letter for You, Honorable Sir," and give it to him. It is, of course, the crushing moment of his life.

That night, as usual, I strolled brightly down the path until I reached Tokito. Just as I was about to sing my song, a horrifying realization struck me. "My God," I blurted aloud. "Herr Kammersinger, I forgot the letter!" It was on my dressing-room table. I bolted for my room by the most direct route I knew, which meant plunging through the scenery and vanishing behind the Mediterranean. The audience rocked with laughter, Herr Tauber almost had a heart attack, and I only prayed for the floor to open and let me sink into invisibility.

I cried myself to sleep that night but next day everyone mercifully pretended nothing had happened.

Said Mother, "For the while, the theater is more important than Madame Subilia's." She enrolled me in the Academy of Music and Dramatic Arts and returned to Budapest, three hours' train ride away, promising to come up and visit me. She left me in the care of Louisa, a one-time governess in our household, who moved in as my companion and chaperon. To protect me further, Mother left me with a wardrobe consisting mainly of sweaters and little pleated skirts. The stage-door Johnnies, she felt, would hardly be intrigued by a schoolgirl. But she did not count on a man called Willi. Nor on me.

I saw him sitting one night in the first row, his eyes always on me. He was a wild, passionate-looking man in his late forties, with a square, Mongolian face and a great mane of iron-gray hair. Each time his dark eyes fell on me, the impact was almost physical. It was all I could do to keep from staring back helplessly, like a doe hypnotized by a lion. I was in a curious, electric state in Vienna. I moved in a kind of self-intoxication, as sensitive as a wild animal to everything about me—the excitement, the freedom, the romantic intrigues going on backstage. I was fascinated by the *grand amour* between Tauber and his leading lady, Mary Losseff. Tall, slim as a boy, her golden hair cut in a shingle bob, she was breathtakingly beautiful. Everyone knew that Tauber was her lover, that when he held her in his arms and sang the exquisitely

44

tender "You Are the Entire World to Me," it brought tears to everyone's eyes; this was not make-believe, this was true. I was thrilled to be part of all this, too. Whatever the magic of Vienna, of the stage, it had begun to work on me.

When I saw Willi sitting there like a lion with his wild mane of hair, watching me, I could not help myself. I had to find a way to meet him.

I confessed to Herr Tauber. He had been kind to me. He called me "Sasha"—he gave pet names only to those he liked —and now and then as I passed him backstage, he would pat me approvingly on the rear. "Solid, solid," he would say teasingly, and burst into laughter when I whirled with an indignant, "Please, Herr Tauber!" I was not so much insulted as hurt. He treated Mary Losseff as a woman to be wooed and won, but jested with me as if I were a child. I hated to be patronized. I might not yet be sixteen, but the *femme fatale* in me was outraged.

Now, when I described the man in the first row, Tauber stopped spraying his throat. "But that is one of my dearest friends, Willi Schmidt-Kentner, the German composer," he said in surprise. Yes, I thought, he looks like Beethoven, a wild, untamed Beethoven. Willi, Tauber went on, wrote music for such stars as Sara Leander and Greta Keller—a very well-known man. He looked at me thoughtfully. "Are you sure you want to meet him?"

"Oh, I'm dying to." I meant it. Beethoven. A German composer. A man of deep, dark moods.

After the curtain that evening Tauber beckoned me. I went into his room in my ever-present red sweater and navy blue skirt. There sat my composer. Tauber said, "Willi, here is Sari Gabor. She is dying to meet you."

I wished I was anywhere but there. I stammered, blushing furiously, "Oh, Herr Kammersinger, I don't know what you can mean—"

Tauber fixed the monocle in his eye. "Now, Sasha, don't put that on. This is Mr. Schmidt-Kentner, the composer." Then, aware of my distress, he said, "But don't you remember, my

45

child? This is my friend who composes the songs you like so much."

In an amazingly soft voice for one who looked so fierce, Willi said, "You are adorable as Violet, Fräulein. And your acting—"

I dared to look at him. Everyone was pulling my leg. But he seemed serious. He went on. "With proper guidance and hard work, you can make a real career." His dark eyes were on me; whatever I was going to say, I forgot.

The two men began to talk. Presently Willi turned to me. What was I doing this evening? Louisa was to call for me: I always returned with her directly to our hotel. But I said, "I am free."

Would I care to join him for a drink, perhaps?

I had never been out alone with a man. I had never had a drink, save wine. I played the *grande dame*. "I would be delighted, but I must bring along my Mother's friend. She is visiting with me."

Tauber looked at Willi as if to say—and I dreaded lest he say it— "She is really very young, you know." But he did not. He clapped Willi heartily on the back, bowed to me, and left.

A few minutes later I introduced Louisa to Herr Tauber's distinguished friend who had been kind enough to invite us for a coffee so he could discuss my career.

I was in love with Willi. There had been the boys at Stadtwaldchen. Every girl on the rink, when I was eleven and twelve, had her string of admirers who tightened her skates and ran her errands. I liked the boys. But when in a dark corner or around a distant turn they seized me and stole a quick kiss, it was giggly, little-boy-little-girl play. I played it because the other girls played it, but it meant nothing to me. When Philip, the tall, handsome Romanian secretary held my hand through the garden fence, I had been thrilled. I was not aware of it then, but I was always to be drawn to the man—not the boy. Willi was a man. I respected and admired him; he overwhelmed me. He was so much older, so much wiser, so much stronger. And he *liked* me. I thought: my dear darling mother, she thinks if she keeps me only in sweaters and skirts, nobody will look at me. Here is Willi Schmidt-Kentner, the great composer, and he can't keep his eyes off me! I sensed that I had power, too, and it excited me.

I listened dreamily, yet fascinated, as he spoke about his career. He was soon to go to Rome to write the music for a new film, *Costa Villa,* starring Marta Eggerth. He told me about Tauber and Mary Losseff. Such a glorious love affair! Did I know that *The Singing Dream* was based in part on their life? For Mary Losseff had been born in Vladivostok during the Revolution, and somehow managed to escape to Berlin. There Tauber, already world-famous, had discovered her, penniless and unknown, seen her promise, fallen passionately in love with her, and taken her with him to fame and fortune. As Tokito had done.

Suddenly I could not bear the thought that I was the daughter of a well-to-do family, living sedately with a chaperon. I wanted desperately to be a refugee, too, a penniless waif, helpless and alone, who is discovered one night by a famous composer who falls madly in love with her and guides her to her destiny as a great actress. I play-acted with Willi. I told him all sorts of outrageous stories to intrigue him. I was quite emancipated. I had had many men. Vienna was just an interlude in my career. Someday I would make my name known in all Europe. Had not our Regent, Admiral Horthy, told Father, "Vilmos, we should never export a commodity like Zsa Zsa, we must always keep her in Hungary." Willi listened and smiled understandingly, and ordered more shashlik and more vodka. And each time he smiled at me, I felt I would do anything he would want of me.

When one day our performance was canceled because Tauber was ill, Willi asked, "Will you come with me to Cobenzl?" I said yes, almost humbly. Cobenzl was a tiny village, high in the Alps.

We went there by funicular. I stood to one side, pretending

47

I could not be seen, as Willi bought the tickets. Once in the car I snuggled next to him on the hard wooden seat. We began the slow chain-rattling climb up the steep mountainside. Once or twice we clattered to a stop to take on a few passengers. I averted my head each time. I was sure someone would come aboard, recognize me, and leap off at the next station to wire Father, "Yes, everything you feared has come true. I saw Zsa Zsa with an old roué."

Willi asked, "What is it, my darling?" I was ashamed to tell him.

We reached the top. Willi brought me to a charming inn built in a series of terraces into the very side of the mountain. It was almost lost amid the fir trees. The air was sharp and pure. We were five thousand feet above the rest of the world. White, white snow wherever I turned and always the dark green fir trees pointing to the sky.

Willi kissed me. Then he held me at arm's length and looked at me tenderly, yet searchingly, almost wonderingly, as though he were trying to read nameless secrets deep in my eyes. "I am such a fortunate man," he said softly. I trembled and clung to him. I am wicked, I thought. *Wicked.* "How sweet," he said. He used the German word *süsse,* a word which to pronounce is like a kiss itself. "How very, very sweet you are." He murmured gently, *"Du bist die ganzen Velt zu mir"*—You are the entire world to me. "You are," he said. "You are."

Willi said rebukingly, "Why did you tell me all those silly stories?"

I said indignantly, "What silly stories?"

My indignation was real. Of course the stories were not true, but why should he call it to my attention and spoil everything?

For three months *The Singing Dream* played to packed houses and for three months I was in love with Willi. I would steal a glance, when he was unaware, at his lined intelligent face with its heavy Mongolian cast and think: he looks like one of those wild Tartars of the Middle Ages who swept out of Asia to conquer Europe with fire and sword. I was desperately drawn to him.

Looking back now to this first love, I realize how great a wonder it was to me that a man I loved would want me, and love me, and fulfill me. In years to come, this was the secret I would keep to myself—for all I know, it is the secret every woman keeps to herself: that I never thought of myself as making a gift of myself to a man I loved. He was the gift to me. I was the fortunate one. He bestowed his favor on me. It was all, the most I asked in life: to be loved by the right man, the man I love. I thought if this was being a woman, this was what I wanted.

When Willi told me that he was married—his wife was ill in Switzerland, taking a cure—I did not feel guilty. In the world in which I grew up, one did not marry for love: a man took as his wife a suitable young woman of good family who became the mother of his children, who was skilled in running his home and entertaining his friends. For love he turned to someone else. Love in marriage was a luxury which only the very poor could afford. I remembered overhearing Mother on the phone to a girl friend. "Oh darling, don't fret," she was saying. "He will come back to you, but he simply had to take his wife for a vacation." When Willi told me he was married, I felt only hurt that he belonged to another woman. But one had to suffer for love: this was how life was.

Night after night after the theater we went out. By this time Louisa had accepted the inevitable. (Later she told Mother, "You wasted your money hiring me. Not even a regiment of Hussars could have controlled that girl.") We dined at the Bristol Bar, one of Vienna's most popular night clubs. Willi pointed out Hedy Mandl with her husband, Fritz Mandl, the Viennese munitions king. The girl I was to know later in Hollywood as Hedy Lamarr wore a blue sequined dress which matched her blue eyes, her jet-black hair was set off by a superb diamond diadem, her face was incredible—I had never

49

seen anyone so beautiful. At the bar stood a young maharajah from India, Prince El Barre, tall, slim, dark, a touch of gray at his temples who, Willi said, was one of the finest polo players in the world. With him was his mistress, a blonde film star newly arrived from New York. She smiled langourously into his eyes, and allowed the smoke from her cigarette, in a long crimson holder, to float tantalizingly between them. A cynic might have said they were posing for a cigarette advertisement in *Harper's Bazaar:* I only knew I thought they were two of the most beautiful human beings I had ever seen. On nights I had no performance Willi took me to the Kammerspiel Theatre and we watched plays on the little stage on which Marlene Dietrich, Tala Birrell, and Luise Rainer had begun their careers.

For me Vienna, with all that it meant, was intoxication.

To add to my drunkenness, Alexander Korda, the Hungarian-born film producer, having seen my photograph on a magazine cover, had wired Mother from London that he wanted to screen-test me but had been unable to obtain a British working permit for me. Outraged, Mother dashed off a letter, with my photograph, to King George VI himself. "Does England want to deny Sari Gabor the right to make a brilliant career?" Incredibly enough, an imposing letter arrived from Buckingham Palace, heavy with the seal of the Crown on it, in which one of His Majesty's secretaries explained to Mrs. Gabor that in these difficult times, His Majesty was so very occupied that it was unlikely any change could now be made in the British-Hungarian trade agreements. It was a lost cause, but Mother was very proud of her correspondence with Buckingham Palace.

My Vienna episode came to a close the Saturday night in December that Willi left for Rome to work on Marta Eggerth's film. He said, "Come with me to Rome." I said, unhappily, "Oh, Willi, you know that can't be." Immediately after my performance I saw him off on the train. We said goodbye in his compartment. The warning whistle blew. "One parting kiss, my darling," Willi said. I went into his arms, but when

50

I tried to free myself, he held me, and only when the train moved did he release me. "I have two performances tomorrow!" I wailed. "What are you doing!"

"Wire and cancel them," Willi ordered. "Say you've broken your leg skiing, say anything. I must have you with me in Rome."

I sent the wire.

But at 3 A.M., when the train halted at Klagenfurt, the last stop before entering Italy, I left Willi sleeping in his compartment and stole off the train. This was getting out of hand. I was frightened—not only of Willi but of myself. To have a romance with Willi in Vienna was in the great tradition of the books I had read. But to go with this middle-aged, married man to a strange city—this was something else.

I stood in ankle-high snow, hidden in the shadow of the station until the train pulled away. The next train for Vienna was not due until 5 A.M. I sat over a cup of black coffee in the tiny restaurant, in tears over what was ending. The waitress looked curiously at me. I must make a pretty picture, I thought—hatless, my make-up still on, my mascara running, wet and bedraggled in my sweater and skirt, the snow still melting in my hair.

After a while I wandered into the waiting room and sat on a bench. I looked around. The station was dimly lit, completely deserted, foul-smelling. I shivered. What was I doing here, away from my lovely home, my parents, my family? The *grand amour* was suddenly something tarnished. Until the train came I sat on the bench in the half-darkness, stared at by the ticket clerk and the watchman, thinking, what now?

4

IT'S hard to explain such things. Four weeks later, I was married to His Excellency, Burhan Belge, Press Director of the Foreign Ministry of the Government of Turkey.

Everything happened with breakneck speed. This pattern of reacting to circumstances has saved me in my most difficult moments. Except for one terrifying period in my life when it seemed the bottom dropped out of everything, I have never had time to become deeply depressed. Instead of lamenting, I act—I do something, usually something fantastic. Now, instead of brooding over Willi, within a month I was married, and that excitement carried me past him and past everything that troubled me.

A week after Willi left for Rome, *The Singing Dream* closed. It had played one hundred performances. I was immediately ordered home. I was to be sent back to Madame Subilia's. Father was furious. Aunt Dora, fresh from a visit to Vienna, had walked in on my parents. "Fine theater and fine governess!" she had exclaimed indignantly. "I saw Zsa Zsa the other night in a night club with a man three times her age!" I thought to myself: if they only knew!

Back in Budapest, I pleaded with Mother. After Vienna, how could I return to long black stockings, penances, and psalms before dinner? "I know, darling," Mother said, not unsympathetically. "But what else is there for you to do?"

For a week I wandered aimlessly about the house. Willi was waiting in Rome. I could not get him out of my mind. I was homesick for the theater, the applause, the hot glow of fame. I longed for the gaiety and freedom I had known. With each day the thought of Madame Subilia and Miss McClain, pink and suspicious, grew more unbearable. It would be a prison. I was trapped.

And Father was difficult. I had missed my German shepherd dog so much that Willi had gone into a pet shop on the Kärtnerstrasse and bought me an adorable little Scotty, named Mishka. He was a real Viennese gentleman, warm and affectionate, but he always snapped at Father, who took out on him all his anger. "Get rid of that dog!" he shouted. "I won't have him in this house!" I found myself crying as bitterly over Mishka as over Willi. It was all impossible.

Then I thought of M. Belge. On impulse I telephoned the Turkish Embassy. His Excellency was now in the West but was expected in Budapest momentarily. I left my name.

Two days later I was strolling with M. Belge on the Corso, chattering about my Viennese experience, my near career with Mr. Korda. His Excellency was as I had remembered him—quietly elegant, a little weary, and apparently secretly amused by me. We paused in front of the Hotel Ritz. "A cognac?" M. Belge suggested. We walked into the Prince of Wales Bar—the Duke of Windsor, when Prince of Wales, had often come here—and M. Belge ordered a Scotch and soda for himself. I was impressed again by him. No one I had known was sophisticated enough to order Scotch.

Sitting in a corner sipping sherry, I said suddenly, "Excellency, will you marry me?"

M. Belge choked on his Scotch. He began to cough and had to put down his glass. "Oh, forgive me!" he said, a handkerchief at his mouth. His dark face had grown as red as a beet. "Now, what did you say?"

I was a little taken aback, but I pushed on. I said reasonably, "You promised you'd marry me when I grew up. I think I'm grown up."

He stared at me for a moment, then burst into laughter. "You are quite right, Fräulein Gabor," he said. He picked up his drink and sipped it thoughtfully. He did not look at me.

I went on, "I'll be a good wife to you, Excellency. You need someone like me, anyway. You are always so solemn." He said nothing. Then I remembered. "Just one thing, though. I hope you will allow me to keep my Scotty, Mishka. I'd be lost without him."

M. Belge shot a sharp glance at me. Then his face relaxed and a half-smile began to play about his lips. "May I have a little time to think this over?" he asked.

By now I was completely caught up in the game. Queen Victoria could not have fenced more diplomatically with Disraeli. "How long do you want, Excellency?"

He said, helping me from my chair, "Suppose you permit me to take you to dinner this evening. We will discuss it then."

That night he took me to the Hotel Gellert, where Mother had once fled after a quarrel with Father. We danced to the soft strains of a waltz. I tried to reach M. Belge. Eva had helped me into a tight-fitting black gown and the way other men's eyes followed me on the floor gave me confidence. Surely His Excellency could not be completely indifferent to me. Looking back, I know that I was incredibly naïve—and this even after Vienna, which should have given me a certain sophistication. The measure of my naïveté was not only that I proposed to Burhan Belge, a serious and completely unfrivolous man; it was also that not until after our marriage did I learn that he had been married twice before. It had never occurred to me to ask; and he had not found it necessary to tell me.

Back at the table I said, "Aren't these pretty of me?" I showed him half a dozen photographs I had had taken at Angelo's, the best known theatrical photographer in Budapest. Mr. Angelo had posed me carefully. In one photograph I stood in profile against the light, my blouse partly open, my head back, dropping cherries provocatively into my open mouth. In another, I wore a tight red sweater, a red leather belt emphasizing my small waist, my hair fell to my shoulders, and I looked roguishly at the photographer as I bit hard into an apple.

M. Belge regarded them with interest. "Very, very lovely," he said. "You are most photogenic." He continued to look at them, then at me, then back at them.

I could wait no longer.

"Have you made up your mind, Excellency? Are you marrying me?"

Still holding my photographs in his hand, he smiled at me. "Why not?" he said.

"And Mishka?" I heard myself say, almost idiotically.

"If you wish," he said, gravely. "Of course."

Then—and only then—I blushed at my temerity.

Mother, surprisingly enough, took it philosophically. "My God, I must start getting you a trousseau!" she exclaimed, and was immediately on the telephone to her sisters. Grandmother beamed. "You are so young for him—but he is a fine gentleman." Father couldn't understand it. "A Turk?" he demanded. "A diplomat, yes, that is good—but why a Turk?"

I know now why there was no stronger protest. Father, with three unmarried daughters on his hands, was actually relieved. I think he was just as happy, too, that I was no longer subject to Mother's whirlwind schemes to make me famous. Father might have wished to keep Magda, Eva, and me with him indefinitely. But these were critical days. The future of Europe, of Hungary, was uncertain. Budapest was gay, because Hungarians hate to face reality. But it was impossible, with Hitler on the march, not to know that anything might happen. For me to be the wife of a high-ranking Turkish government official, protected by a diplomatic passport, was no small thing. As it turned out, within a year or so my sisters, too, were married, and like me, to foreigners, living with their husbands in foreign lands—Magda to a Pole, in London; Eva, to a Swede, in Hollywood.

I married M. Burhan Belge. It was a quiet afternoon ceremony held fittingly enough in Grandmother's house. Father's last words—he was gruff, there were tears in his eyes, but he had to maintain his authority to the end—"Don't hurry to bring me back a little Turkish soldier!"

I sat opposite my husband on the Simplon Express, roaring eastward through the darkness to Istanbul, where his parents, his sister Lehman, and her husband Yakob Kadri, Turkish Ambassador to Albania, awaited us. From there we would go to Ankara, the Turkish capital, nearly three hundred miles inland. Watching Burhan as he read one of the stack of newspapers he had piled beside him, I began to realize the enormous step I had taken. The headlines shouted, "Barcelona Bombed," but my mind was far from the Spanish war. The last weeks had been so busy I had hardly had time to think. That morning, only a few hours before the ceremony, I had crept into Eva's bed and we had hugged each other and cried like two eight-year-olds. Through her tears, Eva had choked, "If ever you need help, just wire the word 'Gypsy' and I'll come from the ends of the earth!" And we had thrown our arms around each other and sobbed again into each other's pink linen pajamas. I was leaving home, not as a schoolgirl on a gay lark to Vienna a few hours away, but as the wife of a man I scarcely knew, to live in a strange, Oriental land where only a few years before men kept four wives and women walked the streets with their faces covered.

Grandmother had said M. Belge was an important man. It was true, I learned, at the very first frontier. The mere showing of his diplomatic passport was sufficient: he was saluted, bowed to, and treated with the utmost respect. I was impressed—and frightened. I thought guiltily: I don't love this man. I married him but I don't want him to come near me. It's still Willi. Each time Burhan stirred behind his newspaper, or put it down to smile at me, my heart began to pound. Mishka was curled up at my side. Burhan and my little Viennese gentleman had taken an immediate dislike to each other. Later when Burhan went into the smoking room, I prepared for bed, thinking helplessly: how can I keep him away? My own ignorance saved me. When Burhan entered,

I lay feigning sleep, Mishka curled up in bed with me. Burhan stopped for a moment. I felt him lean over me. He kissed me on the forehead. "Good night, my dear," he said, and prepared to spend the night in his berth. I thought, relieved: he senses how I feel. Then I was suddenly hurt: how could he control himself so easily? How dare he! How could I know that to a Moslem dogs are unclean—that Burhan would never sleep where a dog had lain?

Our honeymoon was spent in his father's home in Istanbul, a white fairy-tale house overlooking the Bosphorus. Servants removed our shoes as we entered and slipped our feet into beautifully embroidered slippers. I was presented to my mother-in-law, a tiny woman with a fiery red Mohammedan *säl* about her shoulders, sitting with her legs crossed under her like an Oriental queen. She might have come out of *The Arabian Nights*. The only modern thing about her was the cigarette she smoked in a long amber holder. Her nails were painted dark red, her eyes were black and enormous with mascara: they gave her an exotic, Egyptian appearance. I almost curtsied. Burhan's father, a slender man with impeccable manners, bowed to me, kissed me on both cheeks, and told me in flowery French how welcome I was in his house and in his son's life. Burhan's sister, Lehman, was a fair, blue-eyed woman of great dignity. My brother-in-law, Yakob Kadri, was a handsome man, with shining black eyes and a luxuriant black mustache that captivated me at once. "Welcome, welcome, welcome!" he said with gusto, and clasped Burhan's hand. "You lucky fellow!"

After much chatting in Turkish, of which I understood nothing, we were led upstairs to a red velvet and gold bedroom set aside for us. On each side of an enormous double bed a dozen kinds of colored sugar candy were arranged. These were Turkish wedding sweets. Little blue pearls were embroidered on each pillow to ward off the evil eye. I was treated like a bride; I was helped to dress for dinner, my hair washed, then rinsed in rose water to bring out its red highlights; then my sister-in-law helped me into a strikingly tailored white satin gown Mother had chosen for me. My jewels were simple—a lovely ruby necklace, a wedding present from my parents, and a diamond pin that Grandmother Franceska had worn as a girl.

After dinner the ladies left the dining room and the men remained for brandy. Presently my sister-in-law took me aside. She asked, with a discreet, almost apologetic smile, did I not wish to retire? "It is not wise to make a new husband wait," she said. "I think I should tell you that my brother has been spoiled by many women. His first two marriages were not agreeable and I am delighted that he has found you." I was shocked, both by her information and her frankness. I had been told Orientals were so devious. She went on, "He seems to be very fond of you. You must submit to him and be good to him. You must learn to know when he is displeased, for he is a proud man—he will never tell you his feelings. He simply walks away, or becomes silent for a long time. You must learn how to please him." She paused, and said in a tone that allowed no dispute, as though the matter was no longer in my hands, "Now I think you should go upstairs. I will send him to you presently."

I grew redder and redder as she spoke. Suddenly the harem was too near. I turned to call Mishka, who was worrying a bone under the table, but my sister-in-law, taking me by the arm, said firmly, "We will make a place for him in the kitchen tonight."

I nodded resignedly. Like it or not, the honeymoon had begun.

A letter from Magda, a month after my arrival in Ankara:

Well, they did it! They finally got their legal separation papers. I think your getting out of the house made Mama decide that now at last she could start her own life. She asked me to come to the courthouse with them. I felt wretched, but I said yes. I never thought they'd go through with it even if Mama has been warning all her life that she would leave him.

58

Janos (our chauffeur) drove us downtown without saying a word. He must have felt as badly as I did. They went into the courthouse and I sat on the jump seat, waiting. I just couldn't believe it. But a few minutes later they came out with the papers, and got into the back seat behind me and we started up. After a little while I heard Papa say, "It's been a long time, Jolie." I thought I'd cry then and there, he was so sad. Mama didn't say anything. Then I heard him say, "I will take you home, Jolie."

We drove without a word for about five minutes. Then the most amazing thing. From where I sit on the little jump seat I can look directly into the rear-view mirror above Janos' head and see them. And what do you think they are doing? Kissing! Madly kissing, like two lovebirds!

I couldn't help it. I turned around. "Mama!" Her face was absolutely pink. Papa spoke up in his Franz Josef voice. "Janos, we have changed our minds. Drop Miss Magda at home. Mrs. Gabor and I are going out to dine!"

Mama just looked up at him—you know the way she has, like a little girl. "Oh Vilmos!" she said.

You see how it is—our crazy family! Do you know what they've done since? Mama's moved into a house on the Danube and Papa took a small apartment by himself, but they're always together. She goes every day to his place to lunch with him, he comes every night to her to dine. I never saw them so much in love!

And then, a P.S.: "How does it feel to be called 'Your Excellency?' " After that, a P.P.S.: "Have you seen the fabulous Kemal Ataturk yet?"

I wanted to laugh and cry. Yes, our crazy family! All her life Mother longed for her freedom from Father, and now that she had it at last, it was clear that she only wanted it so that she could be free to flirt with him!

5

TURKEY to me was hot sun, dazzlingly reflected from the golden cupolas of the ancient mosques; the eerie wail of the muezzin as he stood high in the minaret, chanting "Allah illah Allah" to the four corners of the earth, calling the faithful to prayer. It was dark bazaars stretching for miles under vaulted roofs, smelling of spices, coffee, and unwashed humanity. It was outdoor night clubs on the roofs of office buildings—strolling downtown, you looked up to see couples dancing five stories above the street with only a railing to protect them. It meant exotic delicacies in food: breast of chicken beaten to the consistency of whipped cream, sheep's eyes, and rice pilaff, and goat's meat so strong that even Mishka turned away. It meant the sound of radios blaring into the street from dawn to midnight. It meant the portrait of Mustafa Kemal Ataturk, forbidding and thin-lipped, staring out from every store window, from every café wall, from above the fireplace of every home. It meant Yakob Kadri, shining-eyed and jovial and forever pulling my leg—"Do you know Ataturk is furious with Burhan for marrying a foreign woman?" And it meant my husband, Burhan.

If I wanted a man of mystery, I had him in Burhan Belge. He was addressed as "Your Excellency"—and so was I. I giggled the first time I heard it from my houseboy, Ali. Burhan frowned. As I remember him, he seems to have been frowning all the time. I wrote Mother a long newsy letter telling about our beautiful house on Embassy Row, and how I spent my time riding Fatushka, a white Arabian mare

Burhan bought me, and studying Turkish. I described my husband proudly as Minister of Press and Propaganda. "Please," said Burhan with a dark look, "I am not a minister. There is no Minister of Press and Propaganda in Turkey." His title was Director of Press of the Turkish Foreign Ministry; but since the press *was* government controlled, did this not make him chief of propaganda? Burhan dismissed it. "You exaggerate, exaggerate," he said, annoyed. "I am only a newspaperman." But this did not explain why we traveled on a diplomatic passport, nor why he should broadcast a review and analysis of world affairs to all Turkey every Saturday afternoon, nor why in my first months nearly all of Burhan's friends I met were either in government or the foreign diplomatic corps.

Overnight I had been thrown into a bewildering world of political intrigue. "Be careful what you say on the telephone," Burhan warned. "Don't repeat what you hear in this house." No one knew whose telephone might be tapped, or who was an *agent provocateur*. In those tense years immediately before the outbreak of World War II, Turkey, the bridge between Russia and the West, was one of the most important listening posts in the world. And Burhan played a more important role than he cared for me to know. He told me little about his work. I knew that he was a graduate of Heidelberg, had once edited his own political newspaper, and was a leader of the Young Turks, Turkey's fiery nationalist movement which fought any remnant of the old world of the Sultans. He was full of ambition for his country, and only when he talked about the new Turkey did he forget himself. Then his face grew alive, his eyes flashed, he became almost fanatical. Yet even his own father had once had four wives. When I strolled with my father-in-law of an afternoon, he would glance appreciatively after a pretty girl, then turn to me, "Zsa Zsa, would you like another mother?" It was his little joke—but not so long ago, it would have been possible.

Perhaps it was my fault I did not know more about my husband and his work. At the beginning he tried to brief me. "I know this is a new way of life for you," he said. These

61

were difficult times, in addition. He was very pessimistic. Hitler would not stop in Central Europe; and Britain, said Burhan, refused to recognize the fact. Even worse was the threat of the Far Eastern people, who would one day rule the world. As Burhan talked about these things, I would find myself yawning. He would stand up suddenly and stalk away. I could not help it. At first I had been terribly intrigued. How exciting, I thought, to be married to a man of such intelligence, who goes off on mysterious political missions to Germany, France, and England, who is involved in affairs beyond my understanding, who can't even be bothered to try to explain them to a mere woman like myself. But now as his wife, I was uncomfortable; he made me feel like a silly girl called before a schoolmaster.

Perhaps for that reason I acted the part. When he went to his conferences, I was left with Nadya, the cook, a heavy imperturbable woman who kept to her kitchen, and Ali, my fifteen-year-old houseboy from Turkestan. Ali, until I hired him, had never seen a doorknob, had never worn shoes, had never eaten leavened bread. I adored him because when I sent him to market, saying, "Now, go quick like a locomotive," he would run all the way like a locomotive, chugging his elbows and crying out "Choo-choo!" at the top of his voice. Like two children Ali and I would paint a face on a broom, put a hat on it, a pipe in its mouth, dress it in one of Burhan's suits and set it against the wall. Burhan coming home, would see it in the shadows and pull back, startled— it looked like a man lying in wait for him.

One day Ali and I were walking down Bakanliklar Avenue, not far from the Foreign Ministry, when we passed a Turkish farmer holding out a black battered derby in which was a little ball of fur. "Buy, buy, buy!" he cried. "A little treasure." I peered into the derby. It was a baby bear. "Oh, I must have it!" I cried, and grabbing the hat, bear and all, I ran to the Ministry and up the steps, the outraged farmer shouting after me. I pounded on the door of Burhan's office.

My husband opened it. "Burhan, darling, may I have this

cuddly little bear?" I began excitedly. Then I saw the room was full of men. I had burst into a conference. They rose as one, and bowed. Some managed to keep a straight face. Burhan was black and furious. "Let us, please, talk about this later," he said icily. I backed away, the door closed. I had caught a glimpse of the important government officials there —I thought, in chagrin: what they must all think! Poor Burhan! What a silly girl he had married!

I tried to become a good Turkish wife. I learned how to brew Turkish coffee, rich and sweet and topped with tiny bubbles. I studied Turkish with a tutor, and each day when Burhan came home we reviewed my vocabulary. Then I would take my place on an enormous black and gold hassock while Burhan, in a deep armchair, read to me from French, German, and English literature, so that I would catch up on what I had lost in my schooling. But when his friends dropped over, Young Turks who insisted on speaking only Turkish, I understood very little and felt out of place. At dinner parties Burhan would watch me growing drowsy. "Perhaps you had better retire," he would suggest. And I would excuse myself and trudge upstairs sleepily, like a child sent to bed.

My pleasures, those first months, were riding Fatushka and exploring Ankara. The new city had been built around the two-thousand-year-old village of Angora, a honeycomb of twisting, cobblestoned streets with thousands of cats, the famous Angora cats, prowling about. I stabled Fatushka at the fashionable Ankara Riding Club. Once in the saddle, I would trot up the wide, tree-lined Ataturk Boulevard, past the embassies, up, up to the top of the street where stood the great pink marble palace of President Kemal Ataturk, commanding the entire city, commanding this strange new world of mine. When the President was in Ankara, Ali had told me with great pride, the windows of the palace blazed through the night, and all Ankara was gay and happy because they knew Ataturk, "Father of all the Turks," was there to protect them. But when he left for Istanbul and the palace was dark, the city lay under a pall of gloom. I would ride close to the palace, hoping to catch a glimpse of this legendary man. Often on my ride home I stopped for a coffee in an enchanting antique shop run by six Circassian brothers, with long, narrow faces that could have been painted by Modigliani. I enjoyed browsing amid the ancient coins, the hammered copper, the intricate Oriental jewelry.

Numad, the oldest brother, was a lean little man with puckered brown skin, a long nose, and dark eyes so deeply set that he looked like a tortured Spanish saint. He delighted in showing me his newest treasures, allowing me to try on a necklace or a ring, adding teasingly, "Do you like this, Excellency? Shall I find someone to buy it for you?" I would giggle and joke with him.

One morning he showed me a lovely pearl. "Madame Belge, I'm sure the Afghan minister would like to send this to you, if it pleases you."

"Really?" I asked. I looked at the pearl. "Why should he do that?"

Numad said, "If you would be nice to him—"

I was insulted. "Don't you ever want me to come into your shop again?" To myself, I said: this is what one must expect in the Orient.

A few days later he produced a thick gold bracelet heavily encrusted with emeralds and rubies. "How do you like this?" I clasped it on my wrist and held it this way, then that. "Beautiful," I said. "And who wants me to be nice to him now?"

Numad looked injured. "Please, Your Excellency. This gentleman doesn't even ask to be thanked. It will be his pleasure to know that you have accepted it. Sometime, perhaps—" Numad hesitated delicately. "He would like to come here for a coffee so he can see how beautiful it is on you—"

I dropped the bracelet into his hand. "Not interested," I said, and I flicked my riding crop under his long Circassian nose, smiled at him, and left.

I rode home at a smart trot, pleased with myself. When I walked into the house, still laughing at the look of injury

64

on Numad's saintly face, Burhan was there, going over notes
for his weekly broadcast. "What is so funny?" he asked. Because he asked the question, nothing was funny any more.
I dared not tell him about the Circassian brothers. He had
no sense of humor about such matters. Whenever I came
home in high spirits, he snuffed them out. I thought: he's
only twenty years older than I, but he might as well be a
hundred. He's really three hundred years behind me—or perhaps three hundred years ahead of me. I wasn't sure. The
foolish little games Ali and I played only annoyed him. He
had forbidden me to buy the baby bear: he still detested
Mishka, and my little Scotty bared his teeth every time Burhan came into my room. As the days passed and political
developments grew more serious in Europe, Burhan spent
more time at the Foreign Office, and when he came home he
was even more remote and forbidding. The day came when
I found myself trembling at the sound of his key in the lock.
Not that he would harm me, but that he would, with one
dark glance, one word, one question, take the whole joy of
life from me.

In Hungary I had been afraid only of Father. Here I was
petrified of this somber, unsmiling man who made me feel
guilty when I was not guilty, who when angry simply did not
speak to me for days at a time.

I can't say I was not a trial to him. One evening we attended
a dinner at the German Embassy. I was presented to a tall,
frosty man, Franz von Papen, Hitler's Ambassador. We sat
down to a sumptuous meal. The entree was roast goose. I
recognized that goose; it could only be Hungarian. A fowl so
plump, so tender, had to come from my country, which raised
the finest geese in Europe.

I said, aloud, "This goose is so good, surely it must have
been stolen from Hungary."

There was a moment of shocked silence, then ripples of
laughter. Madame Belge with her outrageous remarks—

Burhan said, "Your Excellency—"

I was not going to be stopped.

"But it's common knowledge, isn't it, that they take all our good food and we have only bad food left?"

Von Papen gave me an imperturbable smile. What he might have said I will never know because Burhan went on to ask a question about Russian-German relations, and the two men were soon deep in discussion.

At the Russian Embassy I was charmed by the Ambassador, Lev Mikhailovich Karakhan. A giant of a man with a huge spade beard, he was married to a Russian prima ballerina. But what fascinated me was the rumor that he in some way had displeased Stalin and any day would be summoned back to Moscow to be shot. M. Karakhan was a gallant man. On several occasions he had chosen me as his bridge partner, and bridge was not my game. After I had ruined his hand for the third time, a friend asked him, "Excellency, why do you continue to play with her?"

"Ah," he replied, "but she has such a delicious décolleté."

I admired such a man. But even at his parties I could not hold my tongue. At one buffet dinner I wandered around a huge table piled high with bowls of caviar, chef's masterpieces in ice and aspic. I could not find a slice of bread. I said, almost without thinking, "Caviar they have . . . but bread they don't have, because the Germans already took it from them." I looked up to find M. Karakhan eyeing me with an amused smile. He leaned over as he filled his plate. "Madame Belge, I should warn you that there are some situations from which even your décolleté will not save you."

After such occasions Burhan would be like ice. "Why did you do that? Must you always be little Madame Sans Gêne?"

I tried to dismiss it. "Oh Burhan, darling, don't be silly. Everyone doesn't take things so seriously."

But despite Burhan's solemnity, I enjoyed diplomatic life: I lived for the Embassy parties, which continued gaily all through the prewar period, and for riding. These were my reffuge from Burhan. One day when I was about to ride off from the Ankara Club, I was conscious of someone staring at me from behind. I turned. Seated beautifully on his horse, a tall, fair, blue-eyed man, his blond hair turning gray, watched me. He was in his early fifties. He immediately pulled up to me and said, in the most beautiful English, and in the most beautifully modulated voice I had ever heard—so, flashed through my mind, King Arthur might have spoken—"Madame Belge, do forgive me for staring at you. I am Percy Loren. I had the honor of meeting your husband the other evening." Would I permit him to introduce himself?

This was Sir Percy Loren, the British Ambassador, formerly British High Commissioner in Egypt, and the ranking foreign diplomat in Turkey.

Once, years later, Sir Percy told me he had never forgotten that meeting. "I saw you on a horse—a perfect little figure in a riding habit, with golden hair under a black velvet cap. I told myself, 'Oh, God, don't let her turn around because I can only be disappointed.' And then you turned around, my dear, and under the golden hair I saw an angel's face."

Sir Percy invited Burhan and me to a small supper for a dozen guests. Of all the embassies in Ankara, the French was the most beautiful. It was a miniature Versailles with mirrored halls and crystal chandeliers. But the British Embassy captivated me. It was an English country house and I immediately fell in love with it. As the English girls at school had impressed me by their lack of temperament, so Percy's house impressed me by its subdued elegance. In Hungary everything was boisterous—sound, color, personalities. Here at Sir Percy's all was chintz and simplicity, yet with its own stateliness: behind every chair a uniformed lackey stood; the dinner was good but there was not enough of it. I liked this. At the German and Russian and French embassies, you were fed too much. How chic, I thought, not to feed you too much.

I found Sir Percy perfect. Once, going upstairs to freshen myself, I passed his bedroom and peeked in. On the bed were three pressed tuxedos. His butler had laid out four; Sir Percy had carefully selected the one he preferred for this evening. Such lordly perfection of dress impressed me; I liked the way he carried himself; I liked his manners, his nonchalance, his healthy, optimistic way of looking at the world. If he was not as easygoing as I had heard Americans were, he was so much more friendly than a Turk, so much less ponderous than a Hungarian. I found Burhan terribly tortured in comparison. Sometimes, thinking of Sir Percy, I blushed to the roots of my hair. I said to myself: why couldn't I have married an Englishman like this instead of a moody, brooding Oriental?

I had been in Ankara perhaps three months when Burhan, reading his ever present newspaper, gave a short contemptuous laugh. He read aloud: "According to a survey, 85 per cent of Turkey's women admit they dream of Kemal Ataturk."

Ridiculous, Burhan said, and yet Ataturk was an extraordinary figure: half man, half god. In one mighty stroke, Burhan explained, he transformed a feudal state into a modern republic. He had done away with slavery and polygamy and the harem; he outlawed the turban and the veil; he Romanized the alphabet, changed the calendar, moved the capital from Istanbul to Ankara. He was El Ghazi—Great Pasha—he was the Gray Wolf; arrested, imprisoned, exiled—nothing had stopped him. He had made and led a revolution, almost single-handed. As Burhan talked I caught fire, too. Imagine what the women must think of this extraordinary man who told them, "Throw away your black veils. Be beautiful. Wear modern, feminine, bright-colored clothes. Show your legs; be women. It is good for a woman to be admired by a man." What must this have meant to women who all their lives had been told by their husbands, "Cover yourself, hide yourself—" who wrapped themselves in shapeless black robes and thought of themselves as little better than cattle? I could understand why they dreamed of him, fell in love with him, thought of him as a god. I had dreamed of him, too, the night after I had ridden up to his great pink palace high on the hill. In my dreams Ataturk strode into my room like a prince. He said, "Now that I see you, I am not sorry that Burhan married a foreign woman. He chose well."

But I had yet to meet him.
Then one evening I met him.

"We'll take Lehman and Yakob to Karpiç's," Burhan said. It was to be a farewell dinner for Yakob, who had just been appointed Ambassador to Switzerland and was to leave the next day for Berne. Karpiç was a Russian immigrant whose restaurant had become a show place in Ankara.

When we arrived, we were ushered into an enormous square room with stately pillars; our table was to one side of a small dance floor. Everywhere was Ataturk's portrait, and above the tremendous entranceway, the Turkish flag. I was studying the menu when the pleasant hum of conversation suddenly heightened, then died away completely. The music stopped. There was complete silence.

I looked up.

The two huge double doors at the entrance had swung wide open and through them poured about ten uniformed police; they immediately took their places on either side, like a guard of honor; then, perhaps half a dozen of the most beautiful women, chatting animatedly, stunning in evening gowns, appeared; then three or four men in tuxedos; and then in their center, a slim man with gray eyes the color of steel. I thought: Prince Serge, the hero of my girlhood!

Everyone rose. Lehman nudged me and I found myself on my feet. The dancing couples stopped where they were; everyone on the floor and at their tables stood facing the entrance. Burhan's voice was in my ear. "Ataturk," he whispered.

I stared at Mustafa Kemal Ataturk, the savior of Turkey. He stood, framed in the entrance, suddenly alone: slim, gray at the temples, impeccably dressed in black tie, his shoulders back, his head up, surveying the room as from a great distance as if seeing everyone there yet utterly indifferent to what he saw. He had just drawn a cigarette from a gold case; he held the case in his left hand and was tapping the cigarette gently against it as he looked over the heads of the crowd. The head-waiter scurried up to him, bowed deeply, and led him to an enormous table. The women and police followed. He was the first to take his seat, and until he sat down, no one else in the room moved. It was odd to see a man seated while women stood. I had never before seen anyone entitled to the prerogative of royalty. Then there was a scrape of chairs and a rustle of dresses as we all took our seats; the orchestra leader waved his baton; the music resumed, and the dancers, who had been immobile, like toys suddenly run down, began to dance again.

Yakob on my left, leaned toward me. "Well," he said, almost teasingly, "now you have seen our Gray Wolf. What do you think?"

I turned to stare again at Ataturk, perhaps thirty feet away. Lehman tugged my arm. "Don't look, don't look," she whispered urgently. "Don't call attention to yourself." Yakob looked at his wife—I could never understand how such a lusty, outgoing man could have married so proper a woman—and grinned at me. "She is right," he said. "If he likes you, he may adopt you."

Burhan, opposite me, looked dark.

I had heard these stories. Ataturk was reputed to have many mistresses. When he took a new favorite, the girl who had been discarded became his adopted daughter. He financed her education, even helped her make a good marriage. I thought of the other tales I had heard. He was the greatest warrior, the greatest lover, the greatest playboy. He could outdrink any man; he was rarely completely sober, but even when drunk made effective speeches; he had incredible vigor, he slept only four hours a night; he had once sent Germany's powerful Franz von Papen weeping like a child from an audience with him. He was aloof, brilliant; in military school he had been given the name, "Kemal"—"Perfection"—a man of sudden and awful decision. Once he was to appoint a fleet admiral. Sitting with his highest naval officers, he announced, "Whoever outdrinks me becomes admiral." They sat ordering raki, the Turkish national drink, which is almost pure alcohol. One by one the men slumped from their chairs. Only a young officer of twenty-five was still able to drink glass for glass with Ataturk. Finally

Ataturk was unable to move; the young man downed a glass. At twenty-five, he became Admiral of the Turkish Fleet.

Could I believe these stories? Some Yakob had told me, and I never knew when he pulled my leg. There were so many legends about this strange man who was the idol of Turkey.

I stole a glance at him again. Our eyes met; I felt the blood rush up my face and I turned swiftly away. Yet I knew, as though this were a prearranged script, what would happen next. An aide bowed at our table. The President would like Their Excellencies Burhan Belge and Yakob Kadri and their ladies to join his party.

I glanced at Burhan; his face was even darker. He was jealous! At my side Lehman was so upset she could hardly keep her seat. But Yakob was all smiles, his black mustache almost twitching with delight. He loved intrigue; he nearly burst into laughter, watching his wife's and brother-in-law's discomfiture. "Come, come," he said to me. "Are you afraid? We are all friends."

We rose and went to Ataturk's table. Whether by design or accident, Burhan seated me and himself at the far end of the table. I sat, looking down, as the waiters hastily set places for us. I heard a deep rasping voice, "Bayan Belge, have you ever tasted raki?"

I looked up and said, abashed, "No, Pasha Effendi."

Everyone roared. In my own Turkish I had said, "No, Excellency Mister."

"Well," he said, "you will taste it now."

He filled a glass with a hand that trembled slightly, and added a little water; it turned cloudy and looked like milk. He sent it down to me. Everyone watched as I sipped. Raki is an anise drink like Pernod, and very powerful. I choked, put it down, and went into a coughing fit.

Ataturk burst into laughter. Everyone followed suit, save Burhan, who sat dour and silent at my side.

"Do you smoke?" was the President's next question.

I said, "Not yet, Pasha Effendi," which brought laughter again. I couldn't understand what I had said that was funny.

71

"This is a good one to begin on, then," Ataturk said amiably. "With my compliments." He sent down a thin, flat cigarette rimmed in gold, with "K.A." embossed in tiny crimson letters. I puffed, inhaled daintily, and coughed again.

"Burhan Bey, your lady isn't accustomed to us yet," said Ataturk. He seemed to be enjoying himself. Our food was served; we began to eat. Burhan said nothing. Lehman was quiet. Yakob was silent, too. Ataturk sat back, taking no food, but allowing his glass to be constantly refilled.

A few moments later, Ataturk turned to the woman on his left. I heard his question. "Madame, do you dance the waltz?" She hesitated, then said softly, "Regrettably, no, Your Excellency." He went down the line of ladies and received the same reply from each. Is it possible, I wondered, that these sophisticated women don't know the waltz? When he reached me, I said, "Yes, Pasha Effendi."

"Good." He rose, a little unsteadily, and the entire roomful of people rose with him. He escorted me to the floor and we danced. He was a strong man; he held me firmly; I had no idea how much he had been drinking, but he was able to lead me heavily, in the steps. I thought, terrified: the whole room is watching me. This is Ataturk, the hero, one of the great men of history, dancing with me. I am dancing with a god, a drunken god. Yet he could make conversation. "How do you like our country?" he asked. I dared look up into his eyes. The pupils were so light blue as to be almost colorless; it was like looking at a blind man yet one whose eyes pierced you through. "I adore it," I said. "It's so different from Hungary." Was I learning Turkish? Yes, my husband had provided me with a tutor. Had I been able to understand, he went on indulgently, why people laughed when I spoke? I shook my head. When he explained the absurdity of Pasha Effendi and added that Pasha was a banished word which belonged to the old Turkey, I tried to cover my confusion by asking if the waltz was so unknown here. Ataturk smiled. "No, Bayan Belge, but because I specified the waltz my ladies understood; they deferred to our Hungarian guest." I thought admiringly: yes, these women know how to handle a man. I grew a little more confident, but I was wretched because of my dress. Burhan liked simple clothes and so I had come in a long black sheath with a plain white collar; compared with the other elaborately gowned women, I must have looked like a schoolgirl. If only I were wearing décolleté! But Ataturk did not seem displeased by what he saw. And it came to me again with whom I was dancing. If Mother could see me now! Mustafa Kemal dancing with *me!*

We returned to the table when the music stopped but instead of taking me to my seat, he had an extra chair placed next to his. "Please," he said, still standing. I sat down.

Ataturk surveyed the table. "I have a proclamation to make," he said. "From now on Turkey and Hungary are brother and sister. Is not our history alike?" He pointed out similarities. "We have even the same words. 'In my pocket are many apples.'" Pocket, knife, boot, apples—both peoples, he said, used identical words.

When he had finished he sat down heavily. We all ate in silence. He said suddenly, "We shall leave now." He gestured to Burhan and my husband, unsmiling, left his chair. "Burhan Bey," said Ataturk, "I will drive Bayan Belge home."

Burhan's face was a mask. "If you please, Excellency, I should prefer to do that."

"And you may take home any of my ladies you wish," Ataturk went on, as though Burhan had not spoken.

My husband shook his head and said expressionlessly, "If you please, Excellency, I will take my own wife home."

"What?" demanded Ataturk. I was not sure if he was serious or not. "You don't care to escort any of these very lovely ladies?"

Burhan did not reply. Ataturk burst into laughter. "Good, good," he said. "This is a man." He rose, turned unsteadily, the policemen surrounded him, the ladies smiled and bowed a gracious good night, and the President's party left.

We drove home in near silence. Lehman said, "Really, when he is drunk—" Burhan said nothing. He was never to mention

73

this episode. I sensed rather than knew his courage. I had heard that Ataturk had three men beheaded because they would not discard the fez. He was an absolute monarch and completely unpredictable. Not so many years before a Turkish ruler could have said to anyone, "I want your wife for this night." And the latter would have bowed deeply and replied, "As you wish, Pasha. It is my honor." Indeed, any other man would have served his wife on a silver platter to Ataturk. But Burhan had stood up to him.

In the back of the car Yakob said to me softly, "My dear, you handled yourself well." And then, stroking his mustache as though it were all his doing, "I think he approves of you."

For days I was intoxicated by the thought. But if Ataturk liked me, there was no evidence of it in the next weeks. I was presented to Ismet Inonu, the Prime Minister, and his wife, and to his mother, a bubbling little old lady who refused to give up her veil. "I am an old Turkish woman and I stay as I am," she would say. "If Ataturk wants to behead me, let him. What will he get? Only an old woman's head." On Wednesday afternoons she served tea for the wives of government officials, and I would sit at her feet, chattering in broken Turkish while she listened, chuckling. There I learned that in Turkey one never said all went well; one only complained about one's house, one's servants, one's husband. Otherwise Allah punished you for the sin of pride. Each morning I rode Fatushka, sometimes to the very grounds of the palace, wondering what I would do if Ataturk himself suddenly appeared at a window and beckoned to me. Sometimes I had tea with Sir Percy and Lady Loren and listened entranced as he told me dramatic stories from British history, or of his days in Cairo. Outside Turkey, events moved swiftly. Hitler took Austria, Chamberlain and Daladier went to Munich—Burhan grew gloomier by the day. I received long, chatty letters from Mother. Hungary seemed in another world. Though Europe might be going down the drain, Budapest's night clubs were never gayer.

Her letters made me very homesick.

In front of his shop Numad the Circassian sat taking the sun. As I passed by, he said with a smile, "Come down from your horse, Excellency. I have something that might interest you." I followed him into his rug-draped office. He clapped his hands and a moment later a small boy hurried in with coffee. Numad opened a drawer and took out a square of white tissue paper, which he carefully unfolded. Glittering in the noonday light was a miniature hand fashioned of gold. Numad bent over it lovingly. He handed me a magnifying glass. "You must see it through this, Excellency—such workmanship, such beauty."

I looked through the glass. It was an utterly exquisite thing. "Not the Afghan minister, I'm sure," I said, watching Numad's face. "He would not have such taste. Who is it this time?"

Numad picked up the tiny hand and dropped it into my palm. "It is yours, because you are so pretty," he said. Half-amused, half-annoyed, I began, "Please—" but he said solemnly, "Excellency, listen to me. This is no ordinary piece. It is modeled after the hand of Fatima, daughter of Mohammed, and whoever possesses it will be granted good fortune forever."

I stared at it, intrigued. Numad's soft voice went on, "Somebody wants you to have it because it is known that beauty with good fortune is a blessing, but beauty without good fortune is a curse."

I found my voice. "You mean it is mine, to take with me?"

"Well—" said Numad. I must not jump so quickly. He had a key. The key opened a door in the old city of Angora. He would tell me where the door was, but no more. To possess the golden hand of Fatima, I must show my good faith by using the key. I would not be compromised. "I assure you, it is not what you think," he said. There was nothing more he could tell me. He sat looking at me and I sat looking at him.

"Oh, this is ridiculous!" I exclaimed. "Take back your magic."

He accepted it soberly. "Think it over, Excellency, please," he said, and bowed me out.

That night I could not sleep. Who wanted me to have this magnificent gift—simply because I was pretty? And a secret door in old Angora? This was like the Caliph of Bagdad, and Sinbad, and Ali Baba and the Forty Thieves. I was terribly intrigued. Could it be Yakob Kadri's mischief? But he was in Switzerland. Lev Karakhan? I couldn't imagine it. Burhan, testing me? Burhan would never play with me like this. By the time a week passed I was burning with curiosity. Each morning I went riding and on the way I stopped at the shop and looked at the hand of Fatima and went home and thought about it. I could not endure the suspense. I *had* to know who wanted to give it to me.

All right, I thought. I'll find out. I said to Numad, "Where is the key?"

He produced a small key. On a slip of paper he wrote the address in the heart of the old city. "At four o'clock to-morrow afternoon," he said. "Do not be late."

Surely I was not the cleverest girl in the world then. I was very young; I was bored with my husband; I was not interested in what Ciano said to von Ribbentrop, or that a French mission was to visit Turkey, or in Burhan's dark predictions that Europe was finished and the Japanese would rule the world. I was lost in this strange Moslem country. I had no real confidante. Most wives in the diplomatic colony were at least ten years older than I; Burhan's friends, like him, belonged to Mother's generation, not mine. I was treated as a child and I thought as a child. It was humiliating to be the wife of an important man yet not at home in his society. And Numad the Circassian, with his sad, martyr's face, had said again and again, "Excellency, go. You cannot let this pass—"

I found the address in a tiny street that wound like a cork-screw through the old city. It was hardly more than an alley, so narrow that no automobiles, only carts, could pass through.

Its shops were little windowless cubbyholes in the wall, in the depths of which I could barely make out the shopkeeper. As I went by, there were calls to me: "Come in, Effendim, come inside!" The Turks thought it was good luck if a blonde woman set foot in their shop. I passed a butchershop; the carcass of a cow hung head down, blood dripping, almost covered with flies. I shuddered. Then, so narrow that I could easily have missed it, I came upon an ornately carved wooden door. This was the number Numad had given me. I fitted the key in the lock; the door swung open and I stepped over a high wooden sill into a small cobblestoned courtyard, brilliant with sunlight. Lying in the sun, their great green oval eyes blinking, were the cats of Angora—huge, their fleecelike fur blue-white as the moon. In the center of the courtyard a gigantic olive tree twisted upward. On the far side, facing me, was a covered staircase. I picked my way among the dozing cats and climbed the wooden steps; at the top a door was ajar. Automatically I pushed it open.

In the gloom at first, after the brilliance of the courtyard, I saw nothing save a huge window whose light was shut out by heavy hangings. Then I made out a table and beyond it, the dim outline of an armchair. Someone was sitting in it, back to me. A voice said, "I knew you would come."

I stood like a sleepwalker. I would recognize that voice anywhere. "Woman was not made to resist temptation," it went on. The figure turned in the chair to face me and it was Mustafa Kemal Ataturk.

Of course, I knew it all along, ran through my mind, I have known it all along, but I dared not believe it.

Aloud, I stammered, "Pasha Effendi, it is not the way it appears—" I was deeply humiliated. He had caught me, this man I admired so tremendously. I had taken the bait like anyone else. "I only wanted—" I was on the edge of tears. "It was curiosity—"

He smiled. "I believe you, my dear, but it is well that you

77

are not trying to convince Burhan Bey at this moment. Now come forward where I can see you." I advanced a few steps. "Sit down." He indicated a chair by the table, which had been set for two. On it was a bottle of raki and a large tray of Turkish sweets. "We shall take tea together," he said. He gave a signal and a servant slipped in with tea.

What room this was, I had no idea, save that it must have been a private house he maintained in the old city, a place no one would dream of finding him. "Now, tell me about yourself," he said, pouring a drink for himself. At first I fumbled, trying to explain again, but he swept that aside. "Come, come," he said. "I understand." I began to talk, and he listened as I told him about my parents, my brief stage career, my marriage to Burhan. I told him about my pets Mishka and my Arabian mare Fatushka, about Ali, about the way I had embarrassed Burhan with the baby bear, about the Wednesday afternoon teas at Madame Inonu's and her challenge. He laughed a great deal as I talked. When I had difficulty with my Turkish, I used French, which he understood perfectly. He would stop me. "Speak Turkish. I want to hear you speak Turkish." Then he began to question me about my impressions of Turkey. Which appealed to me more—Istanbul or Ankara? Did I think Ankara modern enough? Did I find the Turkish women well dressed? He had established a school for women to learn make-up and European styles. As he talked, he drank steadily.

After a while he glanced at his watch. I had been there nearly an hour. He seemed suddenly very tired. I realized that my audience was over.

He did not rise but watched as I left. "Goodbye, Pasha Effendi," I said. He nodded. For all I knew, he had already dozed off. His glass had never been empty.

As in a dream I descended the narrow stairs and found myself in the courtyard again. It had begun to grow dark, the sudden, swift darkness that falls almost instantly in the Near East. The cats were up now, prowling silently back and forth over the paved stones. I had to be home by 5:30, before Burhan arrived. In the half dusk I hurried through the crowded little streets, smelling of coffee and spices and a thousand and one tantalizing odors, and suddenly, I jumped. A man, passing, had pinched me. I began to run, not afraid, but thinking: little does that man, whoever he is, know that I just came from Ataturk, and that if I told Ataturk, he would be beheaded. I felt a terrific grandeur about myself as though I were a queen who could order a man beheaded.

Then I found a taxi and came home to discover Burhan already there, in his study, reading.

"Where were you?" he asked, from behind his newspaper.

I still see myself standing guiltily by his chair like a schoolgirl. He was sullen because he had not found me at home, but I knew that whatever he was reading was far more interesting to him than anything I might say or do.

"Where were you, Zsa Zsa?" he repeated.

I said, "Well—" I started to stutter. I was so full of Ataturk I could think of nothing but to blurt out, "I was with Kemal Ataturk."

Burhan put down his paper and stared at me. Then he burst out in one of his rare laughs. "Don't tell me such a story," he said.

"But it's true, Burhan," I protested. "I had tea with Kemal Ataturk. Just the two of us. In a secret place in the old city."

Burhan said indulgently, "You're sure you haven't been to one of those silly American films and are pretending you're a movie star again—"

I said, and I couldn't help smiling because it *was* so unbelievable, "No, no, I saw Kemal Ataturk and he asked me all about Turkey and if I think the Turkish women are modern enough—"

Burhan laughed and said, "I'll find out what you've done," and returned to his paper. I was dismissed. "All right, Burhan," I said, "It's a story. I made it up." I walked away, thinking: if I tell the truth, nobody believes me. If ever I have something to hide, I'll simply tell the truth because people will laugh it off. Why not?

79

My visit to Ataturk was the first of many. I never spent more than an hour; I always had tea; he would sit in his deep easy chair with a glass; I did nearly all the talking. I spoke about whatever popped into my mind: the costume ball given by M. Poncet, the French ambassador, to which at Sir Percy's suggestion ("In any other century, my dear, you would have been a queen.") I came as Helen of Troy; the behind-the-scenes gossip on Embassy Row, the dinner parties I attended, my latest gowns—Mother often sent me evening dresses because *"haute couture* you surely won't find in that Godforsaken Ankara"— who our dinner guests were, and what they said, and what I really thought of them. Ataturk laughed a great deal—I always seemed to amuse him. "Do you know," he said, "you have the life of practically all my officials in your hands?" Not because I knew any state secrets but because when he asked me idly, "And what do they say about me?" I told him. He knew I could not lie to him. It was impossible to lie to him; those terrible, colorless eyes looked through you. They had an Oriental cast, for they seemed to turn obliquely upward at the outer corners, and when he laughed his eyes crinkled, the corners turned up even higher, and I was suddenly reminded of a laughing Chinese mask. He loved intrigue. He told me of a busy morning in which he received a steady stream of ambassadors, half of them not speaking to the other half. It required the greatest skill to avoid a diplomatic incident. "But Pasha Effendi," I asked, "wouldn't it be embarrassing if they met?" "That was impossible, my dear. I had each man ushered into a room and the door locked." He took a drink and mused. "I wonder how those pompous men would have felt had they known I had each of them under lock and key?"

I don't think I jeopardized anyone's position by my reports to Ataturk; but my heart swelled at the thought that I was his confidante and had a place so near the throne.

One day, toward the end, I learned that an important mission was to be sent to Cairo, to explain Turkish nationalism to leaders of the Egyptian independence movement. Burhan very much wanted the appointment. For days he walked about alternately hopeful and dejected. I said to Ataturk, "Please, Burhan dies to go to Egypt. Won't you do this for him?" A week later my husband came home jubilant. No, he would not tell me. "You blab everything," he said. I begged and nagged and finally he almost whispered, "I'm being sent to Egypt on a mission, but don't breathe a word to anyone." Not to tell him what I had done was one of the hardest kept secrets of my life. I thought triumphantly: what have the great women of history—Pompadour, Du Barry, Marie Antoinette—what have they on me?

On Thursday afternoon in late autumn, 1938, I emerged from the Ankara Riding Club and stopped short. Everything about me on the street seemed subtly changed. Then I realized: I was surrounded by silence. People stood in front of their shops, in little clusters on the sidewalk, whispering; some were weeping. As I walked on, like a rustle the words came to me, "El Ghazi—El Ghazi, he is dead."

Kemal Ataturk had died in his Marmora Palace in Istanbul.

Burhan came home, pale and wan. "We have had a great loss," he said heavily. I had tears in my eyes. "I know," I said. He looked at me, almost as if I were a stranger. "How can you possibly know?" he asked. "How can any European?"

I went to my room.

A pall of grief fell over Turkey. In the hours that followed I stayed by my radio. A score of people were crushed to death in the hysteria that swept crowds waiting to enter the palace where his body lay in state. He was to be brought by battleship and funeral train to Ankara.

Burhan was at the Foreign Office endlessly, repeatedly on the air, broadcasting to the world in many languages. I stayed in my room, staring at the golden hand of Fatima, with its promise of good fortune forever. I thought he was a weary, tired, sick man, and he wanted to be amused. And I had amused him in the last months of his life.

6

FROM the London *Times*, May 31, 1939:

VISIT OF TURKISH JOURNALISTS

Six well-known Turkish journalists and their wives arrived in London yesterday on a visit to this country as guests of the British Council.

The visitors included M. Burhan Belge, Director of Press, Turkish Foreign Ministry; M. Falih Rifki Atay, editor of the Government newspaper, ULUS; and M. Mufaffak Menemencioglu, director-general of the Anatolian News Agency . . .

On Wednesday the guests will be received by the Prime Minister . . .

My English visit stays in my mind not for meeting Prime Minister Neville Chamberlain, a thin, icy man who whistled through his mustache when he talked, or Anthony Eden, then Secretary for Dominion Affairs, but for two other events: Burhan and I lunched with George Bernard Shaw and his friend, H. G. Wells; and I helped Eva get married. The luncheon was not of world-shaking importance, although it pleased the hero worshiper in me; but Eva's marriage marked a turning point in my own life. It was to lead ultimately to my coming to the United States.

London was a delight. Not only did I love everything on sight as a true Colonial subject should, but the newspapers spoiled me dreadfully. I opened the *Daily Express* the morning after our arrival to find my picture under the flattering caption: "Elegance Arrives From Turkey." Next day Burhan with a pleased smile brought me the *Express* to show my photograph on the front page with that of the Duchess of Norfolk. "Compare the beauty of these two women—one a Duke's wife, the other a Turk's wife," the newspaper asked its readers. The *Star* also placed me on the first page, praising the "Parisian sophistication" of my clothes, and Ivor Lambe, the society columnist, wrote, "Mrs. Burhan Belge is, I think, the most beautiful woman I have ever seen . . . most fair, with huge lustrous eyes and a perfect mouth." A day or two later I found photographers waiting for me wherever I appeared: I was snapped as I left our hotel in the morning, at luncheon, in the evening, and my changes of gowns, furs, and hats were described as carefully as though the British people waited breathlessly to learn how I dressed for every occasion. I thought: they treat me as though I were visiting royalty— and who, after all, am I?

What I was discovering was that the press liked to write about me. Enormous publicity was to come to me in the years to follow and I could never convince anyone that an army of press agents were not working day and night for me. I enjoyed, I was overwhelmed by my publicity in the London papers, but I could honestly say I had not asked for it. And with each day the other women in our party, completely ignored by the press, became cooler to me. I accepted their jealousy but I wished they wouldn't blame me. I was beginning to discover, too, that women fall into two classes where I am concerned—if they give me thought at all: those who are jealous of me and ready to think the worst; and those who seem to like me and to whom I am most thankful.

But it was Burhan to whom the greatest honor came in London—an invitation to lecture at Chatham House, the Royal Institute of International Affairs, England's most distinguished forum. He spoke on "Modern Turkey" one evening, and H. G. Wells, who was in the audience, was so impressed that he came up later to introduce himself. "I want Bernard Shaw to meet you," he told Burhan. "He's most interested in Turkey and I'm sure he'd like you very much." As a result, on a pleasant Sunday afternoon Burhan and I found ourselves in a cab crossing the Thames to Shaw's apartment on Adelphi Terrace.

I was as in a dream. I loved reading about myself in the papers. I was going to meet a very great man. Even more, Eva was due in London any day, ostensibly to join me for two weeks of shopping and sight-seeing, but actually to meet the man she was determined to marry, Dr. Eric Drimmer of Hollywood. I knew only that Dr. Drimmer was a Swedish osteopath who treated such film stars as Greta Garbo and Signe Hasso; that Eva met him in Budapest and fell madly in love with him; that Father was violently against the marriage. "I don't care," Eva had written me. "Eric is going to be in London and I'm marrying him and you're helping me."

When we entered Shaw's apartment, he received us at the door, looking exactly like his photographs—ruddy-faced, his skin almost transparent, his blue eyes almost hidden under shaggy white brows. He was very gallant in the introductions. His wife, Charlotte, was a thin, reticent woman. Shaw looked at me quizzically. "Are you Turkish? You don't seem to have a Turkish accent."

I looked at him roguishly. I felt equal to sparring even with G.B.S. himself. "No, I'm not," I said. "I'm a wild Mongolian from Hungary. Can't you tell?"

"Hungarian?" said Shaw. "Well," he added cryptically, "that explains a great deal." He had read that that day in Budapest "they're holding—now, let me be accurate—the Sixth International Congress for Bloodstock Breeding and Racing." He shook his head. "A horsy country, isn't it?" Quite unaware of his irony, I said proudly that I had ridden from childhood; every Hungarian child loved horses. Horse breeding was a national art in Hungary.

"Yes," said Shaw dryly. "But I fear politics is not." He turned to Burhan. In the recent Hungarian elections, he noted, Budapest had given the Nazis their largest number of votes. Meanwhile he was glad to read that President Inonu of Turkey had just announced that should war break out, the Turks would fight on the side of the democracies.

It was beyond my depth and I turned to talk with Mrs. Shaw. At lunch I found myself between Wells, on my left, and Shaw, who sat at the head of the table in a high English armchair. He dominated the conversation, showing an amazing knowledge of Ataturk's career, even to dates and places. Later Burhan said to me, "You see, great men take infinite pains. Mr. Shaw must have read everything he could on Ataturk before we came." By the time coffee arrived, Burhan was speaking brilliantly while Shaw and Wells listened attentively and asked innumerable questions. Since Shaw was a vegetarian, we had been served no meat. He had a huge fruit bowl before him and once, with a paring knife, he carefully peeled an orange and gave it to me. "My dear, hand it down—" It was for Mrs. Shaw at the end of the table. All through dessert Shaw kept supplying his wife with peeled oranges, which I passed on, but not once did he send the bowl down to her.

Later he showed us about the neatly furnished apartment. On the sideboard was a huge scrapbook, filled with loose photographs inscribed to him. With some effort Shaw brought it to the table and went through it page by page. When he came to a photograph of Adolf Hitler, he said shortly, "Charlotte seems impressed with this fellow. She'll learn better." A news report—President and Mrs. Roosevelt were hosts to George VI and Queen Elizabeth in Washington, and had fed them American hot dogs—reminded Shaw of a story. "It's one on me," he said. "I was at a party given by Duchess so-and-so and I found myself maneuvered into a corner by a little woman with a Scotch brogue." She was sweet-faced and most charming, but she talked on and on. "I became annoyed. Who does she think she is, I thought, to monopolize the great Bernard Shaw like this?" He paused. "Can you guess who it was?" he asked, with a chuckle. "That charming little Scotswoman today is Queen of England."

Presently it was time to leave. I had a small camera with me and asked, "Mr. Shaw, would you mind if I took your picture as a souvenir?"

85

"My dear child," he said. "I am plagued by persons who wish to photograph me for posterity. I usually charge a thousand pounds for the privilege. But you may photograph me gratis, and what's more, Mr. Wells, too. I'm sure he won't protest."

Wells smiled. He had talked far less than Shaw. "Of course not." he said. "I haven't had so pretty a photographer in years." The two men posed stiffly, standing side by side. Shaw said, "My dear, you now have the only existing photo of H. G. Wells and Bernard Shaw together." To Burhan he said, with a wink, "You see, we two don't approve of each other." Then he took us onto the balcony of his apartment and pointed out various landmarks of London. As he did so, Burhan snapped the three of us, and our visit was over.

Our host escorted us to the door. He looked at my hat with some amusement. It was the latest Paris creation, a black straw that looked like an inverted bowl with the bottom missing. All afternoon, it seemed to me, Shaw had been slyly enjoying himself at Burhan's expense; it seemed to me that he had immediately sized up this solemn Turk and his gay, young Hungarian wife, and was having his fun. Now he said, "This husband of yours must be a stingy fellow— Can't he afford to buy you a hat with a crown?" I don't remember what Burhan said, or whether I replied. Something had happened during the very last moment of lunch which made it difficult for me not to giggle each time Shaw looked at me. I wore a silk suit and had had the greatest trouble keeping my napkin on my lap. Twice it had slipped to the floor. Each time Shaw and Wells both bent down gallantly to retrieve it. The second time I almost squealed; someone had deliberately pinched my leg. The napkin was back on my lap; I looked indignantly at Mr. Shaw on my right, and Mr. Wells on my left: their faces were the faces of utterly innocent men, whose only interest at the moment was in my husband's complicated explanation of Turkish land reform. To this day I don't know which one it was. I like to think that it was Mr. Shaw.

Eva, when she arrived, could think of nothing but Dr. Eric Drimmer. When I met him a few hours later, on his arrival from Monte Carlo where he had been treating patients at the Sporting Club, I could understand. He was impossibly handsome; he stood six foot four, he was golden-haired and blue-eyed, and he could charm the dead. "I almost didn't meet him," Eva confided to me when we had a moment alone. She and Magda had been invited to a late party at Grandmother's house, but Eva had been too tired to go. Instead she undressed, creamed her face and hands, drew on a pair of protecting gloves, and settled into bed with a book and a plate of salami and scallions. She had been happily munching and reading while the radio blared dance music, when the telephone rang. "Eva," came Magda's breathless voice, "the most beautiful man in the world is here! Get dressed and come right over!"

Eva protested, but in the end went. "And there he was— God, so beautiful, and me reeking of onions." It was love at first sight. In Hungary where men are dark-haired and at most five feet eight or ten inches, Eric caused a sensation. No one had ever seen a man like him before. Eva had returned from the party murmuring dazedly, "I am mad, mad—don't talk to me because I can't see any more, I can only see his blue eyes!"

Obviously there was no stopping her. She and Eric would be married immediately and leave at once for Hollywood. "Someone from the family must stand up with me," she said. If I helped share the guilt, perhaps she would find it easier to face Father. "Of course I will," I said. "If Papa won't give you away, I will."

Burhan and I stood beside them as the registrar droned out the marriage service in a little anteroom outside the Registry Office. We said goodbye at Victoria Station, where the boat train waited to take them to Southampton and America. I will never forget the picture they made, as they stood together: Eric, bare-headed in the bright June sun, towering over Eva and waving to us; and Eva, in her trim little black traveling suit, petite, blonde, and so ravishingly beautiful, looking adoringly up at him, bewitched and mesmerized and drunk with love.

I put my arm in my husband's as we turned away. How I envied my sister!

7

ALMOST two years later to the day, June 3, 1941, I arrived in New York en route to Hollywood to rescue Eva from her unhappy marriage to Eric Drimmer. If this seems ironic, it is the way life unfolds. I helped get Eva into it; now I wanted to help get her out of it. Not that she could not have parted from Dr. Drimmer without my aid, for Eva is both strong-willed and resourceful; but rather, that in moments of crisis, the Gabors are not four or five, but one. Mother and Father would have come, too, but Europe was at war, they could not leave Hungary. Thanks to my diplomatic passport, I was able to travel.

In these two years my own marriage, doomed from the beginning, had begun to crumble. Burhan and I had drawn further and further apart. I spent almost the entire winter of 1940 in Budapest and St. Moritz with Mother, to his intense annoyance. "She takes you away from me," he complained. "I have no wife." He would add bitterly, "She influences you too much—we can't even have a baby unless she approves." He was right. Mother wasn't ready to be a grandmother yet. Poor Burhan! I gave him a difficult time.

It was in the midst of these recriminations that Mother began sending me the despairing letters she received from Eva. Eva was under contract to Paramount, producers spoke of her as a new Madeleine Carroll, but she was unhappy with Eric, she hated housekeeping, she missed Budapest, she was lonely— "If only Zsa Zsa could come for a visit," she wrote. She sent along glamorous stills taken on the Paramount set.

I have always found Eva more beautiful than myself. I looked at her photographs. I thought of Hollywood and there was no living with me. What was I doing sitting in Ankara, Turkey, twiddling my thumbs? Ataturk was dead and with his death a great excitement had gone out of my life. I was bored with my husband, he was bored with me—and Eva needed me.

Mother said, "Why *don't* you visit her? You can travel. If you're not happy, take the trip. It will give you a vacation from Burhan and then you can judge better what to do."

The more I thought, the more attractive the idea seemed. Eva might have been unhappy, but America captured my imagination at this period. I had come to know my first honest-to-goodness Americans, Larry and Peggy Thaw of New York. They came through Ankara on a romantic expedition, following the ancient overland route to India taken by silk caravans before Marco Polo. Lawrence Copley Thaw was a big jovial bear of a man—charming, expansive, generous, a writer-photographer whose wife was chic, darling and independent; they traveled in luxury, in a forty-foot air-conditioned Land Yacht, accompanied by a retinue of trucks carrying ten tons of supplies: drinking water, canned food, camping and photographic equipment. Larry, whose report would appear in the *National Geographic Magazine*, wanted permission to go into the remote Taurus Mountains to photograph tribes who lived then much as they had a hundred years before. The Foreign Office was happy to co-operate; but suppose these Americans, in their eagerness to photograph picturesque, backward Turkey, completely ignored the new Turkey? At the request of the Foreign Office, Burhan agreed to accompany the Thaws. I jumped at the chance. "Oh, Burhan, if you ever loved me, please, please, let me go, too." He finally said yes.

During the two weeks of the trip, a new world opened to me. I had seen Americans in films, I had watched them dance in night clubs, but I had had no real contact with them. The Thaws behaved as I thought no one dared behave—with such freedom, such simplicity, such lack of self-consciousness. They seemed to have come from another planet. They were fresh, frank, warmhearted, impulsive; they laughed and jested and joked. Here was none of Burhan's Prussian formality or Father's outraged propriety or even the tired cynicism of the Hungarian intellectuals I used to meet at Grandmother's. These Americans were completely open—they had nothing to hide—they could be naive, even childlike, without feeling themselves fools or delinquents. They were *free*. If all Americans are like this, I thought, then America is the place for me. That is where I belong. I took to the Thaws with all my heart. By the time we got back to Ankara, I felt much closer to Larry and Peggy than to my solemn husband who carried the weight of the world on his shoulders.

Before I bid them boodbye, I said, almost jokingly to Larry, "Maybe I'll come to America one of these days—I have a sister in Hollywood. Do you think I'll like it?"

Larry put his arm around me. "Honey doll, I'll write a note to some friends of mine, the Rathbones, in Hollywood. Basil and Ouida know everyone and they'll give you a wonderful time. How's that?"

When I got up enough courage, I approached Burhan. "Burhan, please let me go to visit Eva for a few months—she's so lonely there."

Burhan would not hear of it. "If you go to America, you go with me."

We did not talk about it again. But I made up my mind. Once more the pattern showed. *Don't* lament—act! I lied to Burhan. I told him that I wanted to visit my parents for a month. He allowed me to do so. But in Budapest I was faced with a problem if I wanted to go to America: could I, as the wife of Burhan Belge, who regularly attacked the Axis in his broadcasts, obtain a visa for travel across Axis-occupied Europe to Lisbon, where the Clipper left for the United States? And if I was granted the visa, would it be wise to take that route? Or would it not be safer to leave Europe through the back door, by the Orient Express eastward to Iraq, then by plane to India, and then by ship to New York?

The first or second secretary of the German Embassy in

Budapest was a young aristocrat known for his roving eye, who had always insisted privately that he was not a Nazi but a career diplomat. I decided to call on him. Baron Bloch, when he received me, turned out to be type-cast for the part; stocky, blond-haired, with protruding blue eyes, a bull neck, and a fine saber cut on his right cheek. He was the soul of courtesy. "*Bitte schön*, Frau Belge, I would so like to help you, but this is rather delicate—" He lowered his voice and fixed me with his bulging blue eyes. "Perhaps it would be best if we discussed this elsewhere—" He indicated that we could not talk freely in his office. Would I care to have tea with him tomorrow?

When I arrived at his apartment the next afternoon, I thought: only a German would be so obvious. On a coffee table before his sofa was a platter of small sandwiches and an ice bucket with champagne. He was dressed in a blue smoking jacket with a white handkerchief smelling strongly of eau de Cologne. The door to his bedroom, invitingly ajar, showed a lovely room lit by a bed lamp, the shades discreetly drawn.

I sat on the sofa beside him. He questioned me. Why did I wish to go to America? To visit my sister in Hollywood. And my husband had no objection to such a trip in these critical times? My husband was very busy, I said, and agreed with me that a visit to America would provide a pleasant holiday. We drank the champagne. Was I in accord with my husband's political views? "Oh, my dear Baron, he is a Turk and I am a Hungarian, he is a man and I am a woman—what do I know about such matters?" The Baron looked at me thoughtfully and nodded. He put down his drink. Yes, he would cable Berlin for a visa. But should he fail, I would appreciate that the Foreign Office, not he, made the final decision. By his words, by his manner, I knew quite beyond doubt that I would not get my visa. But I said, "Oh, thank you very much."

"Let us drink to that," said the Baron. Now our tête-à-tête become a Grade B movie—silent film style. The Baron's blue eyes grew bolder. He moved closer to me. A finger played tentatively with the shoulder strap of my clinging black dress. "You are so beautiful," he murmured. "I am so alone here—"

He made a plunge for me but I twisted away and was on my feet. I, too, could play. I began wandering about his apartment in my stockinged feet, moving undulatingly like Carole Lombard, the Baron on my heels. "What is this?" I asked.

He said, "A German dueling sword. I love you."

"And this?" I toyed with a jar of tobacco.

"My own brand—I mix it myself, the finest English, the finest Turkish—" Sigh. "I must have you." He was behind me, pressing a hot kiss on my neck.

"Patience, patience," I said, slipping away. "And could you tell me about this?" I had picked up a lovely little ivory miniature from his writing table. "What a beautiful face."

"God damn it!" he roared, and then apologized. "Ah, Frau Belge, forgive me. You drive me mad, and you know it." He controlled himself. "That is my beloved mother." Suddenly he had his arms around me and his mouth was on mine.

I giggled in his face and twisted out of his grasp. "Please —you are such a violent man. And I am so timid—"

"Timid!" His dignity was getting the best of him. "Frau Belge—"

With one swift gesture I snatched up my shoes and was out his door and running down the street.

The die was cast. I would go by the Orient Express. Mother, Father, Magda, and my aunts took me to the station in Budapest. Mother said, "I know you—you will never get around to writing letters." She handed me a small brown notebook. "Write down what happens to you every day—and when you arrive in America, send it back to me. I want to know everything." I promised. Father said suddenly, "But, Jolie, the gangsters in Chicago—I don't like it that Zsa Zsa is going through Chicago." Mother tried to make a joke. "Vilmos, don't worry about Zsa Zsa—worry about the gangsters." But none

93

of us felt like laughing. We were all aware, without putting it into words, that we might not see each other for a long, long time.

The train started. I sat down and began tearfully to write on the first page: "Budapest, three-quarters-after-twelve, February 15, 1941. How my heart aches! I have left behind every one in the world I love. Oh God, have I done right? Mother's beautiful little face was full of tears. Father, the poor darling, was crying too. And not even the redheaded *femme fatale* (this was Magda) could stop crying."

For the next few days I kept my diary faithfully. I wrote that my stomach rebelled because I ate too many oysters when we stopped in Belgrade. I reported that we passed through Sofia only a few hours before Nazi troops entered the Bulgarian capital. I described the frightened, sad-eyed refugees from Eastern Europe who came aboard, who could only speak prayerfully of reaching Palestine, which was closed to them. It broke my heart to see them being taken off the train by police at every border. I wrote, "In a way, I am a refugee, too—" I thought: in a few hours we pass through Ankara and I dare not stop.

When we pulled into the station, I took a seat in the darkest corner of the car. We remained there nearly half an hour and for all that time I huddled in the corner, expecting every moment to see Burhan stalk into the train and order me off. But I knew Burhan believed me safe in Budapest. I thought wretchedly: ten minutes from here are my husband, my house, my clothes, my horse Fatushka—and I hide here. After a little while I risked a glance out the window. I was astonished to see the station decorated with British flags. Anthony Eden had arrived in Ankara the night before, the conductor told me. I felt doubly heartsick. What am I doing on this train of human misery among these unfortunate, weeping refugees? Surely there must be a brilliant ball this very moment at the British Embassy in honor of Anthony Eden. Why am I not there? That is where I belong—with my husband, and President Inonu, and all my friends of the *corps diplomatique* . . .

On the seat facing me were two English boys about twenty, en route to the British Embassy in Bagdad. They tried to catch my eye and I thought: they do not know that I am Her Excellency, Madame Burhan Belge. To them I am just another blonde girl to flirt with. It came to me almost with a shock that a woman never changes by herself: it is always the man who gives her position. It made me feel even worse. I should be at that ball taking my proper place among my distinguished friends, showing off my clothes, the fact that I know Anthony Eden, making the women jealous and enjoying every moment of it . . .

I heard the conductor's high, shrill whistle. The train began to pull out. I had tears in my eyes. "This episode in my life is closed forever," I said to myself. I was full of sorrow for what I was giving up and pride for the great step I was taking. Then I sat there, my face pressed against the cold windowpane, watching the gaily decorated station glide by.

"Look," said one of the English boys. "Good old British colors!" He pulled out a pocket harmonica and began, "It's a Long Way to Tipperary." I had always loved the tune but now I could have killed him! I said sharply, "This is Turkey! Play something Turkish!"

"But, Miss," he said, taking the instrument from his lips for a moment. "I don't know anything Turkish." He went back to "Tipperary." His friend beat time, winking at me.

I sat in my seat and glowered at them. For that minute or two, I was a Turkish patriot. Then, we were in open country. The wheels of the train hummed reassuringly. Imperceptibly, the cloak of "Her Excellency" slipped from my shoulders. I smiled at the boys. I thought: I'm no longer a diplomat's wife, I'm young again as I was in Budapest, I'm no older than they are, I'm a pretty girl to be flirted with. "Please," I said to the harmonica player, "would you do 'Tipperary' again? I just adore it."

I was bound for adventure once more.

95

Book 2

8

EVA and I fell into each other's arms, babbling ecstatically in Hungarian. "What a trip!" I exclaimed again and again, when I caught my breath. It had taken me nearly four months —from Ankara to Bagdad to Basra to Karachi to Bombay and then by the S. S. *President Grant* to New York. In Bagdad I had been held up nearly a month waiting for transportation; I had had to report daily to suspicious police who questioned me as though I were a spy: why was I traveling alone on a diplomatic passport? where was my husband? why was I bound for the United States? I had been on the high seas when the German warship *Bismarck* was sunk; war and the fear of war was all about us. Our ship was crowded with missionaries evacuated from dangerous areas, and each time a reconnaissance plane flew overhead, they rushed to the upper decks and fell on their knees, praying. Somehow the good Lord had looked over me and brought me safely here. In New York, John King, a retired American industrialist whom Burhan and I had entertained in Ankara, greeted me at the pier and took me to lunch at "21." I checked into the Plaza Hotel and fell in love with it. I walked for the first time down Fifth Avenue, and next morning I bought my first American newspapers, to find them as complimentary as the British. There, with "Turkish Beauty Arrives," was my photograph, in the *Herald-Tribune*, the *Daily Mirror*, the *Journal-American!* And now I had flown across the entire American continent— What a glorious country!

So far the American films had not let me down. Yet in

those first days I discovered that if I had come to Hollywood expecting to find a lovely fairy tale made real, I was mistaken. Nothing was quite as I expected it. Even Eva had changed. When I had last seen her at Victoria Station, in London, she had been a cuddly, adorable Hungarian girl, as ravishingly beautiful as only Eva can be. Now I saw a girl so thin as to look emaciated, her cheeks hollow, her eyebrows plucked, her hair bleached platinum blonde, wearing a tight-fitting black satin dress, black patent-leather shoes with red spike heels, a huge-brimmed black hat trailing a long black veil . . .

"Oh, Zsa Zsa, please," she protested. "I've become an American and things are different here." Hollywood liked only thin girls: everyone dieted; she dieted, too. Hollywood liked only platinum blondes; she had become a platinum blonde. Everything had been done at Paramount's direction. If she wanted a career, she must follow her studio's advice. There was nothing I could say. At lunch I had to watch her pick at a dab of cottage cheese and half a canned pear—Eva, who like me, was a marathon eater at home.

The first time we drove down a main avenue in Hollywood, I looked about in astonishment. Above my head an enormous stockinged woman's leg, amputated just above the knee, whirled grotesquely from a scaffold high in the air. "A hosiery advertisement," Eva explained. Further on, a clock hung over an ornate entrance, its heavy black pendulum slowly swinging back and forth. "But it hasn't any hands," I said. No, Eva explained. It wasn't there to tell the time. That was a funeral parlor and the clock was to remind you how time was rushing by. I shivered. Across the street, a gigantic windmill fanned the sky. That, went on Eva, advertised a bakery. Americans understood such symbolism. A windmill meant a Dutch farm, which meant rich milk, which meant good bread. I was still considering this when we passed a tiny lunchstand, crowned by a papier-mâché hot dog and a bun as big as an automobile.

I thought: this is like *Alice in Wonderland*. I am not in a city, I am in a circus, an amusement park. When I looked at the people, the women hurrying by, all thin, blonde, dressed

100

alike in slacks and high heels, I thought: they are not real people, they are movie extras dressed for a costume picture on this enormous set which is Hollywood.

We turned into the residential area of Beverly Hills. Suddenly it seemed to me that we were in a ghost city. As far as I could see there was no living thing. No nurses wheeling carriages, no children playing, no dogs frolicking—nothing was alive, nothing moved. Only beautiful, tree-lined streets, beautiful homes with beautifully kept lawns, clean and perfect, but all so desolate you might believe this a city deserted overnight by its population. It was still a set, but now it was a set waiting for the actors to appear.

For those first days, living with Eric and Eva in their small apartment, I tried to forget my disappointment. I bought American clothes, I learned to drive Eva's little Ford, I began washing my hair with henna to make it red. (Eva had said, "We can't both be blondes.") I tried to become part of Hollywood. But one night when Eric and Eva went to the movies, I stayed home and poured out my feelings in a long letter to Mother. I headed it "Villa Ennui" to lighten it, but I was really wretched. I had come to a desolate, unreal city filled with unhappy, ambitious people. Eva was obviously miserable; and I—I missed Burhan, though I did not love him, I missed diplomatic life, I missed everything I had known. When Eric's and Eva's friends dropped over—nearly all members of the Swedish colony in Hollywood—the conversation was always the same: diet and career, staying thin and becoming a star. There was war in Europe, but no one here talked of war. Today I realize that had my first introduction to Hollywood been through the French or British colonies— people whose homelands, like mine, were involved—the discussions would have been more like those I had known in Ankara. Even Eva's ambition upset me. I was still under Turkish influence. It wasn't chic to be so ambitious. That was for farm girls from Idaho but not for Eva or me. Yet I was touched by the fire, too: part of me wanted to be an aspiring starlet who attended acting school and faithfully followed her studio's orders; the other part wanted to be a great lady, a social leader at those tables sat only ministers and ambassadors . . . I could not find myself.

Suddenly I thought of Larry Thaw. I had completely forgotten his promise—that he would write to Basil and Ouida Rathbone. Had he done so? I hesitated to telephone Mrs. Rathbone. Her parties and her home were equally fabulous. The house had been pointed out to me, a magnificent French chateau-style home high on a canyon above Los Angeles. Because it stood so unsheltered when she bought it, she had imported a score of full-grown elms from France and planted them about the house to shade it; she had covered walls and fences with ivy from England; she had surrounded it all with lovely gardens. I admired such a woman. On a Saturday night, when I felt utterly alone, I took a chance and rang her up.

"Of course, of course" came a rich, warm voice over the wire. "Larry wrote us all about you but we didn't know where you were staying." There was a pause. "Are you busy later this evening?"

I told her the truth.

"Well, then, come over!" she said. She told me the address. "I'm giving a party for the Gilbert Millers—he's the producer—and we'd love to have you."

At ten o'clock I took a cab to Bellagio Road, in Bel Air. We climbed a winding mountain road until we reached her home. When the butler opened the door, she came forward to greet me—a plump, handsome woman. I stood uncertainly for a moment. Over her shoulder I saw an enormous room filled with people.

"Come in, my dear," she said. She looked at me. "Why, you're beautiful!" she exclaimed. "Larry warned us, but I said to myself, he's exaggerating the way all men do." She led me inside. I looked about, wide-eyed. Mrs. Rathbone had assembled under one roof every celebrity I have ever read about. Dazedly I recognized some of them: Ethel Barrymore and Laurence Olivier and Grand Duchess Marie of Russia and Artur Rubinstein. Mrs. Rathbone had me by the arm.

"How shall I introduce you? Mrs. Belge or Miss Gabor?"
I took my first step toward independence. "Miss Gabor,"
I said, but added weakly, "I'm terrified, Mrs. Rathbone. Look
who's here—"

"Nonsense," said Ouida, with a laugh. "I'll let you in on a
secret, my dear. There's no one here as exciting as you. Now,
let me take you around." I regained a little of my confidence
as the introductions flowed. "Lady Mendl, may I present Zsa
Zsa Gabor . . . Mr. Cole Porter—Zsa Zsa Gabor . . . Mr.
Clifton Webb—Zsa Zsa Gabor." I met Vivian Leigh, Sylvia
Fairbanks, Barbara Hutton, David Niven, Florence Vidor,
Cary Grant . . .

I was a success that night. Men surrounded me, women
joined me in laughter. I waltzed with Douglas Fairbanks, Jr.,
and tangoed with Eric Rothschild. I chattered in French with
Igor Stravinsky and in German with Jascha Heifetz, I was
courted, dated, complimented, I found myself in the center
of laughing listeners—everywhere Ouida took me that memorable evening people enveloped me in warmth and cordiality.
When I left, I kissed Ouida. "You can't imagine what this
has meant to me," I said gratefully. "I never dreamed it could
happen in this city."

"I told you," Ouida said. "No one so beautiful should ever
be terrified, my dear. Don't you know that with your beauty
you can storm a fortress and conquer it?"

I meant what I said to her. Hollywood had shown its other
side to me. That night I looked in the mirror. I saw my face,
pale white compared to the faces tanned by tennis and
swimming that had been there tonight. My hair was tawny
red, my eyes hazel brown. "Such coloring!" Ouida had said.
Thinking of her words, thinking of my success, I glowed, as I
had so many years ago when the boys at St. Stephen's shouted
after me. "Zsa Zsa, look at me. . . . pretty Zsa Zsa . . ." Yes,
I thought. It makes me happy to be admired. It is like food
and drink to me.

I think when I fell asleep that night I was content for the
first time in Hollywood.

A few evenings later I went to a Malibu Beach party. It was much as Eva had told me I might expect—up to a point. There were at least eight couples, and Eva and Eric drove me to our host's beach house, an elaborate, rambling, two-story structure with a terrace from which you could see the vast expanse of the Pacific. It was a soft, cloudless night and our host was a famous producer, said to be one of the most powerful men in Hollywood. Mr. Cord, which is not his real name, was known for the beautiful film stars he escorted to opening nights.

We swam in the warm ocean under a full August moon; we sat around a roaring bonfire in our swimming suits, eating barbecued steak. While the others began playing charades, which I did not like, I went into the house for a moment and then, on impulse, out on the terrace to see the moonlight play on the water. I heard a sound and pulled back. "Oh," I said, "I beg your pardon." Mr. Cord was sitting there, staring out to sea.

"Good evening," he said. He rose unsteadily. I saw that he had been drinking. His next words astonished me. "So you found me," he said. "How'd you know I was out here?" I tried to explain, but he went on speaking and what he said was unmistakably clear. He wanted me to make love to him.

I didn't know what to say—he was our host and a distinguished man, and perhaps this was an American way of pulling my leg—so I laughed nervously and began backing out. We were alone, everyone else was down on the beach.

He followed me. "I'm asking you," he said.

"I really must get back—" I began brightly.

He burst into laughter. "Sit down, my dear," he said. He was quite cordial. I thought: it *is* a joke; and rather bravely I took a chair. He made his way to a chaise longue and sat down, hard, on it. He stared at me. I realized suddenly that he was quite drunk. "Look, baby—" he began, and then, unexpectedly, he was red-faced and angry. "How much?" he demanded. "I'll pay it— I'm no piker!" He pulled out a fistful of bills and began flinging them at me. Hundred-dollar bills fell all about me. "Is that what you want? There's plenty more where that comes from—take it!"

I sat there saying to myself: it can't be possible. I am not seeing this, I am dreaming it. Then panic swept me. I found myself on my feet and fled out of the room into the back yard and flung myself into Eva's car. I had taken only a few lessons, my hand shook so that I could hardly turn the key, but I started the car, shot out of the driveway into Pacific Palisades, and drove wildly down the wide avenue, weaving in and out of the heavy traffic. My tears almost blinded me. That this man, this Hollywood man, should think I came to his house and followed him to his room to make love to him —how dared he! That this vulgar man with his arrogance, his money, should think he could buy me as he buys a tart . . . All the grandeur I had built about myself flooded back upon me. I was Madame Burhan Belge, friend of Ataturk and Inonu and Sir Percy, treated like royalty in Vienna, London, Ankara —how dared he! Just because he ruled Hollywood? I had known men who ruled countries!

I cried like a child behind the wheel. I still have no idea how I got home that night, whether I drove all the way as I was, in my bathing suit, or left the car and took a cab. I only knew that I would rather have killed myself with the car than remain in that house one second more.

Three months after my arrival Eva separated from Eric. I encouraged her to go through with what she knew was inevitable. Again and again I said, "Darling, if it isn't working out, why stay?" Eva said, with a sad smile, "You are a fine one to give advice." She was right, of course. The day we moved out and took a cozy, little $75-a-month bungalow in the Hollywood hills, I wrote Burhan asking for a divorce. His reply—I could have what I desired; he, too, knew that our marriage was over—came the week of Pearl Harbor. Now there was no return for me even if I wished it.

But by then I did not wish it. I had met a man.

9

IT WAS a dinner party and I remember the dress I wore: shimmering dark blue satin with turquoise embroidery. As we swept into Ciro's, I was on the arm of Gregson Bautzer, the attorney, one of Hollywood's handsomest bachelors, and Eva was behind me with Bentley Ryan, Greg's law partner and like him, striking enough to decorate a magazine cover. We made an exciting entrance, and I thought: why not? We are an attractive foursome, and it's only right that people should stare and buzz as we take our table. I was in high spirits. Louella Parsons had given me my first notice. "Eva Gabor has every reason to rave about her sister, Zsa Zsa. We've just met Mrs. Burhan Belge and she's even prettier than Eva told us!"

I looked up just as a couple came into the entrance foyer. The girl was a beautiful Hollywood star. I gaped at her. Then my eyes moved to the man. He stood there for a moment: a tall, erect, sun-tanned man with gray hair showing white at the temples in sharp contrast to his dark skin. He stood there looking like a wild Indian, with upturned greenish eyes, high cheekbones—a beautiful, distinguished figure who might have been a diplomat. It flashed through my mind: that is how I first saw Kemal Ataturk, framed in an entrance, surveying the crowd; and I thought: it's absurd but he *looks* like Ataturk —the same finely shaped head, the same almost colorless eyes that crinkle when he smiles and turn up, Chinese fashion, at the corners, the same military bearing, the same air of command—

I found myself thinking: this man I could marry. I was a

little shocked: I have no idea where the thought came from. It was almost as though it had been whispered in my ear. I turned to Greg. "Who is that?" I asked.

Greg said, "That's Conrad Hilton, the hotel man."

I had never heard the name before. Why does he have to be a hotel man, I thought. Why couldn't he be a diplomat, or a political leader?

I watched as the headwaiter led the couple directly to our table. "Connie's a friend of Joe Drown, sitting opposite us," Greg explained, as they approached. "They're joining us." There were two unoccupied chairs to my left. Mr. Hilton looked at me and inclined his head with a quick smile. "Do you mind, Ma'am?" he asked. It was a flat American accent that was new to me. He helped the girl with him into her chair and then sat down next to me.

Greg made the introductions. For a few minutes nothing happened. Everyone spoke to everyone else. Mr. Hilton turned unexpectedly to me. "Would you care to dance?" he asked abruptly.

I rose and danced with him. He was slender and muscular, a tall man who towered over me. He was at least six foot two to my five foot four. We spoke, but I remember little of it. I thought: how familiar he looks, as though he belonged to our family. The same bone structure of the face, like Father, the same strong features and firm jaw, the same color eyes, the close-cropped gray mustache—suddenly it seemed to me that this man looked like Ataturk, like Father, like a wild Indian, like a cowboy, like Uncle Sam—he looked like everything I wanted, and I had met him only a few minutes ago. He said, "They told me to expect a very pretty Hungarian girl tonight—by golly, they weren't kidding!" I smiled up at him, "Oh, thank you." I had been introduced to him as Zsa Zsa —he called me Georgia. "Can't pronounce Hungarian," he said, with a grin. He spoke in spurts, nervously, like a man with tremendous energy. Now I could see that his eyes were not green, they were blue, the eyes of a Viking. "Mother's German, Dad's Norwegian," he said. I thought of Norsemen and the founding of America, and suddenly all the young handsome men around me lost their attractiveness: this young man's collar was too high, he looked too much the movie actor; this young man with the sleek black hair, his dinner jacket was cut too smartly; this young man was too effeminate, this one's features too regular, this one's smile too ingratiating —the man I was dancing with seemed to me everything that was fresh, hard, vigorous, unspoiled America. Though he was in his fifties, he was more vital than anyone else on the floor. He danced energetically, like a college boy, his left elbow straight out, completely unconcerned when he jabbed another man in the back, so that everyone gave us a wide berth and we sailed around the floor as if we were alone on it. I thought: this is a real American, rough, rugged, dominating, a blue-eyed Texan who wears a ten-gallon hat and spurred boots and always gets his way . . . He asked me about myself. I told him I had been in the country only a few months, I still missed Turkey, and my first impressions of Hollywood. I even hated the palm trees: such long, naked trunks, such badly *designed* trees—they were too tall to have such silly little hats on top of them, and if they were short they were noth-ing— He had a wonderful laugh, he laughed like a young boy, throwing his head back and roaring, uninhibited, enjoying himself completely. He took me back to the table. When I said something he liked, he slapped his knee and roared. After a moment I said, because I had to say it, "I think I'm going to marry you."

Years later he remembered how he stared at me, then burst into laughter. "You sink you're going to marry me?" he re-peated with delight, mimicking me. His eyes twinkled. "All right, why don't you do just that?" And he led me out on the floor again. "Georgia, you're a card!"

He was going down to Florida to visit his brother, Lieu-tenant Commander Carl Hilton, a Coast Guard officer sta-tioned at Key West. "How would you like to come along?" he asked, smiling down at me. I wasn't sure whether he meant it, but I was shocked.

"Oh, no," I said. "How can you ask me that? I hardly know you and my divorce isn't final yet."

"Well," he said, "I'll call you when I get back. O.K.?"

"O.K.," I said.

In our apartment that night I said, "Eva, this is the man I marry."

Eva stopped brushing her teeth. "What man?"

"Conrad Hilton."

"But isn't he too old?"

"Oh, no. I find him so beautiful!"

Eva sighed. "First a Turk and now a Texan!" She giggled, and went on brushing her teeth.

Greg and Bentley kidded me. "Is Connie still courtshipping you?" Greg would ask, imitating me.

"Of course he is," I would retort. "Roses every day—"

"Don't ever say 'marriage' to him," Greg had said, when he realized how I felt about Connie. "He's been married once and that's it. He's a confirmed bachelor—been one for years. Mention marriage and you'll never see him again."

"Oh, you silly man!" I had said. "I *have* mentioned marriage and the flowers still come."

Connie courtshipped me in earnest. He telephoned me each morning—he woke at 6 A.M., an unbelievable hour—and took me to lunch every day and nearly every night we went out. Though he was the father of three sons—Nicky, the eldest, was nearly seventeen, only a little younger than myself— I never thought of Conrad as middle-aged. He was too full of life. It was all I could do to keep up with him. Next to golf, he loved to dance, but always with more vim than skill; once he whirled me about so vigorously a buckle on my shoe flew halfway across the room. He never forgot it. Years later he would say gleefully, "Remember when I danced the shoes right off you?" He never knew how I suffered. After a night of dancing I would limp into our little bungalow groaning, "Oh, my feet!"—and Eva would have a basin of hot water

109

and Epsom salts ready, and help me carefully strip my stockings from my bruised toes, and I would sit there soaking my feet and laughing at her woebegone face.

She worked long hours at Paramount and needed her sleep, and Connie's energy was making a wreck out of her. His 6 A.M. telephone calls to me— "Georgia, I'm having breakfast, and gosh, I miss you!"—made her desperate. We slept in a huge king-size bed and as I reached blindly for the telephone, she would moan, "For God's sake, marry the man so I can get some sleep." The injury to her was double; for when Connie brought me home late at night after a party, we would sit in his car, parked just under our bungalow, and follow an old American custom: we spooned. At least once each evening Connie would manage to lean on the car horn and send a terrifying blast that all but shot Eva out of bed, just above us. "Oh, God, that clumsy man!" she would say. "I can't sleep at night and I can't sleep in the morning. Marry him or I die!"

A few weeks later, Connie took Eva and me to El Paso, Texas, to meet his mother, Mary, a tiny white-haired woman in her eighty-first year, with the same direct blue eyes and wonderfully expressive face. "But you're so little to have such big children!" I exclaimed. For in addition to Connie and his brother Carl, who also stood over six feet, there were four sisters, each a tall woman. "Why, you're Norwegian Vikings!" I said.

Mrs. Hilton smiled. "And you're so lovely—and so young," she said, with a sharp, sidewise glance at Connie. He had blushed like a little boy when he introduced me. "Mother, this is Georgia. She's just come over from the other side." His mother had been born in Fort Dodge, Iowa, and reared by very pious German immigrant parents, and although her English was as breezy as Connie's, I always thought of her as a European mother. He had told me fantastic stories about her, his family, and his early days in New Mexico and Texas. He had been born on Christmas Day, in a little adobe house in San Antonio. His father, Gus, who came to America as a young boy, began as a peddler, going from town to town selling whisky and tobacco to the miners and trappers. Later he opened a general store in Tasco, New Mexico, in which Connie helped sell everything from flour to coffins. The entire family lived above the store. When times got bad, his mother took in boarders. This was Connie's first introduction to the hotel business. All this, to me, was as from another world. No one in Europe rented their rooms to strangers, or had them at their table; and Connie's colorful yarns about gold prospectors and wild cowboys were like the Jack London adventures every child in Budapest read and loved. In those dangerous pioneering days his mother actually used to sleep with a gun under her pillow, he told me. I told this to her. "Used to?" she demanded. "Why, girl, I still do!" She stamped up to her bedroom and pushed a pillow aside to show me. There lay a small, pearl-handled revolver.

I sat fascinated when Conrad told me about his own career, in his quick, nervous manner, now and then slapping his knee gleefully as he remembered something that amused him. I was amazed at its variety: he had been a prospector, an innkeeper, a merchant, a banker, an army officer abroad during the war, even a lawmaker, elected to the New Mexico legislature. I thought: he *is* a political figure, after all. He had been poor, then rich, then poor again. I was overwhelmed by his trading genius; when he told me of his exciting business deals, investing in what others thought valueless, making successes of others' failures, risking millions on this venture or that, and going on to buy one hotel and then another, I thought: he is an Ataturk in his own right, a leader of men who is building an empire too. Everything about him fascinated me. Even his clothes I found as from a storybook. They were so outrageously different from anything I'd seen in Budapest or London or Ankara: his tweed suits pinched at the waist with a belt in back; his high-heeled, pointed, leather boots; his big, wide-brimmed, white Stetson hats, his ties with horses' heads painted on them—even one incredible tie with three hotels painted on it in color—

111

I must take him to a tailor, I thought. Will I dare suggest it?

I read and reread a letter from Mother:

My darlings, this letter will probably be the last I can write in Hungarian. It is being sent through the good offices of the American Embassy. When you write again, do so care of the Portuguese Embassy which is taking over for the Americans. I am sure this war can't last long and when it's over I'll take the first Clipper to fly to you, or perhaps you to me . . .

Please be happy, my children in the faraway distance. My greatest happiness is that you are together. But I worry that your overabundant energies will be even more stimulated by the rush of American life . . . Remember, it is not urgent for either of you to become Greta Garbos in a matter of months. The longer it takes you to reach your goal, the better; you know anticipation is almost better than fulfillment. Don't be in such a great rush. Come to a halt every once in a while, take each other by the hand, disassociate yourselves for a while from that Hollywood vortex, betake yourselves to some beautiful beach, take a dip in the ocean, bury yourselves in the sand, and think back to all the good moments in your lives . . . Consider that you two together are so ravishingly beautiful and so rhapsodically young that you can dismiss that treacherous, cursed, miraculous city built on bluff which is the dream of thousands of beautiful young women! You are only visiting there, you are superior to it, you are free to leave whenever you have enough of it and come back home to us . . .

I have been so terribly busy in my shops and now I am taking a well-earned rest. You should see me, dictating this letter from my bed to Ilonka, who is nice enough to sacrifice her Sunday afternoon. Here I lie on my beautifully decorated neobaroque rattan and green brocaded chaise longue. My bedding is pink silk, I am wearing a lacy, seductive light blue silk nightgown. I have an Antoine hair-do with a light blue velvet ribbon in it. I am surrounded by a powerful radio, also an automatic record player, a lot of new records, mostly hot tangos and love songs . . . It is such a gorgeous room! My bar table is a dream in baroque, holding golden cocktail

112

and liqueur sets, golden demitasse cups, all from Crystello, divine liqueurs in gorgeous containers, Gerbaud bonbons, vases of flowers—a modern still life!

We are having a party Sunday night. There will be only fifteen of us, for the rest of the family is invited to Grandmother's. Grandmother, thank God, is more beautiful than ever, as you can see from the enclosed snapshot, and sends you all her love, as does Magda . . . I am inviting a few new, dear friends: the Minister of Portugal . . . and of course my latest beau, Vilmos de Gabor . . .

Eva and I were delighted with Mother's letter. The war had not yet touched Hungary, Mother and her friends seemed to be living in a dream world which had no contact with reality—and we prayed selfishly that the war would never reach Hungary, that, as Mother predicted, it would all be over soon. It was good to know that things were exactly the same with our parents; that, divorced though they were, Father still courted Mother. Vilmos *de* Gabor! It was like Mother, to knight a suitor!

There was nothing in her light, gossipy letter to indicate that at that very moment Magda, in the guise of a Red Cross driver, was working in the anti-Nazi underground helping spirit Polish prisoners-of-war to Egypt to join the British Eighth Army. Nothing in her gay, affectionate letter to forecast the fate in store for my family: that my beloved grandmother Franceska Kende and Uncle Seby would be murdered, my parents and Magda narrowly would escape death at the hands of the Gestapo, and I would undergo an ordeal that almost seemed to make my own life hardly worth living. How were any of us to know?

I read the postscript: "P.S. Zsa Zsa, my little one, now that you are free of your middle-aged Balkan, don't rush into another marriage, please! Give anything like that your careful consideration. I am sure you will find your Prince, and a young one, too."

I wrote Mother about Connie. Eva said, "What will she think?"

113

"But he *is* a prince," I said dreamily. "A prince without age."

The week after Easter, 1942, Eva began catching up on her sleep. Connie and I were married in Santa Fe, New Mexico. As once I had stood up for her, Eva stood up for me at my wedding. The date was April 10, 1942. Connie and I had known each other less than four months. Eva hugged me. "And Mama said, don't rush into another marriage!" And she echoed Magda: "Oh, this crazy family . . . !" The wedding took place in the Santa Fe Hotel, a lovely Spanish hacienda which Connie's friends almost smothered in white lilies, hyacinths, and bougainvillaea. Greg and Bentley were there, and the managers of Connie's hotels in Albuquerque and Lubbock —tall men with wide-brimmed hats and the same Texan drawl. Connie was in high spirits. He came to the ceremony with the contract for a new hotel in his pocket—the lovely Town House in Los Angeles. "Made a package deal," he always said proudly afterward. "Got Zsa Zsa and the Town House the same day."

Connie never proposed in words. Instead, one night at the Mocambo, in the presence of Eva and Bundy Solt, a family friend from Budapest who was now a Hollywood screenwriter, he drew out two small, black, velvet-covered jewel cases. He put them before me on the table. He said, almost shyly, "Choose the one you like, Georgia." Each case contained an engagement ring, one with a large diamond, the other with a small one. I thought: I know what his golfing companions say to him—weary, cynical, long-married men with their middle-aged, overfed wives, who envy him because he takes me out and suspect me because I am young, European, and flirtatious. How they must tease him: "Oh, Connie, come now, you don't think that little Hungarian number is really in love with you!" I was always aware of this; later it was to drive me almost out of my mind. Now, looking at the rings before me, I thought: the larger ring is more elegant, it really is, and if this were Father giving me a gift, of course I'd tell him I liked the larger. Why shouldn't I? But Connie will feel better if I choose the smaller, and so I will choose the smaller. Connie slipped it on my finger and kissed me. "I knew you'd like that one," he said. "We'll be married in two weeks." We were engaged.

Connie took me to his house on Bellagio Road, a huge, semi-Spanish, one-story stucco home with a red tile roof and spacious terraces overlooking the Bel Air Country Club golf course. It was next door to the Rathbone's. In all the parties I had gone to at Ouida's, I had never known that Conrad Hilton was her neighbor. "Hire a decorator to fix your bedroom as you like," he said. I immediately ordered a four-poster bed, like Scarlett O'Hara's in *Gone With the Wind*, white lace curtains, a violet-printed white chintz bedspread matching the walls which I had covered with chintz. In Europe we only knew ornate French Louis XV furniture, such as Father loved, or equally stodgy English mahogany. When I read *Gone With the Wind* I fell in love with Early American: now I was Scarlett O'Hara herself.

Though as usual everything moved with headlong speed, there came one terrible moment before the marriage. A week before Easter Connie said, "I have something I must tell you." He was very distressed. He almost blurted it out. "We can't get married." I was stunned. Slowly, painfully, he explained. He held his Church very dear. Because of his divorce, he had seen his priest about obtaining a papal dispensation to allow our marriage. Now he had been told that in the time left to us it would be difficult, most likely impossible. We could not marry.

I remember that we were walking in his garden as he spoke, and that I had to kneel suddenly and pretend to fix a plant so he would not see the tears that stung my eyes. I fought to keep them back. I couldn't let him, I wouldn't let him think that I would cry because he couldn't marry me.

I went home heartbroken. For three days I did not leave our bungalow. Nothing Eva could say would comfort me. Then Conrad called. "Georgia, I can't live without you," he said. "I can't live without you, Connie," I said. He took me out that night and everything was as it had been before.

Somehow, in some way, he would obtain a dispensation from Rome after our marriage.

At the ceremony there was a great deal of merriment. Conrad and his business associates were at the bar, celebrating. My sister and her friends were somewhere in the hotel. I walked by myself into the deserted patio. The air about me was soft and sweet—too sweet—drenched with the almost overpowering fragrance of the tuberose, the bougainvillaea. Suddenly a sense of absolute unreality came over me as I stood alone in the darkness, in this strange little city in the desert, in this dark patio with its Spanish arcades . . . I was in a strange, strange land. What am I doing here? This is not me, standing here, wearing something blue, something old, suddenly so desperately American, in this too-sweet atmosphere, while my husband in his ten-gallon hat is drinking with his cronies . . . This is not me. What has happened? I am still Madame Burhan Belge of Turkey. I belong in a land of intrigue and intelligence and sophistication, with people who know me and think like me—not in this countryside, this primitive, simple land with its cowboy jokes and hearty thigh-slapping guffaws . . .

It is difficult to explain. I judge everything by mood and feeling. I had never been in Spain nor in a Latin land. I knew the odor of England, leather and wood; of Germany, a certain coarseness; of France, tart sweetness and chicness, something of champagne and silk—but everything here, the white flowers, the gay colors, the stringed music, it was all too Spanish, too rich, too sweet—too sweet for a Hungarian. What was I doing here?

Next morning we went to Chicago where Connie was trying to buy the Blackstone Hotel. He took me to see it, quite excited because the deal might come through any day. Then he said, "There's another place I'd like you to see." We took a cab to the Stevens Hotel. On the way Connie told me about Ernest Stevens and his lifelong dream to build the largest, mightiest hotel in the world. And he had done it. Now we were going to see it. We got out of the cab across the street

116

from the gigantic building. "No, stay here," said Connie. "I don't want to go inside. I just want to look at it." For a long time we stood there, and I watched Connie; he stood there on the sidewalk across the street from the Stevens, gazing at it in silence. There was a sharp wind from Lake Michigan and Connie's eyes teared. The wind whipped a tear away. He said suddenly, almost hoarsely, "I'm going to own that someday. Georgia, you watch! Before I'm finished it's going to be mine!"

That night Connie and I were truly husband and wife. In Sante Fe there had been too much drinking, too many people; I had felt remote and estranged. In the darkness and in utter peace, I rested in his arms, thinking: now I know how much I love him. I am content. There is nothing more a woman can ask from a man; this man, strong, virile, possessive, is everything I want, everything I admire: lover, father, brother, protector. I am really content. In the silence, in the darkness, I whispered softly, "Conrad, what are you thinking of?" and I waited dreamily to hear him murmur, "Oh, my darling, I love you, I love you."

"By golly!" came his voice at my ear. "I'm thinking of that Blackstone deal!"

10

I SETTLED down to my new position as Mrs. Conrad Hilton. Before the wedding I had redecorated part of the house in Bel Air; now I finished the job. There were four bedrooms: one for Conrad, because he was a man who could never share a room with a woman; one for me down the corridor from his; and in another wing of the huge house, one for the boys, Nicky, and Barron, fourteen; and a guest suite. Conrad's youngest son, Eric, twelve, lived with his mother.

I had each bedroom redone in a different color—save Conrad's. I was impressed when I saw it. The room was almost Spartan, with an old-fashioned Spanish wooden bed such as might be found in a monastery, and to one side, a lovely bedside shrine before which Connie never failed to pray each night. I made a few improvements in the room, adding an orange velvet bedspread and rugs to match, with copper accessories; but I completely refurnished the rest of the house. I hung gay new paintings on the wall; I redid the living room in white wall-to-wall carpeting (this had always intrigued me in American films; in Europe we knew only the reds, browns, and golds of Oriental rugs); I put graceful white wicker chairs on the terraces; I had the house repainted; I hired new servants and interviewed women until I found a superb cook to do justice to the kind of table over which I wanted to preside. I told my friend Bundy Solt, "This is my career—being Mrs. Conrad Hilton."

"And you don't want a career in the movies?" Bundy asked teasingly.

"Only if I became a great actress," I remember telling him. "But just to be another sexy redhead who wiggles across the screen in a tight dress—no, thanks." I meant it. If I could not be Greta Garbo at once, I was satisfied to be the wife of an important man who was growing more important every day, to help him in his career, to run his home graciously, and to take my place in the society in which he lived.

I don't think anyone tried harder than I to make a success of my marriage to Conrad Hilton. Had I been ten years older and Connie ten years younger, had I been less European and Connie less American . . . But when I married him, I married America itself—and it was too much for me. And when he married me, he married the entire European problem—and that was too much for him. And always there was his knowledge that he had married outside the Church . . . But I tried. I realized from the first day that Nicky and Barron might present a problem. They must feel odd with a stepmother not much older than themselves. One evening I greeted Conrad with a warm kiss. Nicky, who only a few years later was to marry Elizabeth Taylor, said with a grin, "Dad, what must a fellow do to get a kiss like that from Zsa Zsa?" Conrad and I both laughed it off but I knew it would take real diplomacy to maintain my position as Mrs. Hilton—and not Zsa Zsa, the Hungarian glamour girl—in this household. I did my best to be a companion to the two boys. Each morning during the summer I went riding with them. Barron was my little page, running errands for me—I came to adore him. When he came into my dressing room one evening as I sat before my mirror and said soulfully, "Oh, Zsa Zsa, may I sit here and look at you while you make up?" I became his slave as well. Though sometimes I thought Nicky spoiled, actually he impressed me: he was a young Conrad, proud, stubborn, hard to control. The very first day we went on the riding path I remarked, "Nicky, your Western saddle is so ugly. You need an English saddle." I thought of Sir Percy Loren. "Gentlemen always ride English saddles." Nicky turned on me as though I had insulted him. "No siree," he said indignantly. "I'd never get

119

an English saddle. You don't understand, Zsa Zsa. We're *American!*" I tried never to criticize him again.

The boys helped me plan a basement playroom which I saw as a bit of Hungary in Bel Air. I always thought Bel Air was like a huge cemetery and needed cheering up: the spaces were so enormous, the houses so far apart. I called in Paul Klemper, a Hungarian artist, to decorate the walls of the room with gay scenes from Budapest, and to paint the bar in a Hungarian peasant motif. Nicky and Barron helped me buy proper chairs and tables and colorful tablecloths. We added a juke box and games—chess, checkers, ping-pong, darts—and Nicky, surveying it, said, unexpectedly, "Let's call it Zsa Zsa Village." From then on Zsa Zsa Village became a rendezvous not only for Eva, Bundy, and my Hungarian friends, but for the boys and their dates.

I tried to keep pace with Connie, too. Each morning I stumbled out of bed at dawn so I could join him for breakfast. I sat opposite my husband, my eyes blurred, thinking: how can anyone be interested in boiled eggs and French fried potatoes at 6:30 A.M., while Conrad ate quickly and efficiently, glanced through the morning newspapers, and was on the telephone to New York, where he and his associates were fighting tooth and nail to break into the Eastern hotel field. After he left for the Town House, where he used a remodeled suite as his office, I tumbled back into bed for a nap before joining the boys on their morning ride.

After lunch I threw myself into the job of becoming a one-hundred-per-cent American. I took golf lessons from William Novak, the Bel Air professional; tennis from the great Bill Tilden, who taught at the Town House and helped me perfect my game; and English lessons from Helen Vogeler, a well-known M-G-M coach. Like most Hungarians I could not pronounce *w;* it always came out *v.* Mrs. Vogeler wouldn't give up. She made me repeat with her, over and over, "I walk westward, watching the wintry wind whip over the wide sidewalk." I did excellently. "See," she said triumphantly, "You *can* say 'w.'" Just then her telephone rang. "Darling, practice by yourself for a while," she said. Halfway through her conversation she paused to call over, "How are you coming on your *w*'s?"

I called back proudly, "I'm vorking on them!"

At tennis I met Charlie Chaplin and his current tennis partner, Gussie Moran. I had only seen Charlie on the screen, in his famous tramp costume. I was astonished to find him such a handsome man, with a quick, darting smile and an almost European courtesy. I played tennis with Charlie and Tilden each afternoon at the Town House. One day when I was in a low mood—Connie had left town on one of his innumerable business trips and I felt deserted—I turned to Charlie and said dramatically, "Oh, Charlie, what shall I do with my life!"

Charlie looked at me, then looked at the Town House rising majestically before us. "Don't you think you've done pretty well so far?" he asked teasingly.

"Oh, silly!" I said, but what lay behind his words hurt me. It seemed an almost universal attitude among Connie's friends. It came to a head one morning when Connie, just before leaving for his office, said, "Georgia, it's about time you had a car of your own to get around out here. What kind would you like?"

There flashed into my mind the elegant picture Mother made when, so beautifully dressed in red and gray, she drove us down Andrassy Ut in her red-and-gray Mercedes. "That copper Cadillac we saw in the window," I said. It was a striking convertible done in a tawny shade that perfectly matched my hair. "I'd just adore having that convertible, Connie."

My husband frowned. "Why must it be a Cadillac?" he asked. "Anyway, I think a secondhand car would do for you." Greg Bautzer drove about town in a blue Chrysler he wanted to sell. Connie bought that for me.

I said nothing. I couldn't explain to Connie why I hated that blue car—that the color reminded me of a kitchen stove. I wailed to Eva. "Every time I drive it I smell potatoes cooking!" I thought unhappily that my eye had been caught by a car that matched my hair. It *happened* to be a Cadillac. And what was so wrong with that? Connie drove two Cadillacs, and each of the boys had his own car.

Years later I brought myself to ask Connie why he had refused me. He said, "You couldn't have known, of course, but the day before on the golf course I said something about getting you a car and someone said, 'Of course, the little woman will want a Cadillac.'"

I looked at Connie and tried to hide my hurt. "Whoever it was, he was right but for the wrong reason," I said.

Now, I think, perhaps it was just as well that I did not have too expensive a car. I was a dreadful driver. Once in heavy homebound traffic I stalled, started the car in reverse, and forced all Wilshire Boulevard traffic to back up for blocks behind me until I got control again. It was like an old-fashioned slapstick comedy. Another time, daydreaming about a dress I'd seen in Magnin's window, I crashed my car into the rear of one driven by Rosemary Lane, the actress. We both leaped out and accused each other. "Of course it's your fault!" I shouted at her. "Why don't you look where you're going?" A week later Connie found himself sued for damages to her car. He was on a trip and sent me a note. "Is it true that you damaged Rosemary Lane's car?"

I wrote him a brief reply. "Dear Connie: I never, never damaged Rosemary Lane's car, but if yes, let the insurance pay."

He never got over laughing about it. In matters relating to money he seemed to think that not only I but all women were like children. "I don't want you using my charge account except for things for the house," he said severely, not long after we were married. "I'll give you a check for two hundred and fifty dollars the first of every month. You are to use that for everything you need personally—clothes, luncheons, beauty parlor, amusements, gasoline, tips. You understand?"

I said yes, I understood.

"Fine," he said. "I'll teach you sound business practices

before I'm through." He walked away, quite satisfied with himself.

A few days later I bought six chiffon housecoats and two dozen hangers. I paid for the hangers out of my allowance and charged the housecoats. Connie hit the ceiling.

"Look at this bill," he said. "You've been charging again. Six housecoats."

"But, Connie," I said indignantly, "the hangers were for my dresses, so I paid for them. But you promised to take care of everything for the house and these are house-coats."

"Oh, Georgia!" Connie shook his head in mock despair. "I give up."

But he did not give up. Each month we had our battle over expenses. I loved to give presents and Connie didn't mind so long as I paid for them out of my allowance. I bought gifts for his mother, his sisters, as well as for Connie himself. But what about gifts for friends—Bundy and others who came to our house—household friends? Connie would look at me suspiciously when I argued this, not sure whether to take me seriously. "You're just afraid your silly little wife will get the best of you in a business deal," I'd tell him, and Connie's eyes would crinkle and suddenly he'd burst into laughter. "Why, you're tougher than those horse thieves in New York!" he'd say. "I always end up with the wrong end of the stick!"

None the less he held me exactly to the letter of the law. If I charged the smallest personal need—a five- or ten-dollar purchase—to his account, I found the sum deducted from my check the next month. The wives of Conrad's associates with whom we were always seen—Mrs. Arnold Kirkeby, whose husband also owned hotels, Mrs. Willard Keith, Mrs. Frances Moody—all wore expensive dresses, spending three hundred to five hundred dollars for them. I could not afford this on my allowance. Once I tried on a gown at Hattie Carnegie's—a black taffeta bouffant with a hood and copper lace cuffs, their "Scarlett O'Hara" number—and the price tag was $500. "All I can pay is a hundred," I said. Miss Carnegie herself came into my dressing room. "Mrs. Hilton, you look so divine in it, you may have it for a hundred."

Nothing I said could make Conrad understand how difficult it was for me to keep up with the wives of his friends—that it was not I but Mrs. Conrad Hilton who needed a generous allowance.

Yet it was not always finances which caused me embarrassment. We spent our first New Year's Eve in El Paso, Texas, in Connie's hotel, the El Paso Hilton. It was a dull dinner, a dull evening. Everyone was so much older—Conrad, his sisters, his friends. I wore my Scarlett O'Hara dress and realized as soon as I appeared that it was not right for El Paso, for this sedate company. What a waste of a dress, I thought; no one noticed it, no one commented.

At 12:30 Conrad rose abruptly. "It's late," he said. "I've got to be up early to play golf." I got up from the table and unhappily followed him. In Hungary New Year's Eve is so festive—I was ready to stay up all night and celebrate. We crossed the lobby, crowded with soldiers; I saw their stares, how they nudged each other. When we entered the elevator three young officers gaily piled in after us. They eyed me, then Conrad, and as the elevator rose, one said, "Come on, Dad, don't take your daughter up yet. It's New Year's Eve— let her have some fun. Why don't you go to bed and we'll take her out?" Conrad said nothing; he did not move a muscle of his face. I pretended I had heard nothing. The elevator operator grew white—*this, to Mr. Hilton!* When we reached our floor, the penthouse, I stepped out, Conrad behind me, the three boys at his heels. Conrad turned and without a word pushed them back into the elevator, the operator promptly closed the door, and the car descended. We went to bed in silence.

I began to learn more about this remarkable man I had married. He was not a man to be controlled by a woman. He never had need to explain himself; he sought no approval from me; he went his own way. I remember what Kemal

124

Ataturk had told me one afternoon: "Yes, I divorced my wife. She began questioning me—where I had been, where I was going. I will not be answerable to a woman."

This was Conrad, too. He put it differently. "Don't fence me in, Georgia," he had said once. I never forgot it.

In those years, 1942 through the end of the war, Conrad was building his empire slowly. When he married me his interests had been in a few small hotels in the West. Now he was spreading across the country, and into Mexico. I never knew where he might be at any hour: now in California, now in Texas, now in Chicago, buying, trading, negotiating. Once I went with him across the continent to New York. We stood before the Plaza Hotel, as we had stood before the Stevens, and Conrad asked, "Georgia, which shall I go after—the Nacional in Havana or this one?" I knew nothing about the Hotel Nacional, but I loved the Plaza; it was massive and gracious, all the hotels of Europe rolled into one. "This one, Connie, this one absolutely. But what will you do with the old ladies in the lobby?" That had been my first impression of the Plaza when I arrived from Turkey: the beautiful, well-preserved, little old ladies who sat forever in the lobby watching everything that went on. Conrad grinned. "I'll put on my ten-gallon hat and pot them, one by one, with my .44!" The picture of Connie, in his big Stetson hat and leather boots, armed with a rifle and crouching behind first one chair and then another to stalk the prim old ladies with their high black chokers and careful little steps struck me so ridiculously that I burst into laughter. But thereafter he went on his trips alone, and I would come to breakfast to find him gone. I would ask Wilson, the butler, "Where is Mr. Hilton?" "He left for Chicago last night, Madam." Conrad had told me nothing. When I telephoned his secretary, Olive Wakeman, an intelligent, understanding woman, she confirmed it. "Yes, he had to take the midnight train to Chicago. If you'd like to join him this weekend, I'll get reservations for you—"

I was always deeply hurt. I could compete with a woman but I could not compete with his hotels.

Left to myself, I fell into a routine. I kept busy with my riding, my lessons, my garden. On moving into the Bel Air house, I found Ranger, a beautiful, sensitive German police dog. Until I began to lavish love on her, she hid from everyone. If you moved in her direction, she bolted like a frightened deer. Little by little she grew to have confidence in me and became my constant companion, sleeping on the chaise longue in my room at night. But she still remained a nervous dog, alert to every sound, showing the whites of her eyes in fear at any unexpected gesture. She stayed with me as I spent hours in the garden cutting flowers, and sometimes, when I walked about aimlessly, she would nudge her wet nose into my palm as if she sensed my loneliness. Often I would get on the telephone for long conversations with friends. Each day, around five o'clock, I visited Eva in her little bungalow. Here Bundy would join us, and for an hour we were back home again, chattering in Hungarian, our plates piled high with Hungarian salami and green peppers. We followed the growing terror of the war in Europe with anxiety; fewer and fewer letters came from Mother; we tried to keep our spirits up, but more and more I found myself thinking of my family. Once or twice a week Bundy came to the house for dinner; sometimes we went to Romanoff's for a late supper . . .

As the weeks passed, I grew more and more puzzled. Often, when Conrad was in town, I'd say, "Connie, we'll have a nice evening at home tonight. I've invited over a few people." Connie, who had been up since dawn, would say, "Oh, do without me, Georgia. I'm getting to bed early." I would entertain my guests in Zsa Zsa Village—Eva, Charles Isaacs, her new husband whom I liked from the moment I met him, the Paul Henreids, the Henry Blankes, the Ernst Lubitsches—actors, producers, and other friends, and make the best of it. Or I suggested to him, "Connie, there's a movie I'd love to see—let's go, please." Sometimes he went; but more often he said, "I'm tired. Why don't you go with the boys?" Then after supper, Nicky and Barron and I, like three children, went to the movies and sat together munching candy and popcorn, and then like three children we came home. The boys returned to their wing; in my room I got into my robe and went down the long corridor to Conrad's door. "Conrad?" I whispered. There was no answer. I tried the knob—the door was locked.

The first time this happened I could not believe it. It was such an overwhelming blow to my pride! So many men flirted with me, so many men made eyes at me, and my husband locked his door against me!

I lay awake most of the night crying, while Ranger on the chaise longue, her head on her paws, watched me with her huge, brown, frightened eyes.

Conrad bought the Plaza Hotel.

Conrad bought the Roosevelt Hotel.

. . . Is it all my fault? Perhaps I don't explain myself to Conrad. Perhaps he doesn't find me entertaining enough. But does he know how I hate Hollywood, its constant sunshine, its lack of change? I'm a creature of mood: it affects me. What was it someone said? "You wake each morning, the sun shines, you go to bed each night, it's perfect weather, the days pass, and one morning you wake and you're sixty years old." When I was a little girl in our beach house on the Balaton, how I loved the changing weather! I was happiest when it stormed and we had to stay in. I disobeyed and ran out into the rainy woods to gather my little green tree frogs hiding under the trees and bring them in to frighten Cuki. Even now when it rains I love the woods. The forest is clean and I love it so. Nothing do I love more than when it rains and there is thunder and I don't know when the next thunderclap will come, but it will, and it will be so scary and frighten me so deliciously—how can I explain this to Conrad? He thinks I'm spoiled and silly. But my temperament is like the weather I adore—it is changeable. I never want to be the same. One day I love to laugh and one day I love to cry, to be upset, to make a scene. Can he understand that? Sometimes I'm wicked to

him. One night I walked into his bedroom as he was praying and I stood in the doorway in my sheer black nightgown. I was challenging him—can I stop him praying? Who will win? I felt like a scarlet woman, and Conrad glanced at me and said sharply, "Dammit, go to your room and wait for me." I snickered like a little idiot and moved away slinkily, provocatively, like Vivian Leigh teasing Clark Gable. Does he understand me? Is it my fault that something is happening to our marrige? . . .

Now I know that I should have understood what I did not understand too well. Despite all his efforts, Conrad never obtained the papal dispensation he hoped for so badly. Years later in his autobiography I read:

> . . . there were Sundays when we went to church for I went as I had always done, and Zsa Zsa went with me . . . When the congregation rose and made its way toward the altar rail to receive Holy Communion, I stayed on my knees in the pew, chained as it were to the side of my beautiful wife.
>
> It made Zsa Zsa sad, but it did more than that to me. To be deprived of the sacraments was a price I had not truly understood . . . I felt adrift, cut off, spiritually forlorn.
>
> In the end it was more than I could pay.

Conrad did not tell me, but one morning in early 1944 he said, "Father Kelly is coming to see you today. He wants to talk to you about an important matter." He was gone before I could question him.

I could not imagine why Father Kelly should wish to talk to me without Conrad. I was troubled and uneasy. When Father Kelly arrived we went downstairs to Zsa Zsa Village, and as we sat there, Father Kelly began. He said, very gently, "You know of course that Conrad's wife is still alive."

I said, "Yes, I know. The mother of his children."

Father Kelly nodded. "I don't want you to misunderstand what I say," he said. "Conrad loves you. But you must realize that in the eyes of the Church, Conrad is not married to you."

I thought: I have known this but I have not realized it. I have known how silent Conrad is when we leave church each Sunday. Now when Father Kelly puts it in words, it takes my breath away. "Conrad knows that he is living in sin with you." The words came relentlessly. "He suffers a great deal from this, but he cannot bring himself to speak to you about it."

I thought: he does not say, "Divorce Conrad." But he might as well have said so. "There is no way out for us?" I asked, though I knew the answer. Father Kelly shook his head. As long as the first Mrs. Hilton is alive, Conrad is not married to you in the eyes of the Church."

When Father Kelly left, nothing had been resolved. Am I to divorce Conrad so that he can return to the Church? Are we to separate? Is our marriage to be ruined?

I did not know. Conrad said nothing. I said nothing.

Night after night, now, I spent in my room. It was eight o'clock, nine o'clock, ten o'clock. If Conrad was home, he had already retired. Or was away. Nicky and Barron were in their wing studying, or they were out for the night with their dates. I sat on my bed reading, putting down my book, thinking, brooding. Ranger lay curled up on the chaise longue, watching me. She watched me so intently, so intelligently, as if she knew the thoughts racing through my head.

It was very quiet. All the West Coast was under blackout, and darkness was everywhere outside.

I began to hear sounds. All night there were sounds. They came from the quiet, dark garden outside my window, they came from the long, lonely reaches of the golf course beyond. As far as you looked from my window, no house, no habitation, no light; only the darkness of the golf course and far beyond the gray opaque darkness that was the Pacific Ocean.

I sit on my bed, listening. Suddenly Ranger lifts her head, her ears are up, she listens, too. At any little noise she begins to tremble, and I with her. What does she hear that I cannot hear? We are two frightened creatures, she on the chaise, I on

129

my bed, each of us listening, trembling, to the unexplained noises of the night.

I am frightened. I can't bear to be alone in this wing. Even if Conrad is home, I am alone. I can't reach through to him. He frightens me, too. I remember the very first morning of our marriage when I came into his room to join him for breakfast. He was seated there, in a red velvet robe, remote and austere—like a king, like a potentate, like anything but my husband. I could not imagine that I was his wife. In his red velvet robe he was suddenly the Cardinal of my childhood who stared down at me so sternly from the wall. This is not my man, this is not my husband, I thought, this is a high priest sitting opposite me eating soft-boiled eggs. I could have been his handmaiden, his attendant—anything—but not his wife. When I see him in his easy chair of a late afternoon, his glass empty beside him, it is all I can do not to run to refill it for him, to serve him. He is such an honorable man, such a religious man, and he suffers because of me. What did I do that was wrong? Was it wrong to marry a man I loved? I cannot understand. In some dark, inexplicable way the guilt is mine . . .

I shudder. It is like an island, this wing of the house. In my mind it seems to separate from the rest and move away, and I am lost. Fear sweeps over me. I jump from my bed and lock my door, and then I am even more frightened. How will I escape if there is a fire? It is the one fate I fear, to be burned to death. My windows look out on the terrace, and the wide, empty terrace gives onto the garden, and the dark garden leads to the dark, deserted golf course, and that to the cold, frightening sea . . . I am petrified. I can leave this room but it means unlocking my door, and even if I muster enough courage for that, then I must steal through the many dark rooms of the house and out the front door into the gloomy cemetery that is Bel Air . . .

I think of Gustav Romner, the producer. He looks at me always as a man looks at a woman. He is warm, European, cynical, intelligent. When he came as a guest to our house he took in the entire picture at a glance, and being a wicked man, he liked what he saw: the busy, preoccupied, older husband so much away, the wife, young, pretty, at loose ends . . . Gustav flirted with me. "My dear, I live in Malibu— you'd love my beach house." A few times Eva and I went to his luncheon parties. His house was beautiful, furnished in exquisite taste, in sea-blue and white, with bedrooms of beige leather, in his bedroom a riding whip of beige leather on the dresser . . . a wicked man! How he flirted with me! "Will you drive down to me some night?" he asked, looking at me with that cynical, understanding smile. "I will wait for you."

"You'll wait a long time," I said, laughing. I play-acted the coquette with this European man. I teased him. "I'm too much the woman for you." He smiled like a devil. "I know the kind of woman you are," he said. "I know how to treat you." I almost saw him, whip in hand, waiting for me.

"Yes, you'll wait a long time," I repeated, laughing up at him, "until I drive to you."

Now I thought about him. I wanted to escape from this room. I could not endure any longer to sit on this bed, imprisoned, shaking with fear, listening to noises I could not determine, while Ranger trembled beside me. I saw myself climbing out the window silently, stealing across the terrace, walking barefoot lest I make a noise on the gravel driveway, slipping into my car, letting it roll down the incline with no motor running so it could not be heard by Connie, or Wilson, or the boys, or the maids. I saw myself driving petrified the fifteen, twenty miles to Malibu, through the pitch-black darkness, through the frightening blackout, over the mountain in the darkness to the sea, and I saw him in my mind's eye waiting in the doorway of his house, the light behind silhouetting him as he stood there, slowly slapping his riding crop against his palm. I heard him say, "Why did you come?" and my shocked reply, "But you asked me to! You begged me!" "Yes"—his voice, cool and mocking—"then I wanted you. Now I do not. You can go." I saw myself turn, crimson with shame, and then heard him say, "But now that you are here,

131

I don't mind if you stay a while, if you wish." In my mind's eyes I saw him taking me upstairs, soothing me, not making love to me but comforting me. This type of man I knew. One little thing I might say—one word—and he would hate me and beat me. But whatever it was, I understood this man. I knew his reactions. I understood them as he understood mine. I could fence with him. But with Conrad I never knew where I was. I did not know his reactions, he lived in another world with his guilt and his pride and the empire he was building, and I could not reach him . . .

This night I thought: I will go to Gustav. He will understand. He will be the worried, comforting father, taking care of me, giving me affection and understanding. I can confide in him, I can speak to him about Europe, about the war, about my parents, about my fears, how lost I am. I thought: this night I so desperately need someone's arms about me. I don't care what he does to me so long as he loves me in whatever way he wants, but he must love me and be good to me.

I sat looking out the window and could not move. I knew that I would not go to Gustav. I would never go to him.

Somehow on such nights I fell asleep.
But they began to take their toll of me.

11

I STARED at the headlines: NAZIS SEIZE BUDAPEST!

"What is it?" Conrad asked.

We were dressed in evening clothes, bound for a dinner party, and I had driven to the Town House to pick up Conrad. He had come out of his office carrying the early edition of the morning paper, which he tossed into my lap without glancing at it.

Out of the corner of my eye I had seen the black headline, and under it:

> BUDAPEST, March 19, 1944—Hitler's storm troops began marching into this Hungarian capital at dawn today and by noon the entire city was occupied . . .

"What is it?" Conrad asked again, seeing the stricken look on my face. I was thinking of Mother, Father, Magda . . . I could only say, "My God, this is terrible!" For weeks there had been no letters from home. Half of Europe was in flames, under bombardment from the Allies, and now the Nazis were in Budapest. This meant the Americans would begin bombing Budapest—and my parents were there! Fire in the streets, fire from the skies—my imagination went wild. I began to cry.

"Now, now, Georgia," Conrad said gently. "Come, it isn't as bad as you think, it can't be. Let's go on to the party."

He took the wheel. I tried to be gay and bantering that night, but I did not do a good job. Our host, an expansive insurance executive, put his arm around me. "Zsa Zsa, what's happened to that smiling face?" he demanded. "Baby, you can't do that to us. You're a fun girl. Here, Sweetie, have a drink—" He forced a Scotch and soda on me. "It's good for whatever ails you—"

I thought: to everyone here Europe must seem so far away, and Hungary—Hungary might as well be on the moon! These headlines mean nothing to them. Here is gaiety and prosperity, here cocktail parties and dinner parties, and what Louella said and Hedda said and Cobina said, but in my country, all is death and destruction. As far back as anyone remembered Hungary was in revolution or in war, or trying desperately to recover from revolution or war.

I could not rest, I could not sleep. I said to Conrad finally, knowing he would not miss me too much, "Connie, I've got to go to Washington and see if someone can't help my parents get out of Hungary." I had no plan, but I knew people in Washington who knew friends in the diplomatic corps in Ankara; perhaps they could help me. "Of course," said Conrad, "Go ahead. Do what you can."

I flew with Eva to Washington, where we conferred with Dr. Vasco Garin, First Secretary of the Portuguese Embassy. Could he not be of help since Portugal represented foreign interests in Hungary? Early in the war I had been able to communicate with my family through the Portuguese Embassy in Budapest. Dr. Garin explained that it was a most difficult matter. Portugal accepted war refugees only if the United States guaranteed their admission into this country. But this was impossible in the case of enemy aliens. He shook his head.

For the next two months, Eva and I knocked on doors to no avail. I called on dear friends, the Turkish Ambassador to the United States, Dr. Munir Ertegün, and Mrs. Ertegün. "Don't you worry, my baby," said Mrs. Ertegün comfortingly, "I'll introduce you to Gwen Cafritz. She knows everyone important in Washington and she'll help you meet the right person." At one of Mrs. Cafritz' famous parties I was passed from celebrity to celebrity, like a dancer twirled from partner to partner—the young Mrs. Conrad Hilton, so gay, so effervescent—but to no one could I talk about my mission. Mrs. Cafritz pulled me down next to her on a sofa and began a spritely conversation—her children, their school, her servant problem, war scarcities—and I chattered away with her, as was expected of Mrs. Conrad Hilton, talking about everything imaginable but what was on my mind. A waiter approached with tea and cake, heavy with whipped cream. "Darling, do have some—" Mrs. Cafritz deftly fixed a plate for me. "Thank you," I said, taking it, but I had to fight a wild impulse to dump the cake, whipped cream and all, on Mrs. Cafritz' perfect coiffure and shout, "Dammit, don't feed me cake and tea, tell me, can you send me to someone who will save my parents?" Yet how could I blame her? She was warm and hospitable, but I had an obsession and nothing else mattered.

A few moments later a courtly Senator held my hand. I managed to tell him my problem. He interrupted me. "Young lady, perhaps—just perhaps—I may be of aid." But this was no place to discuss it. "Would you care to dine with me, say, Sunday night, and we'll talk about it?" I dined with the Honorable Gentleman from a State I do not remember, and all evening he nuzzled me, but no one to whom he sent me could help.

I lay in bed in my hotel room. I felt at the end of my strength. I had talked to Representatives, Senators, political figures. "Your parents are enemy aliens—there's nothing we can do." I had not heard from Conrad, who was in Texas; Nicky and Barron were in military school in New Mexico; Eva's husband had joined her and they were out visiting friends. I lay there, worrying, brooding—what will happen in Europe? I remembered Burhan's dark predictions: Everyone in Europe will be killed, the Jews will be slaughtered by the Nazis, the Christians will be slaughtered by the Russians, the Japanese will take over the world.

The radio which had been playing softly, was silent for a moment. A man's voice broke into my thoughts, droning the latest news ". . . and a famous Bel Air show place was gutted

135

by fire tonight. The residence of Mr. and Mrs. Conrad Hilton on Bellagio Road—" I sat up, shocked. The details came. One wing—my wing—had burned to the ground. My clothes, my possessions, my precious photographs of Mother, Father, Magda, Grandmother, the family—all destroyed! The voice went on: " . . . the only casualty was Ranger, the Hilton's German police dog—" His words tore at me. I could not believe it: my poor, sensitive, frightened Ranger burned to death! Had she run to my room thinking I would save her?

It had been Mrs. Basil Rathbone who first saw the flames and called firemen. Almost distraught, I got Ouida on the long-distance wire.

"Zsa Zsa, it was frightful—" Ouida's voice broke. "I stood in front of your burning house and I heard Ranger howling and I couldn't do a thing. She was trapped in your room. I begged the firemen when they came, 'For God's sake, get the dog out, save the dog!' But they were too late—"

Fire, everywhere over the world, I saw fire.

All night, it seemed, I heard Ranger whimpering.

I did not know where to turn when, at the last moment, an interview was arranged for Eva and me with Secretary of State Cordell Hull. We were escorted into a small office, and behind a large desk a slender, gray-haired man rose. We begged him to help. I remember that I opened my mouth, and for nearly a moment I could not utter a word. Whether it was the courtliness of his manner, the understanding in his deep-set gray eyes, or the knowledge that at last we were in the presence of a man who had the power to help, I do not know, but for the first time in my life I could not speak. Mr. Hull was very kind: he brought a chair, gave me a glass of water, and presently I was myself. Our conversation was brief. He would look into the matter. We knew the difficulties, he was sure. He could promise nothing. A great deal depended upon my parents' papers. He repeated, he would look into the matter.

There was nothing else to be done.

I returned to the West Coast, my nerves at the breaking point. Eva came back with me to join her husband in their suite at the Beverly Wilshire Hotel. Our Bel Air house could not be lived in. Conrad had already moved into the Town House. When I arrived, he was courteous, he was kind—but he installed me in a separate suite. It was the Bridal Suite. And there, amid the mirrored walls and silken hangings, I became ill.

It began with my jewels.

For hours I sat before my dressing table, trying them on, the lovely rings, pins, necklaces, bracelets. All my life my family had showered presents on me. I had indulged myself, too, buying what I loved, because I adored beautiful and exquisite things, and because lovely jewelry, like lovely clothes, is as necessary and right to a woman as fragrance to a flower. I tried them on endlessly—the pearls Grandmother gave me for my sixteenth birthday, the ruby necklace that had been Father's wedding present when I married Burhan, my keepsake from Kemal Ataturk, the diamond and topaz bracelet and matching earrings Conrad gave me on our first wedding anniversary, saying almost shyly (and hurting me without knowing it), "Darling, my mother never had more than a tiny diamond pin in her life—"

I was alone, alone. The days passed. Now it was Christmas. The Russians had captured Budapest. The papers told of block-to-block fighting, and still no word from my family. I could not sleep. At night each time I opened my eyes I saw myself multiplied a hundred times in the mirrored walls. My insomnia, which began in Bel Air and grew worse in Washington, took over completely. Even now I can't understand why it never occurred to me to take a sleeping pill. Instead I stayed awake until my imagination began to play tricks on me. I no longer knew which was dream or reality. I saw Mother and Father killed, I saw Magda struggling in the arms of soldiers—were they Nazis, were they Russians?— I saw every member of my family tortured time and again. They turned to me, pleading to save them—and I would turn and dance away with another handsome man, or, completely unmoved, try on another necklace. I saw the frightened eyes of Ranger, the whites showing, as she cowered in my room while the flames roared closer . . . A great guilt filled me. Why had I left Europe? Why had I deserted my family in Budapest, leaving them to the fire and the bomb? Why am I away from it now? Why am I not there fighting? Or working in a women's corps, or wrapping bandages, or helping the wounded? . . . My life is sterile, empty, wasted. I have taken everything, given nothing. I have been a giggling schoolgirl while all the world is burning—

I sat at my dressing table, obsessed by guilt, and one morning as I put on and took off my jewels, I looked at my pearls and rubies and diamonds and it came to me. "That's it," I said excitedly. "That's why I can't sleep, that's what is making me sick. My jewels. If only I can get rid of them I will sleep again, everything will be all right again. When I don't have them any more—the wealth, the selfishness, the idleness, everything they stand for—I will be all right again. Hitler won't exist, Stalin won't exist, Mother and Father won't be killed, Conrad will come back to me, our house won't be burned down, Ranger will still be alive— Yes, the jewels. They're to blame, they're why everything went wrong in Europe, they're why people are being machine-gunned to death and burned in ovens, they're the cause of all human suffering—"

And suddenly I scooped up my jewelry in both hands and rushed to the window and cast them out. I watched them glitter as they tumbled through the sunlight six stories to the ground below.

I sat in a chair, wearily. Perhaps I will sleep now.

A few minutes later, Inger, my personal maid from our Bel Air house, came in, as she did each morning, to look after my wardrobe and clean up. A moment later the hotel maid walked in. They spoke to each other as if I were not there. Inger said to me, "Dearie, you sit there." I hadn't the strength to put her in her place. *Dearie!* And ordering me about! Instead, I sat where she told me, saying to myself, "How dare she—"

The buzzer sounded. There stood the doorman, holding my jewels. He had found them on the grass and recognized my ruby necklace. Eva arrived. "Zsazsika," she said, sounding like Mother, "Charles has been called to duty. I want you to move in with me for a little while—there's no point in your staying here alone."

My spirits rose. "Eva, that would be wonderful." We had been happiest, we two, when we lived in our little bungalow, gay and carefree as two puppies in a basket.

I moved that day to her suite in the Beverly Wilshire Hotel.

Each afternoon now, I sat on Eva's terrace, thinking, brooding. My imagination played bizarre tricks. The flies buzzing about me—suddenly I thought of the transmigration of souls. Each fly, I thought, was the soul of a loved one who had been murdered: this was Father, this was Mother, this was Magda . . . *Oh God,* I thought.

Ernst Lubitsch, the great German director and our dear friend, would sit with me, comforting me. A little man with infinite tenderness, he spoke to me. "Zsa Zsa darling," he would say, "it is too much—you must not take on so. There is nothing you can do. You are a good daughter—why do you blame yourself so?"

But I suffered; I suffered in me for all the hurt and pain and cruelty in the world.

One night in Eva's apartment I woke. My sister slept peacefully beside me. I went to the bathroom for a glass of water, uneasy in the dark, but not turning on the light lest it wake her. Suddenly, without warning, without a sound, the bathroom door behind me swung wide open, a blinding light flashed on, I turned, terrified, and there stood Eva, staring at me. I screamed and screamed.

Eva became panic-stricken. "You're sick!" she cried. "You need a doctor." She ran to the telephone and called Bundy.

"Come over, quick," she cried, almost hysterically. "Zsa Zsa's sick, she's screaming, she can't stop!" I sat on the bed, beginning to control myself, as she put the phone down. "Don't say that, Eva, please don't say that." "Yes, yes," she said. "We're getting a doctor, we must do something right away." I sat on the bed like a scared animal. "Please don't say that," I begged her. "I'm not sick, I'm not sick." The more she insisted, the more I felt like a deer who wants to run away and there is no place to go.

A moment later Bundy was there . . .

"You need sleep, young lady," said the doctor. "A good deal of it." He gave me a sedative and for the first time in weeks, it seemed, I slept. When I woke, I was in a hospital room in Santa Monica where I was to stay for a week's complete rest.

Every few hours I was given a sleeping pill. I lay in a lethargy, everything strange and remote. Now and then I sat up, looking out the window. Delivery trucks passed by all day. I thought somberly: will it be a truck like that one, or the one behind it, that will carry me away in a coffin when I die? I was asleep in the middle of the night, when I was awakened by voices. At my door stood two men in white, with an empty stretcher. I heard them say distinctly to my night nurse, "Is that the body?"

They were pointing to me. My heart almost stopped.

"No," said the nurse. "It's in the next room."

Someone had died in the adjoining room. The men had come into my room by error.

Recalling it now it sounds like a ridiculous comedy, but no one can imagine what it meant to me at that moment.

A doctor sat at my bed. "Do you see things?" he asked.

How dare he treat me like an infant, I thought. "Yes," I said. "Of course I see things. I see five balloons, and one is Hitler's head and one is Hirohito's head and the third is your head and the fourth is Eva's head and the fifth is Bundy's head and I'm shooting each of those balloons, just like Conrad shot

140

all the little old ladies in the Plaza Hotel. Isn't that funny, doctor?"

The doctor looked at me queerly, and walked out.

I thought, he deserves it. If he asks silly questions I will give him silly answers.

The day before I left Santa Monica, Eva came bubbling with wonderful news. It was a cable from Lisbon: ALL WELL WE SEND YOU LOVE. MOTHER, FATHER, MAGDA. Within months they expected to receive their papers admitting them to the United States.

It was better than any medicine.

"I'm going to New York," I said. "I want a change of scene. I want to wait there for Mother and Father and Magda." So it was done. I went to New York, to a beautiful suite in the Plaza Hotel, now Connie's hotel. It was spring 1945. I went knowing my marriage to Conrad was coming to a slow end. We had not discussed divorce. But my address was now the Plaza Hotel, New York; Conrad's was the Town House, Los Angeles.

12

THE question that still puzzles me is, was not the cure far worse than the illness? For without knowing it, I was to have even a harder time over the next few months. The doctor who cared for me, an old gentleman, believed in keeping me asleep most of the time. I would sleep away my fears, my guilt, my wretchedness over my marriage. As a result, when I left Santa Monica, bound for New York and a change of scene, I carried with me enough sleeping pills for a regiment. "How often ought I take them?" I asked my physician. He said generously, almost offhandedly, "Oh, whenever you need them." He had great faith in the sleep cure. I can only assume that much less was known then, in early 1945, than we know today about barbiturates and their Dr. Jekyll-Mr. Hyde effect.

Whatever the case, in New York, in a two-room suite in the Plaza, I tried to reorganize my life. I tried to forget. Thanks to the pills, I could sleep. But I remained lethargic through the day, and in the evening I still felt apathetic no matter how bright I attempted to be. At parties, at night clubs, I sat like a zombi, saying nothing. When people began a conversation I stared at them, smiled weakly, and replied in monosyllables. My mind refused to function. If someone remarked: "Wasn't it beautiful today," it was difficult for me to say yes or no. I could not make up my mind. I simply could not think. And I am usually the life of the party, I thought. Now I am dull, I can't talk—I must be the dullest woman in the world. I became desperate, sitting in people's homes, so silent.

"What you need," said a friend, "is a happiness pill."

"A happiness pill?" I echoed.

He nodded. "Benzedrine. Perks you up."

I'd never heard of benzedrine. I went to a doctor. He prescribed benzedrine.

Now I took pills to sleep, and during the day I took pills to keep awake. Sleep pills, happiness pills, sleep pills, happiness pills. I swallowed them as once when I was a little girl I used to swallow chocolate-covered raisins, greedily, guiltily, so Cuki wouldn't see.

The results were marvelous. To be alive, alert, bright again —how wonderful! I had been so apathetic so long, so sure my parents were killed, looking so darkly on the world, that it was a blessed relief to be myself again. Nothing stopped me now. My brain responded—of course, I told myself, I have always had a fast mind. Never opened a book in Switzerland. Knew Miss McClain's questions before she asked them. I knew other people's questions, too, before they asked them. I am Mrs. Conrad Hilton, wife of the hotel magnate. He's not with me much these days, but then, he is so very, very busy, darling. You know he just bought the Dayton Biltmore, and he's buying the Stevens and Palmer House in Chicago, he's considering the Waldorf-Astoria—his empire is growing at fantastic speed. To myself I said: I am relieved. I no longer wake in the morning wondering, will Connie be at breakfast. I no longer go to sleep at night wondering, will he hurt me tomorrow by not telephoning. That was finished.

I swept into my new life. I gave party after party, inviting people by the score to my suite for cocktails and midnight supper. I was full of new, inventive ideas. I recalled the Sunday afternoons in Ankara when Madame Inonu served exquisite hors d'oeuvres which she made with her own hand on a little charcoal brazier, or *mangel,* set on the floor in the center of her salon. I shopped on Third Avenue until I found an authentic Turkish *mangel;* and then I threw a shish-kebab party such as no one had seen in the Plaza before. I roasted the meat before my guests on my own *mangel* in the center of the suite. It was a sensation, though the smoke distressed some of the less sophisticated guests.

Next morning the hotel manager called on me. Had I actually set a coal stove on the carpet? "But that is how we do it in Turkey all the time," I told him, annoyed. "And certainly you don't dare compare your cheap carpeting with our priceless Oriental rugs!" He had no reply. That afternoon I looked about my apartment. I had been right. Nothing here compared to my home in Ankara. I thought of our beautiful Bel Air house, and how I enjoyed redecorating it. Now it was burned to the ground and I lived, like a thousand other transients, in a hotel room. I had always been surrounded by beautiful things. Why should I—really, why should Mrs. Conrad Hilton—live like this? If I could redecorate Connie's home, why couldn't I redecorate one little suite in one of his hotels? My husband had just bought the biggest hotel in the world. Surely his wife should be able to buy furniture for one tiny, little two-room suite?

This became my next project. I redecorated completely. I spent long afternoons in the showroom of the Samuel French Company, importers of superb period pieces. My pride was the bed of Empress Josephine, Napoleon's wife. The price tag read $5,000. It was worth it. I'll have them deliver it on approval to see how it looks, I told myself. It looked stunning with my other furnishings. I was satisfied.

Then I bought two adorable pets: a brindle boxer and a French poodle. I saw the boxer advertised in *Vogue* magazine: she was brought over. She trotted elegantly through every room, sniffed about disdainfully, then leaped on Empress Josephine's bed and curled up contentedly in the middle of the white satin cover. "Well," I told her, "you must be Josephine if you like that bed so much," and I named her Josephine. The poodle, an idiotic, jealous little Frenchman, became Harvey.

I rode high. I was out night after night dancing often till dawn. People whispered when I appeared. I wore copper-colored frocks to match my flaming red hair; a platinum gray

144

mink coat so new that no one else had anything like it; tight-fitting jersey dresses to show off my figure, made for me by Hattie Carnegie—and jewels, jewels, jewels. At other times I dressed with startling simplicity, wearing tailored skirts and little silk shirtwaists, but my buttons were two 10-carat diamonds which I had Van Cleef & Arpels set for me so they could be used as earrings or cuff links as well. People who knew me at this period told me they had never seen such energy, such wakefulness, such vivacity. At parties I was gayer than ever, and when I came home I was endlessly on the telephone. One month I glanced at my telephone bill; it was over $600. My God, I thought, now that I talk again, how I talk! My other bills soared. Decorating my suite cost $15,000. I have no idea what I spent on gifts. I rode the whirlwind faster and faster. If I had difficult moments, I tried to forget them. Sometimes when I entered the elevator the operator refused my command. "I am going up, Madam," he said. "But I want to go down, immediately!" Instead he went up. I protested to the manager. I flew into a rage—the maids were impossibly slow, the telephone operators incredibly inefficient, the chauffeur of my limousine amazingly ignorant of his city, salesclerks unbelievably ill-bred. But I got over my anger just as quickly. The fact that my pills no longer put me to sleep did not especially disturb me. I could not stop myself now even if I wanted to. Often I came home at dawn, having danced all night, and simply changed clothes and hurried right out again, to walk for hours with my dogs in Central Park.

Then came two episodes. I was sitting with actor John Sutton in a night club when a reporter approached us. "Are you and Conrad Hilton considering divorce?"

I nodded.

"Will you ask for alimony?"

I made a grandiose Hungarian gesture. "Of course—I'm going to ask for ten million dollars."

"Ten million dollars!"

"Oh, I don't want a penny for myself," I said. "I'm giving it all to the poor homeless European refugees."

My statement appeared in all the papers. I didn't yet realize that what you might say to a newspaperman as a quip, or to shock, could be taken seriously and make such a tremendous impact.

A few nights later I was at a restaurant with a Hungarian friend. The owner, a friend of my sister Eva, said something to me and I flung my champagne in his face. I was immediately ordered out of the place and asked not to return. No one knew why I made the scene. Actually I had been suddenly reminded of the man's offensive remark months before, when Conrad and I were leaving there. It was just after Eva's marriage to Charles Isaacs, member of a distinguished philanthropic family and one of the finest persons I have known. As I was being helped on with my coat, the man said to me slightingly, "How could you let your sister marry that—?" I almost slapped his face then, but I could not make a scene before Conrad. Now, in my excited state, remembering, I had lost my temper—

I was sitting on my bed a morning or so later talking to Josephine when the door opened and Eva and Bundy walked in. "Children!" I exclaimed. "What are you doing here?" We talked, I telephoned friends, and Bundy and Eva sat on the sofa chatting. The doorbell sounded and Bundy opened the door. A small, slight man with heavy rimless spectacles stood there. "Oh, Mr. Stein. I'm so glad you could make it," Bundy said. He turned to me. This was Rudolph Stein, a Viennese producer, who had told Bundy he felt I would be perfect as the lead in his latest play. "Now that I see you," he said in his soft German accent, "I am certain of it." He approached me—I had just put down the telephone—and said surprisingly, "You're a very tired little girl. Why don't you go to bed?"

I was about to snap, "How dare you!" when it suddenly occurred to me that I couldn't remember when I had slept last. Was it a night ago? A week ago? Yes, I thought, what he says makes sense. I walked into the bedroom and lay down on my Empress Josephine bed. Mr. Stein pulled up a chair next to me and sat down. "You know," he said softly, "there's

146

really nothing so urgent—nothing at all." The light from the window glinted on his glasses and I could hardly make out his eyes behind the lenses. "Nothing is so important. You are tired. You should eat more." I thought again: he is right. I must be quite thin. That stupid maid had been forced to take in my dresses twice last week. Or was it a week before that? Mr. Stein talked on, his gentle voice began to fade away and then I did not hear him. I was asleep.

I did not know that Mr. Stein was not Mr. Stein at all, but a psychiatrist; that Eva and Bundy had flown in a few hours before from California and at Conrad's suggestion brought him to see me; that he had put me into a hypnotic sleep. While I slept they consulted. In his opinion the sleep cure on the West Coast had not helped me. Now I was suffering from severe neurotic tensions. I had to be treated at once. I must go to a sanitarium.

"But she won't accept that," said Eva. "How will you get her to go?"

Mr. Stein explained. He had given me a posthypnotic suggestion. When I woke, I would go with Bundy wherever Bundy said. It would fall upon poor Eva to sign the necessary papers—an agonizing step for her and one she took with the greatest reluctance, knowing the responsibility yet wanting to do all she could for me.

And so it was done.

I remember opening my eyes to the late afternoon sunshine and thinking: what am I doing, sleeping at this hour? Bundy was there. "Well, I'm glad you had your nap," he said. "Mr. Stein wanted to discuss the play with me but had to leave. He's waiting for us at his home now. Why don't we go over?"

It struck me as an excellent idea. I dressed carefully—in my most beautifully draped gray jersey, my platinum mink, my diamond necklace and earrings and solitaire—and with Josephine and Mr. Harvey on a leash, I left with Bundy. On the way out, in the Plaza lobby, a man slapped Bundy on the

147

shoulder. "Bundy!" he exclaimed in delight. Then he grabbed my hand and shook it warmly. "Zsa Zsa!" It was Tibor Varga, a Hungarian friend from London, whom we had not heard from in years. "How glad I am to see you both!" He began a long conversation with me. "I read about your marriage to Conrad Hilton," he said excitedly. "Imagine, this is your hotel!" He went on and on. Years later Bundy told me, "I wanted to kick him in the shins and say, 'Look, I'm taking this girl to a sanitarium, she's under a posthypnotic spell, go away, let us alone.' But finally Bundy extricated us and we were in a car driving along the Hudson River.

After we had been riding for some time, I decided to show Bundy something. I took a folded piece of hotel stationery from my purse. "Bundy, you're a writer. I want to show you what I've put down."

"I'd love to hear it," said Bundy. At any moment he feared I might glance out the window and demand, "Where are you taking me? How far away does Mr. Stein live?"

I began to read to him:

"I was born in Budapest. My father wanted a boy and when I arrived, a little ugly, ash-blonde girl, he was disgusted. But as I grew up and got a little prettier, dear Father began to like me better. I have two pretty sisters. We were well known in Budapest as the lovely Gabor girls—"

I stopped. "That's as far as I've gotten." In the nights I could not sleep, I had thought a great deal about my childhood.

"Wonderful!" said Bundy, then interrupted himself with, "Here we are." The car had entered an enormous park and stopped before a lovely red and white bungalow. Bundy led me to the door. "Go in," he said. I went in.

I was in a completely barren room. A fireplace, a table, two chairs—nothing more. There was a mantelpiece, but nothing on the mantelpiece. There was nothing on the walls. There was nothing in the fireplace, nothing on the table—not a book, a magazine, an ash tray. I thought in amazement: how can a human being possibly live in a place like this?

Suddenly a tall man with a goatee entered. He said, "Welcome to our little place."

"Who are you?" I asked. I was puzzled. A friend of Mr. Stein? Obviously a writer—who else would wear a goatee in the United States?

I heard a sound. I turned—a man and a woman in white uniforms were standing there. They had come in behind me, noiselessly, from the bedroom. The front door opened and a little man entered with a tray of food. He placed it on the table and left.

The man with the goatee said, "That's your dinner, my dear."

"My dinner?" I echoed.

"Yes. You're going to stay here with us for a little while."

I backed up slowly. Where was Bundy? Then it came to me. I'm kidnaped! That's it! For my diamonds! From one side the man in white uniform, a hypodermic needle gleaming in his hand, advanced slowly toward me. The man with the goatee stood near the door, watching me. Suddenly I grabbed a teapot from the tray and threw it at the goateed man with all my might, thinking: if he ducks I'll rush by him and out the door—

I heard, "Look out, she's violent!" They leaped at me, I struggled, the man with the needle shouted, "Get that necklace off or she'll hurt herself—" I began to strangle, I could not catch my breath, everything went black . . .

13

SLOWLY, painfully, I came to consciousness.

I was still in my gray dress, but I lay on a bed, soaked in my own perspiration. I tried to move: I could not. My hands and legs were tied: I was in a strait jacket! At the foot of the bed my boxer, Josephine, lay growling. Then I realized there were other persons in the room.

"Somebody take that damn dog away—" It was a man's voice.

"Not me—" said the woman.

I heard the soft voice of Mr. Stein. He approached me and I stared up into the almost opaque lenses of his glasses. "*Liebling*," he was saying, in his German accent—to me, who had in my mind fought the entire Nazi terror—"tell your dog to get off the bed."

Weakly I ordered Josephine away.

I felt a sting as a needle entered my thigh, then agony—and blackness.

How shall I describe the nightmare of the next weeks, days and nights and horrors that might have been invented by a Dante? I lived in a world of strait jackets, insulin shock treatments, endless injections—and always the unreal, terrifying realization that though I saw what went on and I knew and heard and understood the enormity of what was happening, no one would listen to me. No one came to visit me: not Conrad, not Eva, not Bundy—no one. I felt rejected, utterly abandoned.

For nearly six weeks I was watched day and night by my guards, the couple in white. They literally lived with me in my bungalow, and all day long they played cards. Sometimes I painted. I sat before an easel, while they sat in the room playing cards. I painted, remembering how proudly I brought my prize canvas back from Switzerland, and Mother's "Darling, hang it in Cuki's room—" I wept.

The couple talked about me as though I were not there. They would burst into mocking laughter. Desperately, time and again, I sought to escape. I screamed, "I must get out!" If I was not watched every moment, I made for the door. Sometimes I struggled with the woman: she would strike me across the face, I would fall back, I would leap on her, she would seize a pillow and smother me with it until I was helpless. For days I fought, until I realized I could not escape that way.

I slept. I woke. Mr. Stein sat by my bed, asking questions. "Who is Ali?" I thought: I must have been telling him about my houseboy in Ankara. I did not trust Mr. Stein. "I don't know any Ali," I said.

"Come now—of course you do."

I looked at Mr. Stein. How could he know the hours I had spent questioning myself, to assure myself that I was not like the others here: repeating to myself my name, my birthplace, my parents' names, when I had come to the United States, what day this was, what had happened to bring me here, the fact that I was here. All these were clear to me.

"Come now—you know Ali," said Mr. Stein.

Very well, I thought, I would lie to him. I play-acted with him as I had once play-acted with Willi. I told him the most incredible stories about myself, taken whole from the forbidden books I had read as a girl. Serge, the Russian prince, my father's chauffeur—he had been my lover. How my father had wanted to horsewhip him! I told Mr. Stein every wicked tale—German, Hungarian, French—that I had ever heard. Willi, Tauber, Ataturk—all were confused with Hungarian cadets, the Bagdad police, the surrealistic world of my dreams.

When he left, I alternately wept and plotted. How will I get out of here?

It was my night nurse who saved me. She said, "Sweetheart, don't worry, I'm an Irishwoman and I have a heart. You don't belong here—I'll help you."

I said, "Darling, darling, pray for me, please pray for me."

I managed to give her the telephone number of a couple I knew. She telephoned them; they came to my aid with a lawyer. I was released through a writ of *habeas corpus*, charging that I was being wrongfully detained. There would be a hearing in the New York Supreme Court. I remember being taken from the sanitarium and the long drive to the Supreme Court in the Bronx; I remember sitting in the chambers of Supreme Court Justice Lloyd Church. The lawyers talked. I felt I sat alone on a mountain peak, utterly alone, with no one to touch, to lean upon, to help me. The judge questioned me. Everything I replied sounded like lies to me. Who was I? "Mrs. Conrad Hilton." This sad, bewildered girl in sweater and skirt, begging to be freed from an institution, claims she is the wife of Conrad Hilton, the millionaire hotel owner? If that is true, why is he not here? Why is her family not here to help her? Why is she all alone? I trembled. I thought: what will the judge think? Will he think me insane and send me back? "Where were you born?" "Hungary." Hungary? Is there a Hungary? Does it still exist? "How did you come to America?" "I came from India. It took me four months." From India? Four months? "Were you married before?" "Yes. In Turkey." "To whom?" "To His Excellency, Burhan Belge, friend of Kemal Ataturk." His Excellency? Kemal Ataturk? What *is* this girl talking about . . .

I almost could not believe it when Justice Church ruled for me. "The writ is sustained," he declared. I was released and discharged. I was free.

I emerged, a stranger in the world. When I called the Plaza, no one knew anything about my clothes, my jewels, my suite.

152

It was as though all evidence of my existence had vanished. I was too hurt, too proud—too frightened—to call Conrad or Eva or Bundy. I learned through the lawyers that my jewels had been put into a bank vault. It would take litigation to get them out. I had no money. I could only think of Tibor Varga, who had come upon Bundy and me in the lobby of the Plaza the day I left. I asked Tibor if he would lend me three thousand dollars. With the money I bought myself clothes and was able to move into a small apartment on Long Island, overlooking the sea, with my two dogs. They could give me love —and silence. That was all I wanted. Like a swimmer exhausted after an impossible race, I wanted only to tread water now, and recoup my strength.

Across the street was a small lobster bar, owned by a pleasant Polish couple. It was the only place I visited. I spent evenings sitting in a wooden booth, lingering over my coffee, my sandwich, listening to the hum of conversation. It was strangely reassuring, as it had been when as a child I fell asleep to the murmur of voices and warm laughter from Mother's guests in the salon. The wife of the owner of the lobster bar, a tall, buxom woman, grew to know me. One Saturday night, when her husband was ill and the bar became crowded, she said, "Wouldn't you like to help out?" I put on a little apron and waited on the customers. I thought: this is a kind of therapy, too. Sometimes I felt as I had on the little streets of Ankara, as though I were a caliph of Bagdad, incognito. No one here knew me as Mrs. Conrad Hilton. I was a Hungarian girl, nameless, without identity, wearing a little white apron over a sweater and skirt, serving clam chowder and broiled lobster to people I never saw before and would never see again.

During the day I went marketing with my dogs. I painted and walked a great deal. Sometimes I played Hungarian records for hours. I spoke to no one; I read no newspapers; I felt I belonged nowhere. I was a spectator in a strange world, thinking nothing.

One afternoon as I walked slowly on the boardwalk, a man's

voice sounded behind me. "Zsa Zsa!" I turned around to see a face I recognized vaguely. "Don't you remember me?" the man demanded. I looked at him, embarrassed. So much of my memory seemed gone. "Zsa Zsa—Stephen, Stephen from Vienna!" Slowly it came back to me. When I was in Vienna, Stephen was a young voice student, an admirer of Richard Tauber. He had been in the audience when *The Singing Dream* opened. "How is everyone?" he asked, taking my arm and falling in step with me. "Is your family still in the old country? How is Mr. Hilton?"

I managed to make some reply. I desperately did not want to be questioned. After a little while he tipped his hat and went his way. I hurt his feelings, I thought wretchedly.

I recuperated slowly. From my room I could see the sandy beach and a solitary stone pier stretching a hundred feet or so into the sea. Sometimes, when I woke in the early morning, I would sit by the window and watch the dawn come. I faced directly East; the sun would rise out of the water, a burning yellow ball of fire, and light up my entire room. One morning about five o'clock, as I sat staring dreamily out the window, my heart froze: I saw what appeared to be a gigantic man rising out of the sea, like a sea god, towering, enormous, striding naked out of the sea, out of the flames of the rising sun. My God, I thought, is my imagination playing tricks again? I was dazzled, I could not see him clearly, nothing was real in that hazy dawn, the sun so blindingly bright, the sky dark blue as a painting. Then I saw that it *was* a man, wearing blue jeans, naked from the waist up, standing on the stone pier fishing. I watched him for a long while; when it was full daylight, he was gone.

Next morning at the same time I slipped into a dress and, barefoot, went down to the beach with Josephine. The fisherman was there on the pier, the sun gleaming and shining on his sun-tanned body. I strolled toward him, kicking the sand with my bare toes. I could not see his face: he stood directly in the sun. When I was near, I ventured, "Hello." He looked up, and as though it was nothing extraordinary to see a bare-footed girl walking the beach with her dog at 5:30 A.M., he said, "Hello." I sat down, cross-legged, on the sand, Josephine beside me, and watched him.

He said nothing more. I said nothing more.

When full daylight came, he took up his rod and bait, nodded to me, and left. We had not exchanged another word.

The next morning I went down again. We nodded to each other and that was all. I sat on the sand with Josephine, watching him. There was no one else in the world at that moment—only the two of us, the sea, and my dog. I felt strangely content.

The third morning he was not there. I missed him terribly. I did not know who he was, where he came from—all I knew was that he was a quiet, silent man who came before dawn each morning to fish on this lonely stretch of water. I thought: the whole world is empty because this stranger is not here.

The fourth morning he appeared. I sat on the sand again, watching him. He came over and sat beside me. He said in broken English, "You are American?"

I said, "No, I am a Hungarian."

He pointed to himself. "I am Yugoslav." He had blue eyes, the powerful rugged face of the Yugoslav mountaineer with furrowed lines in his cheeks. I had always admired the Yugo-slavs. Father said they were the finest soldiers—a solid, honest people. We sat silently for a few moments, then he rose. He inclined his head jerkily and left.

Thus began the most curious relationship of my life. Each morning he fished, and I watched him. We met tacitly. I never learned his name. He never learned mine. He asked nothing. I volunteered nothing. I thought of him as the only friend I had. Suddenly it was as though I had been put before the basic facts of life. Everything was gone from me—Europe, Turkey, Hollywood, my husband, friends. It was as though we were the only two people left in the world: I was Eve, the first and last woman in the world, without name, without history; he was Adam, the first and last man in the world, without name, without history. He fished, and I sat next to him, protected, saying nothing, looking at the sea, waiting for the fish to strike. He did not ask me, "Where is your jewelry? Where is your husband? Where is your sister? What are you doing here? Are your parents safe?" He asked nothing, and so I was content with him. He never said, "Take me to your house." I lived a hundred steps away. He never said, "I want to make love to you." Yet at this moment he was the only man in the world I cared to be with. It was not physical attraction, it was not sex; we were two human beings alone in the world. This man knew nothing about me; he was my only friend, yet he was not even a friend. I thought: he is like something that comes up out of the sea each night, stays on the beach to look after me, and then vanishes into the sea again. I never saw him in full daylight, so that he was never real; he existed only in darkness and dawn.

And I went to him each dawn like a grateful dog who goes to his master and sits next to him wherever he is.

Then, quite as unexpectedly, I was brought back to reality. It was Eva, back from the West Coast, with news that Mother, Father, and Magda were on their way to New York.

14

ALL the silly, wonderful nonsense began again the moment
Mother arrived from Lisbon. Although she, Father, and Magda
received their American visas the same day, each had to come
by a different route. Mother had been too excited to wait a
week in Lisbon for a plane; instead she rushed aboard the
first ship bound for the United States—a Portuguese freighter
carrying a cargo of cork—and then impatiently paced the
decks for the next twenty-eight days until it finally landed in
Philadelphia. Eva and I greeted her at the dock. Two days
later the three of us went back to Philadelphia to meet
Magda's French poodle, Canou, which for some reason had
become separated from her and made the trip alone by ship.
Three days later Mother, Eva, Canou, and I drove to La
Guardia airport to meet Magda coming in by plane; and a
week after that Mother, Eva, Magda, Canou, and I formed the
Gabor delegation that waited at the pier in Philadelphia for
Father's ship to arrive.

Thus, at last, we were all together again!

Mother, rushing down the gangplank from the freighter
that first day, was Mother as only she can be. Her blonde
hair was beautifully coiffured, and when she swept me
in her arms I smelled again the divine perfume she always
used. Amid the kissing and the hugging and the tears,
she suddenly remembered. "My God, I must give something to the steward, we were only six passengers and he was
a darling to us." She pulled a hundred-dollar bill from her

purse. "This is all the money I have left in the world. Children, how much is this? What will it buy?"

Eva, laughing, said, "About two hats—the kind you like."

"Two hats I can do without," said Mother, and with that she turned and dashed up the gangplank again. "Here," she said, pushing the hundred-dollar bill into the hand of the astonished steward. "For you and the crew." She hurried down again. "Darlings, I'm so happy—"

"Mother," I ventured. "If that was all the money you have—"

She shook her head. "We have lost everything. All I own is what is on my back. So—" She kissed me. "I might as well begin with nothing in America as begin with a hundred dollars."

Seeing her in that spirit, I marveled, the more so when we called for Father. His hair had grown white, though he was still vigorous; but it was obvious he had taken their experience in Europe far worse than Mother. But I fell in love with him all over again. He arrived, a man who had lost everything he possessed, uncertain of himself in this country because he could not speak English and stubbornly refused to learn it. For the first time, however, he was not too busy to listen to me; he no longer roared and thundered; he had become mellowed, and I found him perfect. Neither he nor Mother said anything about the fact that I lived by myself in the Madison Hotel. From Eva's letters they knew that Conrad and I had separated. But here Conrad proved himself admirable and generous. He came to New York to meet my parents, and gave them and Magda a suite free at the Plaza for as long as they needed to get on their feet again.

The day after Mother's arrival, we dropped in on Bela Leonard, a Hungarian friend who also lived at the Plaza. I remember that Eva and I were in the living room chatting with him when suddenly there was a piercing scream from Mother in the anteroom. We rushed in to see her faint and a letter drop from her hand. It was a terrible moment. The note had been written to Leonard a short time before by Magda, just as she was leaving Lisbon, telling him how Grand-

1. Magda, Zsa Zsa, and Eva, ages approximately 7, 5, and 3, in Budapest.

2. Eva, Zsa Zsa, and Magda, ages approximately 3, 5, and 7, in a Budapest dance studio.

9. Zsa Zsa and her husband, Burhan Belge, in Ankara, Turkey, in 1940.

10. Zsa Zsa Gabor Hilton photographed with Eva at the Hilton Bel Air home, some months after Zsa Zsa's arrival in the United States.

16. Zsa Zsa, Errol Flynn, and George Sanders at the Cannes Film Festival in 1953.

17. George Sanders and Zsa Zsa, after their divorce—and still friends.

18. Francesca Hilton in Paris, 1953.

19. Zsa Zsa in her first film, *Lovely To Look At*.

20. Zsa Zsa with Jean Pierre Aumont in rehearsals for *Lili* in 1952.

21. Francie imitating her mother, posing as Zsa Zsa posing as Jane Avril.

22. Zsa Zsa as Jane Avril in *Moulin Rouge,* 1953.

23. Francie, Bundy Solt, and Zsa Zsa in Rome while Zsa Zsa was making *For the First Time* with Mario Lanza.

24. Mother and daughter after costume birthday party given by Zsa Zsa for Francie in 1958.

25. After Francie's confirmation in 1960, Conrad Hilton takes Zsa Zsa and Francie to lunch at the Beverly Hilton.

26. Alfred Hitchcock presenting Zsa Zsa with a trophy as "The Most Glamourous Actress of the Year" at the Coconut Grove in Los Angeles in 1958.

27. Porfirio Rubirosa in Hollywood.

28. Rubi at the door of his favorite Mercedes racing car in Le Mans, France, in June 1954. Left to right: Bernard Boyer, Zsa Zsa, Rubi, and Rubi's co-driver.

29. Night-clubbing at Maxim's in Deauville. Left to right: Bill Cavanaugh, Zsa Zsa, Baron Elie Rothschild, and Rubi.

30. Mr. and Mrs. Edmund de Szigethy (Jolie Gabor) at Zsa Zsa's party for Ramfis Trujillo.

31. Confrontation in Zsa Zsa's Bel Air home at her party for Ramfis Trujillo. Left to right: Kim Novak and Ramfis Trujillo (partly hidden); Zsa Zsa, Rubi, and Rubi's wife, Odile.

32. Zsa Zsa and the Aga Khan in Cannes shortly before his death.

33. Watching Rubi play polo at Deauville. Left to right: Cy Howard, Bill Cavanaugh, Gloria Graham, Derek Goodman, and Zsa Zsa.

34. Ingrid Smadja, Zsa Zsa, Rubi, Pierre Smadja, and
Mrs. Jean Roi at Longchamps.

35. Reunion in Vienna in October 1958—Francesca Hilton photographing the Gabor family—Zsa Zsa and Vilmos seated in front, Magda, Jolie,
and Eva behind them.

mother Franceska—Mother's mother—and Uncle Seby—her only brother—had been trapped with others outside the Portuguese Embassy in Budapest and killed. No one knew whether it had been the Nazis or the Communists, for it happened on the day the Russians liberated the city and there had been hand-to-hand fighting in the streets, room-to-room fighting in the buildings. Leonard, not expecting us to walk in on him that afternoon, had left the letter on a table. Mother had recognized Magda's handwriting . . .

That was Mother's greeting in her first forty-eight hours in this country.

When we could, Eva and I tried to bolster her spirits by painting a beautiful picture of the future we planned for her in America. "Look, Mother," I said, "you've worked enough in your life. There's no reason for your working any more. Eva and I will give you an allowance each month, we'll help you buy a little house, find you a good Hungarian maid, and you can live without a worry."

Mother looked at us.

"Are you both out of your minds?" she demanded. "Do you think I would ever depend on my children? Come to you for a hundred dollars and then another handout of a hundred when I need it? No, I want to be independent. Just give me enough in one sum to start a business and I'll support myself from then on."

There was nothing to do but agree. Mother set out to conquer America. She and Magda shopped New York's finest stores. The three of us pored over the fashion magazines, and listened to conversations at jewelry counters. Mother decided that American women wore more costume jewelry than any other women in the world, but nothing here boasted the careful workmanship of genuine jewelry. This had been the secret of Grandmother's success. She had created exquisite copies of Empress Maria Theresa's crown jewels and of other royal pieces, using synthetic stones instead of diamonds, pearls, and emeralds. Once Mother's mind was made up, she knew exactly what to do. She looked for a shop location and with unerring instinct chose Madison Avenue, in the Sixties, where she opened "Jolie Gabor"—a costume jewelry boutique, charmingly decorated after her shop in Budapest. It became the first of a chain of shops and from the day she opened it, a success.

Sometimes in those first days, Magda took me aside and told me, little by little, my family's experiences in those last terrible years.

When war broke out on September 2, 1939, with Germany's invasion of Poland, Magda was married to John Bychowsky, an Englishman of Polish origin. With the fall of Poland, thousands of Polish soldiers began fleeing into Hungary, where they were interned in prisoner-of-war camps outside Budapest. The Polish Embassy in Budapest closed; its interests were taken over by the British Embassy. Magda promptly volunteered to serve as a Red Cross driver. Her assignment was to take medical supplies from the Embassy to the newly created prisoner-of-war camps, fifty to seventy-five miles from Budapest. She soon found herself smuggling civilian clothing to the camps and returning with a truck full of Polish army uniforms, which were at once burned in the Embassy stoves. An underground operation had begun, in which Magda played an important part. While it was impossible for uniformed Polish soldiers to escape from the camp, once a soldier was in civilian clothes, he could steal out, be put on a train to the East with a Hungarian companion to speak for him in case they were stopped, and go on to Romania, Turkey, and finally to Egypt to join forces with the British. At the beginning, Magda told me, her shuttle dealt only in clothing and uniforms, later, as she grew bolder, she actually smuggled men out of the camp in her truck. "The Embassy gave me directions, telling me when I could bring in men, when I could only transport clothes."

With Pearl Harbor Day, December 7, 1941, the Allied countries closed their embassies in Budapest. Their interests were taken over by the neutral Portuguese. Magda became deeply involved in the underground in the next two years. She not only smuggled men out of the camps in order to continue her work, she served as aide to the Portuguese Ambassador, Dr. Carlos de Sampayo Garrido, a liberal on the side of the Allies. Dr. Garrido was a brave but ill man: he had suffered a heart attack and carried with him a small vial of medicine; his staff were instructed that if he was seized by an attack again they must break the bottle and pour the contents into his mouth. Magda admired him tremendously; she assisted him in deciphering the Embassy code and even helped put out an underground newspaper. In early 1944 bombs began to fall on the city and the Embassy moved for safety to Tahy Castle in the village of Galgagyork, about thirty miles from Budapest.

"Then," said Magda, "came Sunday, March 19, 1944."

I remembered that day. It was the day Conrad had tossed the Los Angeles *Examiner* into my lap and I read the headline, NAZIS SEIZE BUDAPEST!

"Saturday night, the night before," said Magda, "Mother gave a dinner party. Everyone was there—Papa, Grandmother, Seby, our friends—you'd not think there was a war, we'd all lived with it so long.

"Next morning, Sunday morning, about nine I'm awakened by my bell. Outside I see the Embassy car with the Portuguese flag. The driver is at my door. 'The Ambassador wants you to come to the Embassy at once.' At the Embassy Dr. Garrido is pale. 'The Germans are marching on Budapest,' he tells me. 'They began at 5 A.M. They'll be here in two hours. No one knows it yet.' He had heard it through his own channels. 'You're deep in it, Magda,' he says. 'You know the code, too— The Gestapo will be looking for you. You must hide here.'"

Magda could only think, "My parents—"

Dr. Garrido said, "Get them. Hurry."

Magda dashed into an Embassy car, the doors were locked, and they rushed back to Budapest to Father's house. "Papa," she told him, "something's going on and Dr. Garrido thinks it best if you come to the Embassy with me right now." For once Father didn't try to control the situation, but went with her. "It was as simple," Magda said, "as if I'd told him, 'Papa, let's go for a ride.' He came in the clothes he wore, and with nothing else.

"Then we drove to fetch Mother." Magda paused for a moment, then began to laugh. "Our crazy family!" she exclaimed, using her favorite phrase. " 'Please don't bother me now,' Mother says, annoyed. 'How can I go with you? I have a luncheon date at the Hungaria and it's eleven o'clock now.'

"I say, 'I'm not supposed to tell you, Mama, but for God's sake come with me. The Germans are marching in!'

" 'Oh, they won't bother me,' she says. 'Now let me go to my luncheon, Magda.' "

Finally Magda persuaded Mother to come with her. That, said my sister, was how our parents left Budapest, with only the clothes on their backs, leaving behind them everything they possessed—their homes, their businesses, their jewels—everything.

In the Embassy, crouched about their radio, they heard that the Germans had reached the city outskirts; then they were in the town itself. Later Magda was told that Germans seemed to pop up everywhere—in the center of town from the streets, almost from behind every tree. It had been perfectly planned. They had marched in so quietly, so secretly, occupying Budapest without a shot. That is what is so unforgivable, I thought—that my country should have accepted German occupation without a shot! By Monday morning the Germans had taken over every newspaper, every radio station, closed every bank—they had captured Budapest.

For weeks my parents and Magda lived a dangerous day-by-day life in the Embassy. Each morning Magda, riding in the locked Embassy car and driven by the Embassy chauffeur, ventured into the occupied city to "collect" others of the underground—"everyone who was a known anti-Nazi, everyone who had worked with us, everyone who was in danger or could put us in danger." They had more than seventy people living in the Embassy at one time. Only Mother's refusal to face reality kept their spirits up. When the Embassy became

162

so crowded that she and Father had to share not only the same room but the same bed, she made an outraged protest to Ambassador Garrido. "I'm divorced from this man," she said with great dignity. "How can you order me to sleep with him?"

The Gestapo had not forgotten Magda. "The morning of the twenty-seventh of April I was awakened by Canou, barking. That little dog saved our life because he awoke everyone." The ominous sound of heavily booted men echoed through the building. "A moment later there was a pounding on my door and the Gestapo came in—three men in black glasses, hats, civilian clothes, boots. 'You are Mrs. Magda Bychowsky?' one said. I was only able to nod. 'You will come with us quietly. Now.'

"That was how they got me," said Magda bitterly, "in my nightgown, at five in the morning."

But Canou's barking had awakened Mother and Father, a few rooms away. They ran into Magda's room. Mother said, "If you take her, we come, too!"

The Gestapo man said, "Then come, too. But quick!"

"Father, in pajamas, dragged on a pair of riding boots. Mother had a long flannel robe over her nightgown and as she went out she grabbed her gloves and a high fur hat and stuck it on her head. She looked like a Cossack, but none of us thought it amusing.

"As we passed the Ambassador's room, we saw him lying on the floor, gasping, half-dressed. He had been awakened by Canou, started to come to our aid, and suffered a heart attack. On his dresser stood his vial of medicine. I ran over and shattered it against the wall. My hand bled but, blood and all, I poured the contents into his mouth. One of the Gestapo grabbed me, but by this time Dr. Garrido came to. He managed to whisper, 'If you take these people, I go with them.'

"Here the Gestapo leader made the mistake which saved our lives. 'All right,' he said, 'If you insist, come, too.'"

By the time the little party reached the courtyard, however, one of the three must have realized how embarrassing a prisoner the Portuguese Ambassador might prove. They pushed Mother and Father into their car, then pushed Magda inside, but just as Dr. Garrido was about to enter, one of the men slammed the door shut.

"I don't know what strength God gives to people in danger," Magda said. "I didn't think, I stuck my leg between the door and the body of the car just as he slammed the door. He slammed it again and again, my leg was bloody and half crushed, I almost fainted from the pain, but the door didn't close. By then Dr. Garrido managed to get in with us.

"We had gone about ten miles when the car halted, and to our astonishment the Gestapo men leaped out and ran off into fields. Then we realized we had been followed by the uniformed Hungarian police. They were all apologies when they found Dr. Garrido with us. 'Mr. Ambassador, we are so sorry —we received a report of a holdup in the Embassy—'"

Dr. Garrido said, "Take us back, please."

"I regret," said the police captain, "I must take these people to police headquarters and make a report."

Magda's heart sank. To be returned to Budapest, away from Dr. Garrido's protection, meant death. They would torture her first, to learn the code and the names of others in the underground; Mother and Father would certainly be killed as well.

Dr. Garrido pretended to misunderstand. "Are you saying that I am to consider myself under arrest?"

"No, no—" The police captain turned to Magda to have her translate. "Tell him no—"

Dr. Garrido grew more angry. "Am I to understand that you dare arrest me?"

The police captain was not only stupid but short-tempered. "All right, tell him he's under arrest," he told Magda. "Give him his wish."

All four were driven to Budapest and jailed. The Ambassador demanded a telephone and promptly called the German Ambassador. Again, it was brilliant strategy. He knew that his colleague would be outraged to learn that the Gestapo had tried to seize the Ambassador of a neutral country. The German Ambassador telephoned the Chief of Protocol of the Hungarian Foreign Office, who, infuriated by the stupidity of the Hungarian police in arresting Dr. Garrido, ordered his instant release.

Now Dr. Garrido played his trump card. "I do not leave alone," he said. "You have also arrested a Portuguese citizen and her parents. They must leave with me."

Magda said, "This was payment, full payment, for everything I had done for the Allied countries and the underground. From that moment I was Portuguese. It meant giving us our lives."

At six that evening—their terrible day had begun at 5 A.M. —they left the police station. The police had provided a car. But Dr. Garrido said, "No, we shall not drive. We will walk. Let the Hungarian people see what indignities the Germans do and how the Hungarian police conspire with them."

Said Magda: "We walked in the street as we were—Mother and I in nightgowns and bedroom slippers with robes over us, I limping, my leg one mass of pain, Mother wearing her gloves and high fur hat, Papa in pajamas, robe, and riding boots, the Ambassador in dressing gown, trousers, and bedroom slippers. An enormous crowd followed us to the Foreign Office, where Dr. Garrido lodged an official complaint; then we got into cars and were driven back to the Embassy."

In the end it was with Portuguese passports that Magda, Father, and Mother escaped from Hungary to Portugal. There, on money Eva and I sent them each month, they lived until they could come to this country. One evening Mother received a cable from Hungary just as she was about to sit down to dinner in their little apartment in Lisbon. A direct bomb hit had completely destroyed her villa. Silently she picked up her spoon and went on to sip her soup. Then she said, "I used to get hysterical if a maid dropped a plate. Now my whole house vanishes—everything, paintings, china, crystal— and it does not touch me."

I asked about Grandmother and Seby.

"Mother blames herself," Magda said. "Grandmother refused

to leave Hungary because her other children were there. Father insisted that we put her in a convent where she would be safe. Mother said, 'Oh, she'll be so much more comfortable in the Portuguese Embassy—' And then she and Uncle Seby were shot to death."

Magda tried to tell me, too, something of what she had seen in Budapest in the last days: the slaughter in the streets, the yellow badges, the men and women—our family physician, our lawyer, merchants we knew—taken to Tattersall, the famous riding academy where as a child I learned to ride, and there machine-gunned to death like animals. She saw frantic mothers begging strangers in the streets to take their babies . . .

"No," I said. "Don't tell me any more. I have seen it all in my own nightmares."

Mother's vitality, Mother's buoyancy surmounted everything. Having re-established her shop, within months she had re-established the world we had known in prewar Budapest. We found ourselves going again to dinners and parties, we began again entertaining friends—from Budapest, Vienna, Paris, London. Every boat, it seemed, brought people we had known in Europe, grateful that they had escaped with their lives and eager to rebuild their community again. I was caught up in the activity; I began to feel myself once more. Conrad had taken an immediate liking to Mother and Father; he and I began to see each other again, although we still maintained our separate residences—as a matter of fact, our lawyers had begun discussing a divorce settlement. I was five months pregnant when I flew to the coast with my lawyer, Ed Falk, and asked for a divorce from Conrad.

When I first learned that I was going to have a baby, I met with Ed Falk and Mother. An enormously kind, warm-hearted man, Ed advised me to wait. "You should not divorce with a baby on the way," he said. "You don't know what a bond a child is between two people. After the baby is born, perhaps you and Conrad will get together again. Even if that

166

doesn't happen, it's my duty as your lawyer to tell you that if you then divorce, you will find yourself in a far more advantageous position."

Mother said, "No, Ed, don't change her mind. The important thing now is that she have no more worries and no more emotional pressures. Nothing else matters." I decided, myself, that whatever happened I could not, I would not, go back to Conrad. But, divorce or not, I wanted my baby.

It was a good decision. The knowledge that I was to have a child did more, I think, to restore my spirits completely than anything that had happened since my parents' arrival. I would have something of my own, something warm and living and loving that I created—something no one could take from me. All at once there was purpose in my life.

In the end I obtained a California divorce with a cash settlement of $35,000 and alimony for me of $25,000 a year for ten years, unless I married. Other provision was made for the baby.

Mother showed great understanding. She said, "Well, you certainly can't continue to live in a hotel. We need a house." We found a lovely five-story remodeled brownstone at 8 East Eighty-third Street, overlooking the Metropolitan Museum. The neighborhood was quiet and the green of Central Park reminded me of the little park opposite our apartment on Muzeum Korut when I was a child. A museum stood there, too. Mother liked the house; Conrad came down and looked it over, even to the ceiling fire extinguishers. "Seems good to me," he said. But had I enough money for a down payment? It was not cheap.

Connie patted my hand. "Of course you have. Remember those Stevens bonds?"

Two years before, when he had been negotiating the purchase of the Stevens Hotel, I had sat in his office while he telephoned one associate after another, seeking to raise the millions of dollars necessary. I heard him say in one conversation, "Very well, if you don't think it's a good deal, don't put your money in it." He hung up angrily.

167

I broke into his thoughts. "Conrad, I have seventeen thousand dollars. Take my money. I'll invest with you."

Conrad stared at me, and burst into laughter. Years later he would say, "She trusted me when all the big shots didn't. She gave me her seventeen thousand—but I did all right for her." He bought me Stevens Hotel bonds and now he could tell me they were worth several times what I had paid. I used the proceeds to buy the house. I turned the top floor into a lovely penthouse apartment, decorating it in gray, red, white, and gold. I had an adorable nursery built. My bedroom had antique mirrored walls and apple-green velvet upholstery and hangings. I hired a pleasant Finnish couple—Mrs. Lulu Barth and her husband, John—and there I waited for my child to arrive. It was a happy pregnancy. I walked every day in Central Park; I dated almost every night; I went to the theater, I read, I painted. I felt calm and content, waiting. My house was beautiful, and French, and everything was dreamy . . .

From that penthouse in the Christmas week of 1946, when I was seven months' pregnant, I went with Mother to a neighborhood movie to see Somerset Maugham's *The Moon and Sixpence*, starring the British actor George Sanders. Sanders played the painter, Charles Strickland, based on Paul Gauguin, who at forty, without warning, deserts his wife and children to go to Paris and paint, because that is the one thing he must do. I listened to the dialogue between Strickland and the narrator who comes to Paris to plead with him to return to his family. Strickland refuses.

"Does your wife deserve to be treated like this?" he is asked.
"No."
"Isn't it monstrous to leave her?"
"Monstrous? Yes."
"One can't leave a woman without a penny."
"Why not? I supported her for seventeen years."
"Don't you care about the opinion of people?"
"Not a bit."

"Your children?"

"Somebody will always look after them."

"Would it bother you that people will think you're a swine?"

"No," says Strickland indifferently.

I watched as Kirk, a painter who worships Strickland's genius, finds him near death from starvation, brings him to his home, nurses him to health despite his insults—only to have Strickland seduce his wife, take her with him and later desert her, showing no remorse when she takes her life by poison. I sat in the dark little movie house entranced as Sanders moved through the story like a disdainful prince, cool, remote, sardonic, elegantly contemptuous of everyone. I listened to the suave British voice: "A woman can forgive a man for the harm he does her but never for the good he does her . . . Women are strange little beasts. You can beat them like dogs. Beat them until your arms ache—still they love you." I sat in my seat like a woman mesmerized.

At some point in the film—I do not remember when—I turned to Mother. "Mother," I said, "there is my next husband."

Even Mother was a little shocked. "This is no time for you to think of a next husband!"

When we came home I telephoned Magda. "Magda," I said, "I'm going to marry George Sanders."

Magda said, "Who in the world is George Sanders?"

I said, "I saw him in a movie tonight."

She was still laughing when she hung up.

15

FATHER sat in my room at Doctor's Hospital, while I held little Francesca in my arms. "Not even a grandson!" he lamented, blowing his nose, pretending he wasn't overjoyed, trying vainly to make himself heard over Mother, Magda, Eva, and half a dozen Hungarian friends. That morning I had telephoned Mother. "Come over," I told her. "I know I'm going to have my baby today."

Mother, more excited than I, drove me to the hospital. The more excited she became, the calmer I grew. My doctor, who had been teasing me for weeks, saying, "Triplets, Zsa Zsa, nothing less than triplets," finally said to her, "Mrs. Gabor, perhaps you'd better go home. I'll call you in plenty of time."

Mother went home, got in the tub for a hot, relaxing bath—and only when she began to soap herself discovered that she was sitting fully dressed in the tub full of water.

My room was decked with flowers, there was a delighted telegram from Conrad somewhere in the West, telephone calls were pouring in, but I was too full of my own wonder to be concerned with anything. I am sure every new mother must have the same experience, but I will never forget how I felt the first time they brought Francie to me. When they put her in my arms I was flooded with such warmth as I had never known. I still remember how powerfully my heart beat as I took her in my arms. I loved that helpless little thing as I had loved nothing in the world. To think that I was holding close to me something alive that I created! I thought: this baby is a present from God, to calm me, to make up for what I have gone through in these last years.

Ten days later I took Francie home to my beautiful apartment and put her in the fairy-tale nursery waiting for her. When we arrived Josephine, my boxer, leaped up once to kiss Francie, then assigned herself to watch over the baby. Each morning she walked into the nursery and curled up on the floor next to the crib, and guarded her with absolute ferocity. No one could get near except Lulu and me. To anyone else she showed her teeth and growled as if she would tear them apart.

Now, when I came home, it was to something wonderful, warm, lovely, my own. I took care of my baby. On Lulu's day off I stayed with her from morning until night caring for her myself, taking no one to help me. A friend sent me a high, black, English baby carriage. I put Francie in it, dressed like a doll in pink lace, and on the first pleasant Sunday I presented her to the world, wheeling her down Fifth Avenue, Mother on one side, Lulu on the other, Josephine on a leash behind us. I was as proud as if I had defeated the Spanish Armada. Mother said, "Never, in all my life, have I seen a more conceited mother than you!"

"Mr. Serge Semenenko requests the pleasure of your company at a cocktail party Saturday evening, the 29th of April, 1947 . . . "

So read the invitation from the well-known banker. On a soft spring evening I went to Serge's charming apartment in the St. Regis Hotel. It was already full of people. "Zsa Zsa!" he said fondly, "how nice to see you!" It was one of the first times I had gone out in the evening since Francie's birth, six weeks before. I pressed my lips against his cheek and looked around the enormous salon. I thought: no. Then: of course. It is my fate.

There, sitting in a chair like a pasha, listening to a pretty woman, his head inclined, polite yet obviously bored, was George Sanders. "Serge," I said almost breathlessly. "I must meet Mr. Sanders. Please bring me to him."

Serge obediently maneuvered me through the crowded

room. "George—" he said. Mr. Sanders looked up. His blue eyes swept over me and he rose slowly. He was even taller than Conrad—three or four inches over six feet—and heavier, a tall, powerful man of great elegance, and in his black tie and perfectly cut evening clothes, very handsome. "Mrs. Conrad Hilton—Mr. George Sanders," said Serge, and vanished. In a strange way the pretty woman also seemed to melt into the crowd. Mr. Sanders and I stood facing each other. He gazed down on me: cool, cynical, detached, a man prepared to be bored and ready to endure the ordeal like a gentleman.

I blurted out, "Oh, Mr. Sanders, I have been wanting to meet you for so long. I have such a crush on you!"

Mr. Sanders smiled as though he had not heard this so very often. "Indeed," he said, in his impeccable British accent. "How very understandable." I looked at him laughingly, pretending to be outraged, thinking: he's just as impertinent as I expected. He indicated the place vacated by the pretty woman. I sat down. "I'm such a fan of yours," I went on. I had to talk. "I saw *The Moon and Sixpence* and I cried in all the right places—I thought you were wonderful."

"You did?" asked Mr. Sanders, with a tired smile and a voice that suggested I had just said something idiotic. I didn't care. I told him about myself—I had a baby, I was getting a divorce, it was odd that we hadn't met before in Hollywood. As I chattered on, Mr. Sanders looked at me appraisingly, at my tight-fitting Alexis black jersey dress, my diamond and emerald necklace, my red hair, and I gathered that he did not dislike what he saw. He cleared his throat. "You're—ah—a very pretty girl," he said. I blushed as though no man had ever complimented me before. I found George Sanders as irresistible in person as I had found Charles Strickland irresistible on the screen.

That first evening George and I met, at Serge Semenenko's cocktail party, he was all I wanted him to be; he sneered at me, he was properly contemptuous, he did everything I expected him to do, and he did everything the right way. I was

172

like a little kitten at his side. I never left him. I sat there, and though now and then he turned to speak to others and I gossiped with friends, my eyes always returned to him.

He had come to the party with Erich Maria Remarque, the writer, whom I knew from Hollywood. When the party broke up I found myself escorted home by Mr. Sanders and Mr. Remarque.

At the door of my house I said, "Won't you both come up for a drink?"

"An excellent idea," said George. I led them to my penthouse. Mr. Sanders looked around with an appreciative eye. "Lovely apartment," he said. "Lovely house. Is it yours?" I said yes. "You must both see my baby," I added. I took them into the nursery where Francie lay sleeping. "Isn't she adorable?" I asked proudly.

Erich went to the crib and looked at Francie with interest but George, who had taken only one step into the room, paid no attention to Francie. He glanced about. Josephine, curled up on the floor, growled. George looked at the dog distastefully and backed out. He turned to me. "My dear, do you, ah, have some vodka? And caviar?"

We went into my red-satin-decorated living room. I hurried to the refrigerator—luckily I had both vodka and caviar, of which I was to feed George endless amounts in the next few years—and I served the two men.

It was nearly 1 A.M. We sat about, talking. Erich had just published his latest book, *Arch of Triumph,* and was working on another. He and George discussed it. We spoke about Eva and her career, then about Marlene Dietrich, whom I had often seen with Erich. Now and then I excused myself and tiptoed into the nursery to see if Francie slept undisturbed. After a while Erich looked at his watch. It was nearly 1:45 A.M. George, unconcerned, sat in a deep chair, sipping his vodka. I went into the kitchen and replenished the caviar. The two men talked, paying no attention to me. It was 2 A.M. George was speaking brilliantly about the human voice and the problems which singers face. At 2:15 Erich suddenly rose.

173

"It's late, George," he said. "I think we must go now and let Zsa Zsa get some sleep."

George kept his seat. He twirled the vodka gently in his glass. "You go, old boy," he drawled. "I'm staying."

Erich threw a swift glance at me, but I had risen a moment before to make one of my visits to the nursery and was already halfway across the room. I pretended not to have heard, but I felt the back of my neck flame. I thought: That—! No diplomacy, nothing. He dares tell that to Erich in my presence! But who else would have had such impertinence? Who else would have dared it?

Erich left. I closed the door after him and turned to see George calmly lean forward and carefully spread caviar on the last piece of toast. "We need more toast, my dear," he said, as he popped it into his mouth. "There was really, ah, nothing fit to eat at that dreadful party." I turned dutifully toward the kitchen. I heard him again. He had stretched comfortably back in his chair, his eyes closed. "You might bring me a glass of milk, too, my dear," he was saying. "Just be sure, ah, to take the chill off it."

"I will call you Cokiline from now on. Not Zsa Zsa. Co-kiline."

"What does Cokiline mean?"

"It is a term of endearment. It comes, my dear, from cooky —little cooky. It means, 'my little sweet cooky,' my cooky with a little spice . . ."

In her sleep Josephine growled. All was silent at 8 East Eighty-third Street.

"Cokiline?"

"Yes, George?"

"Do you suppose you, ah, have any more milk in your refrigerator?"

16

THE trouble with George Sanders was that he never knew who or what he wanted to be—an English duke, a beach-comber in the tropics, or the greatest woman-hater of his time. In his indecision he gave me some of the most wretched—and happiest—hours of my life. Since, until I met him, I wasn't sure what I wanted to be—my career began only after I met him and because of him—I gave him some of the most wretched—and happiest—hours of his life.

When we met that spring of 1947, I had no idea that I was falling in love with a man whose screen roles really reflected himself; that the words Somerset Maugham and other writers placed in his mouth—"Women are such strange little beasts" and "All women strike me as being so incredibly stupid . . . it's impossible not to despise them"—expressed his own beliefs. Nor did I know that I was becoming involved with the most difficult, the most complicated man I had ever known. I was too excited by him, and what he told me about himself only fanned my excitement. He had been born in St. Petersburg, Russia, of a family related to the nobility who were forced to flee to England in the Bolshevik revolution. A Russian aristo-crat! Who grew up in England! What more could I ask! His life had been crowded with adventure. At twenty he had gone as a tobacco salesman to South America, had wandered through the jungles and the backwoods towns; he had been wounded in a duel with a jealous husband; he had been on the London musical comedy stage, had understudied Noel Coward, and had made a name in British films before coming to Broadway and then Hollywood.

We had met at the psychologically right moment. George, like me, had just gone through a long, painful divorce ending a marriage of seven years. He was now between pictures; he lived in Hollywood but was staying temporarily in New York "because my psychoanalyst is here."

"Oh," I said, all sympathy. Suddenly I saw George in an even more attractive light. Suddenly there was so much to tell this man. Until now I had no one in whom to confide, no one to talk over my illness with—no one who would understand. It was difficult to discuss it with Mother. Each time I tried, she all but threw up her hands. "I won't listen to that nonsense!" she would cry. "It wouldn't have happened if I had been here. I'd have taken you for a vacation to the Riviera or on a cruise—" Beyond that we could not talk. It was uncomfortable to bring it up with Eva and Bundy; they had been too involved, Conrad was too remote . . .

I told George everything. He listened intelligently, understandingly; it lifted a great burden from me to be able to talk to him. I thought: we can communicate—almost without words. I felt that Burhan, and later Conrad, never really knew what I was talking about. To them I was far away on some distant, absurd tangent; they discounted what I said, they did not know when I was really pouring my heart out to them, and when I played make-believe. But George understood. We found we had much in common, not only in ourselves but in our unbelievable families. I told him about Grandfather Gabor ending an argument by majestically walking out the window, and Aunt Jennie swimming contentedly amid the ice in the Danube; George told me about his father, who still maintained the Czar was alive; and his uncle Jack, who smeared jam on the ceiling, then, lying on his back on the floor with a rifle, amused himself shooting the flies attracted to the jam. We agreed that we had both been married to persons of loftier character than ourselves. "We're two of a kind, Coki-line," George said with great satisfaction the morning my

176

father walked in at 10 A.M., discovered George in bed with a glass of warm milk and a platter of fried eggs, and promptly walked out again. I tried guiltily to explain to Father that George, even as a visitor, was so lazy that he never used a chair if a bed was available. Although this was true— "I'm too tall to stay upright," George always complained—Father was so outraged he never even mentioned the episode to me.

We were two of a kind. We both lived in a special world. In time I was to discover that I saw things not as they were but as a play within a play, in which I was always the heroine, waiting for the prince to awaken me with a kiss, to lead me away from sadness, suffering, and the terrible truth that beauty vanishes and youth grows old. And George? George, too, did not belong with everyday people. He was a sixteenth-century nobleman, an Elizabethan rake who, if he had lived then, could have seduced his best friend's wife or run his sword through an enemy—with equal style. George was superior to both good and evil. He once wrote about himself, "My moral sense scarcely exists." He was not boasting or apologizing. He simply stated a fact.

But nothing mattered to me. I was very much in love. When George a month later took off for Hollywood, I waited twenty-four hours, then put Francie in a little basket, carried her aboard a plane, and accompanied by Lulu and Josephine, followed George to Hollywood. Mother said goodbye to me at the airport. "To fall in love with an actor—" She sighed unhappily. "It can only mean trouble, Zsa Zsa." She might as well have been warning the baby.

George had rented Gene Tierney's house. I moved into the Bel Air Hotel. I bought George a 24-carat gold cigarette case engraved, "I am so glad I met you." George accepted it with a charming smile, kissed me—and allowed me to buy the cigarettes to keep it filled. I cooked for him. I made breakfast in the morning for him and waited for him at night.

Two months later I put Francie in a basket again, carried her aboard a plane, and accompanied by Lulu and Josephine, flew back to New York. I was furious. In Gene Tierney's house,

George had entertained one of my friends, a beautiful young woman. He denied it; she denied it; I was sure of it.

Mother greeted me at the airport. She said, resignedly, "I see ahead of me taking you and fetching you, taking you and fetching you—"

"Oh, no, Mother," I said. "I love him but I can't endure a man who does that to me."

To forget George, I went gaily on the town, dating every night. I gave parties. I attended every theater opening, every charity ball. My escorts were some of the country's most eligible young men. When I looked through my date book— Stewart Barthelmess, Count John de Benden, the Prince of Hanover, Jack Kennedy, Herby Klutz, Franchot Tone, Bob Topping—I said to myself, "Why do I need George Sanders?" One evening Bob Topping took me to dinner at "21." I wore a slim black jersey dress—you can wear only the simplest frock if you wish to cover yourself with gems—and I displayed my diamond necklace, three diamond bracelets, my 10-carat diamond earrings, my 20-carat diamond solitaire . . . It was as though by dazzling everyone I could dazzle away George Sanders' face.

I struggled slowly to wakefulness next morning. A man stood by my bed wearing dark sunglasses, a dark hat, and holding in his gloved hand a black pistol pointed directly at me. "Get up," he said. "This is a holdup." I murmured, not knowing what I was saying, "Come back later, I'm sleepy."

He took a step nearer. "This is serious. Get up!"

"But I've got nothing on," I protested. It was just dawning on me what was happening.

"What do you think I am—a sex maniac?" he demanded. He sounded insulted. Oh, I thought, a gentleman burglar. "Now, get up!"

I looked at him. "I don't go out if you don't give me something to cover myself," I said. He swore under his breath, looked around hastily, saw my black negligee over a chair, and tossed it to me. "O.K.," he snapped. "Quick!'

I hurriedly slipped it on and walked into the other room

thinking: what can I do? My self-service elevator was open at my floor; with a sinking heart I realized that no one could use it until he went down again. He had made sure he would not be interrupted. Just then I heard Francie cooing. The nursery door was open. "Oh, my baby, my baby!" I cried. I dashed into the nursery, and screamed. Lulu lay on the floor in a dead faint. Apparently the burglar surprised her as she was diapering Francie and now my baby lay unprotected on the bathinette, cooing and gurgling. The dogs were nowhere about—the maid must be walking them.

The man's gun poked my back. "The jewelry," he said impatiently.

I flared up. "Even if you shoot me, I'm going to put that child in her bed before she falls off."

He let me put Francie safely into her crib.

I felt the gun in my back again. "The jewelry, lady," he said. "Get moving—" Suddenly I realized the gun could be loaded. I led him into my bedroom again and pointed to a dresser drawer. "There," I said. I hardly recognized my voice; it had suddenly gone up half an octave. Keeping his gun on me, he scooped up the jewels with one hand and stuffed them into his coat pocket. He turned just as a white-faced Lulu peeped from the baby's nursery.

"Come here," he said roughly, "both of you." He ordered us to sit on an iron love seat in my foyer, and began tying us with a cord. My diamond necklace, hanging halfway out his pocket, hypnotized me; it was all I could do not to snatch it back. But now we were tied. He looked us over. I was wearing my diamond earrings, in which I always sleep, but oddly enough he paid no attention to them. Instead he examined a ring on my finger, a band of sapphires, diamonds, and rubies fashioned into two intertwined flags, the Hungarian and the French. Grandmother had given it to me for good luck and I wore it when I went riding or did anything I thought daring. "This ring you can't take," I said. "It's my good luck ring."

He let me keep it but began going through my closets. Now that we seemed no longer in bodily danger, I breathed easier.

179

I began to lecture him. "Really," I said, "why do you do this? There is so much opportunity in this country—you might even become President, I can tell how you talk that you were born here. Why do you take these chances?" He grunted and went on opening and closing my closet doors. "If they catch you, you will end up in jail. Don't you want to do something better than that?"

For the first time he grinned. "Well, lady, for a young woman you did O.K. in this country." Apparently there was nothing else he wanted; he backed away, stepped into the waiting elevator, and was gone.

In a few minutes, working on the rope with our teeth, we freed ourselves and the police were there. For the next month I had the police, the FBI, the insurance investigators—the jewelry was valued at $250,000 and insured for $185,000— and various other persons as guests. They took my fingerprints, they took Lulu's, they even fingerprinted a photographer who had been in the apartment a day before. I discovered my telephone wire was tapped—someone, it seemed, thought I had robbed myself. Mother came over and we seemed to spend most of the day serving coffee and refreshments to investigators who swore us to secrecy. The FBI warned me, "Now don't tell the police what you told us." The police said, "Don't tell the FBI."

I was almost grateful for the excitement, for no word—nothing—had come from George Sanders.

But one midnight my telephone rang. It was the overseas operator. And then: "Cokiline? Are you there, Cokiline?"

My heart began to pound.

"I don't want to talk to you, George," I said, but I talked to him. He was calling from London. "Darling, I've just finished a film, I'm flying to Bermuda. I want you to meet me there in three days."

But I don't want to meet him, I thought. I don't want to be hurt any more. I want to go out with all the charming, attentive men about town and have fun—

George's voice came over the wire, rising and falling as

though the sea moved under it. "I know this will sound absurd to you, but I can't live without you, Cokiline," he was saying. "Please come. Please, please, please!" When we hung up I had told him I would think it over.

Next morning I visited Mother. I sat on the side of her bed. I remember how I looked: I had dressed carefully, in a black paper-taffeta dress from Traina-Norell, and a natural straw picture hat; the boys had whistled at me as I hurried down Fifth Avenue, and everything had been sunshiny and bright. "Mother, George called me."

"Yes?" she said.

I asked her, "Shall I go?"

Mother said reluctantly, "Well, if it will make you happy and you don't take that man too seriously—"

I literally flew out of her room to Bergdorf Goodman's on a buying spree. I assembled a complete Southern wardrobe. When I arrived in Bermuda, there he stood in the airport, waiting.

Each night we danced under a full moon, George in his British whites, I in my blue and pink and white organza gowns. Each day we swam in the bluest waters of the world in a tiny cove that seemed only our own. One morning we looked out our window; as though painted against the blue water, a white British cruiser lay in port. We went aboard; George was more British, more naval, more imperial, than any officer who bowed to us. In the afternoon George joined them on shore in a game of cricket. "Be delighted to play," he told them, "but I'm an old fellow, so I'm sure you chaps won't mind if I appoint lovely Mrs. Hilton to run for me."

Why not? I thought. I kicked off my shoes, and each time George was at bat I poised like a sprinter, and the moment he hit the ball I was off. They found it hilarious. I loved being a tomboy again. Once George slammed the ball and it flew through the air and whacked me on the arm. Everyone rushed to me. "It's nothing," I said heroically, though the pain brought tears to my eyes. I wore my black-and-blue bruise like the Victoria Cross when we danced under the moon that night.

At the end of two perfect weeks George said, "Darling, now we must go. I'm going to Cuba and then to Mexico. You may come with me to Cuba but I must go to Mexico alone."

Why? George gave me a smile. "I promised Dolores del Rio that I would visit her." He hastened to add, "Now don't let that imagination of yours go wild, my dear. It's purely business. She's a big star down there and she can be of immense help if I start my own studio there. I've been thinking of moving to Mexico—I can't take these American taxes. You know how I hate to part with money."

I knew. In Hollywood, when he stopped at a corner to buy a newspaper, he never had change and I had to pay for it; and though I kept George's gold cigarette case full, he refused to give me a cigarette when I asked for one. "I can't afford it," he would say. I had to buy his cigarettes and mine as well.

Now I said nothing. I accompanied him to Havana. After two lovely days, which we spent exploring the city and adventuring in out-of-the-way restaurants, George took me to the airport, put me on a plane to New York, and went off to Mexico and Dolores del Rio, with "Darling, we'll see each other soon, of course." I was too proud to play it any other way. "Of course we will, darling," I said brightly and went aboard my plane as though I were going to my coronation.

But back in New York, all the charming, glamorous, uncomplicated young men who flocked about me again were not as exciting as before. Compared to George they were little boys. Stewart Barthelmess, Richard's son, an adorable escort, took me out triumphantly my first night. "I felt awful when you went off with that rickety old man," he said, "but now that I've got you back, you're staying." I smiled gratefully at him, but it was George's mocking face that remained in my mind.

I had been home five days when George telephoned me. He was once more back in Los Angeles. Sonja Henie was giving a lavish dinner Saturday night. "My dear," said George over the long-distance telephone, "why don't you come here? I'd very much enjoy taking you to Sonja's party."

I said to Stewart, "I'm going to Hollywood."

"Not to see that man again!"

I lied. "Sonja Henie is giving a fabulous party and I don't want to miss it."

Stewart drove me to the airport and I flew to Hollywood, leaving Francie with Lulu. George took me to Sonja's party. When he saw the place cards at dinner—I was to sit between two men—he had them changed so that we sat together. He insisted on this thereafter, no matter how often we fought, how often we separated, when we attended a social event, we must be seated together.

The party was in full swing when the door opened—and there, to my astonishment, stood Stewart. He came smiling to me as George and I were about to rise and dance. "Zsa Zsa," he said, "you forgot your sunglasses." He handed them to me.

George was unimpressed. "Very gallant of you, old boy," he said. "Now, if you'll step aside, I'd like to dance with Mrs. Hilton."

George lived in a small apartment house he owned on Shoreham Drive. One apartment was empty; he gave it to me. Now I made breakfast, lunch, and dinner for him. Dressed in my peasant outfit, I worked happily over a hot stove. We decorated the apartment, buying paint in a neighborhood hardware store, then spraying the walls red, gray, and gold, as in my penthouse in New York. In the basement George had an elaborate workshop where he spent hours turning out everything from lamps to telescopes. He actually ground the lenses himself, after directions in the *Encyclopaedia Britannica*. He had also invented a number of gadgets—one was a non-twisting ski—but he was most proud of a bell which rang an alarm when I forgot to turn off the water in the tub. "A most annoying habit," he said, and proceeded to tell me the names of three beautiful Hollywood stars who always let their baths overflow, too. "I found it necessary to install bells for each of them," he said. "I'm not interested in the details," I retorted coldly. He was happiest in his workshop, but I

183

found him a completely unpredictable man. When we walked, he took enormous strides; I had to trot every few steps to keep up with him. He never slowed his pace; I never said, "George, wait." It became a clash of wills between us—and he always won. I always had to run after him.

Once, after a furious argument, I left the apartment and moved to a hotel. George telephoned. "Cokiline, my darling," he said contritely. "I was beastly—I'm really sorry."

"Oh, George, I forgive you." He so rarely apologized. Words poured from me. My voice began to quaver.

"Cokiline," he said tenderly, "are you crying?"

"Yes," I sobbed.

"Good!" he said, and hung up.

Yet when I remarked one day, "I miss Francie terribly," George flew to New York that night and brought Francie and Lulu back with him. When, in this period, I was rushed to the Cedars of Lebanon hospital with an attack of acute appendicitis, George never left my side. As they wheeled me into the operating room, I saw his face, pale as mine, above me. "Cokiline," he said, with a gentleness I had not imagined he possessed, "don't worry about anything because if anything happens to you, I will die, too."

Next day my room was full of his flowers. He came in, saw me sitting up, gay and smiling, and glanced around the room at the roses and lilies everywhere. He looked very unhappy. "Cokiline, I can't afford this—spending all my money on flowers for you." He sat down. "I wish you would send out for a pack of cigarettes," he said crossly. "I haven't had one all morning."

17

WHEN George and I were married on April Fool's Day, 1949— "How delightfully appropriate," George had murmured —Hedda Hopper, the columnist, asked, "Zsa Zsa, where will you go for your honeymoon?"

"Such a silly question to ask me, Hedda," I said, blushing. "We just came back from it."

I don't say this to shock, but because it was the honeymoon which actually led to our marriage. George and I were in love, but marriage frightened both of us; it had meant only unhappiness. For me, too, marriage posed a practical problem. It would mean giving up my independence, my alimony from Conrad would shrink from $25,000 a year for ten years to $12,000 a year for three years. Not once had George discussed my personal finances. Not once had he asked, "Darling, how do you manage? What do you live on?" He took it for granted that there was inexhaustible money. I had no career then to support me; my only income was my alimony and I was going to lose most of that if I married him.

None the less I said to George, "I want to marry you."

George sighed. "Better think twice about it, Cokiline. I'm being psychoanalyzed. I don't know the sort of a fellow I'm likely to be at any given moment. I might make you miserable."

"Make me miserable then," I said, "but I want to live with you."

George kissed my ear—or it might have been my diamond

185

earring. "Sweet," he said. "But think it over anyway on the trip to New York."

It had been George's idea that we motor by easy stages from Hollywood to New York. "I want to show you America," he said enthusiastically. "We'll make a classic cross-country run." It took us two weeks. We ate on the road like campers; George would stop his car before a grocery, I'd hurry in for bread, milk, ham, and cheese, and then off we went again, George driving while I fixed sandwiches for him, held his glasses of milk, and lit his cigarettes. When we reached Palm Beach we spent a delightful week attending parties, and then went on to New York.

In New York we announced our engagement. I telephoned Conrad, busily negotiating to buy the Waldorf-Astoria. "I'm going to save you much money, Connie," I said. "I'm marrying George Sanders."

"Really?" Conrad sounded surprised. "Are you sure you love that fellow?"

When I told Mother, she said, "Are you sure?"

Eva said, "Are you sure?" and Magda, summing up the general Gabor reaction, added, "But what can we do about it?"

Usually when a new man is about to come into our family, if we are not all enthusiastic about him, he has little chance because we influence each other so strongly. But George was different.

"Nothing," I told them. "Nobody can do anything about it. I'm marrying George Sanders if I have to hit him over the head."

There was really no way out for him. He had to marry me.

I had no chance to ask Father's opinion. Long before, he had called us all together to announce that he was returning to Hungary. He refused to listen to protests. He was lost and unhappy in this country. He had stayed with me, with Magda, and most recently with Eva in Hollywood, but it had not worked out. "I can't find a place for myself here," he com-

186

plained. "I am too old to learn English, and I just will not be another refugee sitting in Hungarian restaurants and talking about the past." It was true. Mother and Magda had made lives of their own, Eva was busy with her career, I was completely involved with my baby and George Sanders—poor Father, he was out of everything. What finally led to his decision was the news that Hungary had become a republic, and that Hungarian citizens who repatriated themselves would have returned to them some of their confiscated properties. We all knew, too, that Father's secretary, who had been in love with him over twenty years, still waited there for him.

At it turned out Father's decision was a good one. He married his faithful secretary shortly after he returned, and though his fortunes rose and fell again, when in 1958 we had a family reunion in Europe—all of us meeting in Vienna—we found him at peace and content. He who had once been so prosperous now lived in a small co-operative apartment we bought for him—but he was happy, among his friends and his own people.

Now George and I drove back to California. In Los Angeles we had to separate. George explained that since we both looked forward to our American citizenship, we must be sure that our conduct was spotless, or the Government might refuse to make us citizens. Consequently I moved into the Beverly Hills Hotel, and George went alone to his apartment.

That did it. Next morning he was at my door. "It's no use, my dear," he said glumly, "I can't live without you. We'll get married tomorrow."

We were married in Las Vegas the next day. It happened so quickly that none of my family had time to get there. With an unexpected generosity, George chartered a plane and flew the wedding party there: his brother, Tom Conway, the actor, as warm and outgoing as George was cool and restrained, was best man, and came on the plane with a shotgun over his shoulder. "Just in case the old boy gets cold feet," he said. The other wedding guests included Bill Shiffrin, George's agent; his close friend, Allan Shute, also a British actor; and Mrs. Jill Lohman, my friend.

At the ceremony George got as far as, "With this ring—" He stopped, and a pained look came over his face. "I seem to have forgotten the ring," he said. On my right hand I still wore the good luck band I'd saved from the jewel thief. Since it seemed to fit this occasion perfectly, I removed it and gave it to George. "Thank you, my dear," he said. "It's very thoughtful of you." He slipped it on the third finger of my left hand. "Now," he said, with a pleased smile, "you're no longer the glamorous Mrs. Conrad Hilton. You're plain Mrs. George Sanders." He tilted my face up for a kiss, only to draw back suddenly. "Cokiline," he said, alarmed, "now I'm not sure I'll be able to make love to you any more."

Chapel, friends, and all, I felt like slapping my new husband on his handsome, impertinent face.

We spent our first married night playing chess. "An excellent mental exercise, Cokiline," George said. "And since it's full of kings, queens, castles, and the like, you should love it." I didn't mind playing chess. Had it been parcheesi or tiddly-winks, it would have been the same. I preferred being home with George to being taken about town by anyone else.

We lived the quietest possible life now. Each night we retired at nine, for George demanded twelve hours of sleep— "Obviously an escape, my dear. I'm trying to find out from what"—and we lay in bed watching wrestling matches on television until our eyes grew heavy. Sometimes Mother, visiting California, might telephone at 10 o'clock, full of vigor, eager to do the town, only to find the entire household fast asleep—George, me, Francie, Lulu, even Josephine, the boxer.

George had meant it when he said, "plain Mrs. George Sanders." A few weeks after the wedding he took me with him to Mallorca, to make a French film, *Captain Blackjack*. When we landed at Madrid Airport we were surrounded by photographers. I posed happily with George. "Cokiline, don't be difficult," he said. "I am making the film, not you." He pushed me gently but firmly out of the camera's range, and posed alone. I watched, furious at first, thinking: I don't like this. I'm his wife now, not a woman to be pushed away. But I smiled when the photographers finished, and slipped my arm into my husband's. "Señora—" A reporter tipped his hat. What were my plans in Spain? Had I any comment on Spanish women, Spanish fashions? George brushed him aside. "My dear fellow," he asked languidly, "why on earth would you wish to interview her? She is nobody. She is just my wife."

This time I laughed despite myself. Part of me enjoyed this play-acting—this rude, superior man who never showed his affection in public. No one had ever treated me with quite the same mixture of arrogance and desire; though others might not know it, there was as much of the hot-blooded Russian in George as the icy Englishman, and when we were alone he was anything but allergic to me.

The picture was to have taken two months. I wanted to bring Francie with me, but George said, "It will be difficult—and you know how uncomfortable I am with children. I find it hard enough to communicate with adults, but with babies—" I had left her behind with Lulu, feeling quite guilty. The picture stretched on to six months, and I missed my child terribly. Yet I hadn't the strength to leave George and fly back to California. Instead I spent most of my time on the balcony of our suite at the Hotel Mediterraneo, painting the harbor and the blue Mediterranean beyond, while each morning George went to his set and returned in the late afternoon, exhausted, complaining about the script, the heat, the director. In the evening we prowled about the island, visiting friends in ancient palaces with alabaster staircases and rooms furnished in crimson and gold, or we sat in the medieval plaza at dusk watching men and women with faces that might have been painted by Velázquez.

When we returned to Hollywood, George announced, "I've decided you must buy a house." This meant selling my brownstone in New York, but since George's career was in Hollywood, I would have no use for it. In any event, George explained, New York was a dangerous city. "The air is full of exhaust fumes," he said. "One whiff—and off you go." I sold my house at a loss. I had had a Bentley car in New York. "Sell that, too," said George. "You don't need it. I have a car." I did as I was told. Then, shopping for a house, I fell in love with a magnificent fourteen-room mansion on Bellagio Place, in Bel Air, complete with three acres of gardens, a guesthouse, a courtyard, and a swimming pool. It was furnished in expensive Chinese modern, with painted screens, ornately carved black mahogany tables, and luxurious potted plants, and it stood high on a mountain peak with a breath-taking view of Los Angeles spread out far below. At night when the city's lights went on, it was like being suspended above an illuminated fairyland. So Budapest at night, strung with lights on both sides of the Danube, looked from the heights of the Hotel Gellert when I was a little girl. I couldn't wait until I owned it. With the proceeds from the sale of my New York house and the jewelry insurance I bought it at a cost exceeding $100,000. I remember that when I had signed the proper papers and we drove away, George said, "Do you think we've made a mistake?"

"But George, it was you who told me to buy it!"

"Only because I thought it was a good investment," he said. He was silent as we drove down the long, twisting mountain road leading to the city below. Then he burst out. "Cokiline, I'm happy in my little apartment. I don't like a big house. I won't like living there." And then: "Anyway, it's too damn Chinese!"

We finally compromised. He would move in but maintain his apartment. "I must have a place to commune with myself," he said. "And my workshop is there." There was nothing I could do. I decided this was one of his neuroses. He and his first wife had lived in nearly a dozen houses during their seven years together. Possessions trapped George and he resented them.

In this period he was very difficult, going from one psychoanalyst to another. He came home one afternoon from a session to say, "You know, I told you I'm not going to be easy to live with. You'll have to have a great deal of patience, Cokiline." It was true. I rarely knew what kind of a husband I would greet in the evening. Sometimes he would sit for hours brooding, staring out a window. Or he would strum his guitar and sing sadly to himself in his beautiful baritone voice. At parties he could change from a somber, hostile man who could turn to his guests at 9 o'clock with "Have you eaten enough? Goodnight, then," to a gay delightful host who sat at the piano and entertained us for hours with hilarious, off-color songs. Or, in a complete reversal of mood, at dinner his face would suddenly get gray, he would stop eating and exclaim, "I can't take it! Dammit, I don't want to be an actor! I want to live!"

"But darling—"

"These damn teeth!" The first time I heard it I laughed, but it was not funny to him. He had had his teeth capped when he came to Hollywood, and hated it. "A man's not a man without his own teeth!" He'd rise from the table and collapse into an easy chair. "Why did I do it? To be photogenic? Who needs to be an actor?" When he was calmer he would explain. Acting was for children. "Who else can take this posturing seriously?" In any other profession, too, a man built an equity through the years. A physician, an attorney, an architect—all commanded higher fees and greater respect as they grew older. But the aging actor— "It's the ash heap for him," George would say gloomily. "A lousy profession." He would sigh. "All I want out of life is a fisherman's cottage on the Costa Brava —and to be let alone." He would sigh again. "Let's face it, Cokiline. The only sensible thing for a man of taste and intelligence is to marry a rich woman—and look how I've allowed you to thwart my purpose."

When word came that Ezio Pinza was going to leave *South Pacific,* George said, "You know, I could do that part." Day after day he practiced singing "One Enchanted Evening," until even little Francie was humming it. He began negotiating for the role. He recorded his voice and sent the record to Dick Rodgers and Oscar Hammerstein in New York, who

191

had him fly there and sing for them in person. They promptly signed him to a fifteen-month contract. George flew back, elated. I was absolutely delighted. "George—it's the greatest part on Broadway!" The day the contract arrived in the mail, George became agitated; his back ached, he could hardly walk. "I don't want the part," he said suddenly. "I'm calling them up and pulling out." He did so. The backache vanished.

"I don't understand, George," I said. "You worked so hard to get it, you studied the part so long, you wanted it so badly—"

"Cokiline," he said, "I can't explain it, but I can't face a live audience. It appalls me—"

"But you have such a beautiful voice, and you *can* do it."

No, he said, no. And then, suddenly, "Sit here with me and hold my hand." So we sat together, holding hands.

I was sorry for George. I knew he was a very complicated man. Now, when he said he wanted to keep his apartment, though I felt badly, I did not insist. I remember the day we moved into our new house. The van arrived from New York with all my possessions, and I was directing the men when the front bell rang. There stood George, two suits over one arm, a painting I had bought him under the other, and carrying his favorite ash tray. "I'm moving in, my dear," he announced.

In his autobiography, *Confessions of a Professional Cad*, George has his fun. He writes that while we were married, "I lived in her (Zsa Zsa's) sumptuous Bel Air mansion as a sort of paying guest . . . allotted a small room in which I was permitted to keep my personal effects . . ." The fact is that George had his own bedroom suite next to mine on the second floor, but kept many of his personal effects in his apartment. It was more than a place to commune in—it was his refuge. Whenever we quarreled, he promptly moved back to his apartment, taking with him his two suits, his painting, and his ash tray. Once we made up, he moved back again, bringing his suits, his painting, and his ash tray. One of his first acts after I bought the house was to survey the living room and say, "We need a piano." He played the piano, as he played the guitar and the saxophone, beautifully, and I enjoyed having him accompany himself when he was in his good moods. We drove to a dealer in Los Angeles who supplies pianos to the studios. George spent an evening trying the various instruments until he found one that pleased him—a little black upright that perfectly matched my funriture. He bought it for $400 and moved it into the salon.

From then on, my husband took over the house. When the telephone rang, it was for him—business calls from his agent, his studio, his producer. When telegrams arrived, they were for him—offers to appear on TV, radio, or endorse various products. When we gave parties the guests were nearly all George's fellow actors and actresses. Hardly a day passed that I wasn't reminded that I was the nonprofessional wife of an acting celebrity. At my parties I always began the evening as the gay, bright hostess, but the moment an actress arrived, the conversation turned to her latest film and I was lost in shoptalk. I sat by, trying vainly to think how to get into the conversation, but it was clear that I was to see that the drinks were passed around, the food kept hot, and to direct the way to the powder room.

I tried to be content, to be the *Hausfrau* George wanted. When I telephoned Mother to report that all was well, she was full of Eva's triumph in a new Broadway play, *The Happy Time*. She read the glowing reviews to me. I hung up, thinking: Eva is making a career and I—I bring my husband's slippers to him, I rub his back, I flatter his ego. "I'm a very helpless man," George would assure me. "That's what I need—a woman like you to mother me."

One day I came home from shopping to find the house full of photographers. George had been cast in a new film, *All About Eve,* in which he played a cynical dramatic critic. Twentieth Century-Fox was preparing a magazine layout—"Actor George Sanders At Home"—and George, handsome and elegant, was in the midst of posing. I managed to catch his eye. He came over. "Shouldn't I be included in the pictures?" I asked. "When you're at home, you're at home with me." My husband looked at me and sighed, "My dear, I know it's hard for you to understand, but this story is not about you, it's about *me. I* am the actor." I grew angry. I thought: he's posing before my paintings, he's mixing drinks at my bar, he's lounging in my armchair—I burst out, "George, this is my house. If you want to be photographed in my house, you include me. I'm your wife!"

George glanced at the photographers. "Let's go upstairs, shall we?" he asked suavely. In great dignity, but in utter silence, we stalked up the stairs together to my room. There, behind closed doors, we had words. It was a bitter quarrel. "Why can't you be like James Mason?" I cried. "When he poses for layouts he insists that Pamela be in every picture. When he made a beer ad, he even had her sit at the table with him! When—"

George suddenly burst into laughter. "Cokiline," he said, "you never cease to amaze me. We will do it your way."

We went downstairs to the waiting photographers. This time I was in the layout, too.

Each time I lunched with George at the studio commissary, I realized again that there is no more lonely human being than the wife of a movie star. I was accustomed to notice, but I seemed invisible there. Into the dining room came some of the world's most beautiful women direct from their sets, wearing their striking make-up, dressed in divine gowns, their hair with every curl perfectly in place, each woman more dazzling than the other, while I sat there completely overlooked. I thought: everyone knows who they are, everyone turns to look at them, and here I sit and no one notices me. And George doesn't help me—he's not a man to show off his wife . . .

I could never understand George's indifference, his alternate warmth and scorn, the way he played with me as a cat with a mouse. Often there would be a dinner party. "I'd love to go," I'd say. George would shake his head. "I've got to be at the studio early tomorrow. You go ahead."

"No," I'd say. "I won't go without you."

I stayed home with him.

Then we were invited to another party. Again I had to turn down the invitation. Friends said, "What's wrong with you? We never see you anywhere." I remember a year after our marriage opening my closet and staring at my beautiful Lanvins, Rodriques, Balenciagas—dozens of frocks I had bought in Paris, Madrid, New York. I had not worn a single one. Beautiful clothes are beautiful only if you can show them off, and if they are not worn, they seem to wilt in your closet. And night after night George and I had been going to bed at nine.

One night the James Masons, who lived not far away, said, "If George can't make it, why don't you come to our dinner party alone—we'll take you home." I liked the Masons. I thought James one of the world's most distinguished men and I loved how he looked. I admired Pam's outrageous frankness and wit. In addition, their daughter, Portland, was about Francie's age and the two little girls often played together.

I said, "George—"

"Of course, Cokiline, you go."

Thus, for the first time in our marriage, I went out without George and it was perfectly all right. I fell into the practice. Sometimes George's brother, Tom Conway, took me to Ciro's or the Mocambo; or his agent, Bill Shiffrin; or Bundy Solt, when he was in Hollywood, said, "Zsa, Zsa, can I take you to a movie?"

"Certainly, Bundy old boy, by all means take her," George said.

Then one night Wilson Linnett telephoned. "Zsa Zsa, wouldn't you like to go to the opening of the Coconut Grove tonight?"

I tested George. "George, do you allow me to go out tonight with Wilson Linnett?" I asked because Wilson was a rich, handsome ladies' man.

"Of course, my dear," said George. He was in bed watching TV. "You're young—you two enjoy yourselves. Of course you'll be bored without me, but go ahead. I'll be waiting right here when you come back."

195

My very attractive escort called for me and took me to the Coconut Grove. He was charming, he exuded sex appeal, but as the evening wore on I desperately missed George. I went into the powder room and telephoned him. "Georgie-Porgie, I'm so bored—"

"Didn't I tell you, Cokiline?" he said. "You just stay there with your young man and be bored a little more."

"No, no," I said. Now I could not wait to be with George. "I'm coming home right now."

I made some excuse to Wilson and rushed home to my husband. He was where I had left him. He snapped off the TV switch at his side and held out his arms wide. "Come to papa, baby," he said.

In the end George was to win an Oscar for the best supporting performance by a male actor in *All About Eve,* but I knew only how wretched I was during its shooting. In the cast, with Bette Davis and Anne Baxter, was a striking blonde with an unbelievably divine figure named Marilyn Monroe, who played George's girl friend. Whenever George made love on the screen, I was sick with jealousy; he had only to shake hands with a woman, let alone kiss her. It seemed to me he always meant it. I had seen Marilyn first at the James Masons, where she had been brought by Johnny Hyde, the agent. Pam had said to me, "Look at that pretty girl—she sits there all evening without saying a word. She'll go far, my dear, because she knows how to listen."

George took me with him when the cast flew to San Francisco for exterior shots. On the return plane I sat at a window seat, George beside me. Directly across the aisle from him sat Marilyn. She had not had time to remove her make-up, she wore a very tight sweater, and each time I glanced in her direction, it seemed to me she was making eyes at George, who appeared quite pleased by it all. I was furious, but I said nothing. Then I discovered, back in Hollywood, that George lunched nearly every day with Marilyn at the Twentieth Century-Fox commissary. When I brought this up, George looked at me. "But the commissary is so crowded, the only place the poor girl can sit is with me, so I make room for her. And you know," he added, with admiration, "she writes quite good poetry."

Poetry! I thought. How can I fight her poetry?

Things came to a head when George began another picture *The Light Touch*, for M-G-M, with Stewart Granger and Pier Angeli. Stewart and George, both beautiful in white tie and make-up, lunched with me one noon. "George," I ventured, "I'd like a cigarette."

"No," he said. "I can't afford it."

Stewart Granger looked at him, not sure whether he meant it, but George sat there imperturbably studying the menu. "You—" said Stewart. "I'm going to get a cigarette for your wife if you won't." He rose and bought me a pack.

Later George took me on the set and introduced me to Miss Angeli, who had just arrived from Italy. When we left he said, "Isn't that a pretty child? Isn't she lovely? And without a touch of make-up! Angelic is the word, really angelic." The more George spoke about her the more annoyed I became, especially since I could see that she had make-up.

That night we were invited to a cocktail party at the home of George's psychiatrist. Before leaving we sat for a moment on the edge of my swimming pool, watching the lights go on in the city below. I had been peeved ever since we came back from the set—peeved at how George had belittled me. Now I could not help myself. I turned on him; I told him what I thought, bitterly.

"Really, Cokiline—"

"And you behaved so badly to me before Stewart Granger! You and your showing off! Who do you think you are! You're just a character actor, you're—"

I went on and on. I accused him of every infidelity. He had been up since six that morning, he had worked the entire day at the studio which he hated, for nearly twelve hours he had been in make-up which he despised, he had been smiling at people he loathed—and I nagged him unmercifully. I didn't

197

understand then. Now when I return from the studio, if someone nags me, I'm ready to explode—

George was ready to explode, too. Suddenly he jumped up, his face pale. "I've had it," he said hoarsely, "I'm going to kill you." He advanced on me. I began to back away. "George, Georgie-Porgie," I stammered. "No—no—"

He grabbed me by the throat and began to choke me. "I'm killing you," he muttered between his teeth. "You're not going to do this to me! I can't take it!"

I fought, trying to break his hold. "But you'll be electrocuted—I'll never see you again—this is a serious thing—"

"Oh, no, I won't! I'm throwing your body into the pool, and I'm going to asphyxiate myself in the car—"

"George," I gasped, "it's so silly—don't kill me—don't kill yourself—we have so much to live for—"

I clung to his hand and slowly he strangled me less and less and I don't know what happened but we found ourselves in tears and we apologized to each other and we went on to the cocktail party given by George's psychiatrist as though nothing had happened.

I could happily have strangled George not long after on the night he won his Oscar for his performance in *All About Eve*. We sat together at the Grauman Chinese Theatre. We heard, "Those nominated for the best supporting male actor . . . The winner"—a pause for the space of a heartbeat—"George Sanders!"

I was wild with excitement. I threw my arms around George and kissed him. "Oh, George, I'm so proud, go up, go up!" Without looking at me he rose and walked to the stage. He said into the microphone, "Thank you," and Oscar in hand, he vanished behind the curtain.

I sat alone as the other awards were handed out. The ceremonies came to an end—and I sat there. People filed out, the auditorium became completely empty, and I sat there; a huge, naked electric bulb was switched on: ushers came down the aisles, turning back the seats. I sat alone in the empty, eerily lit auditorium. Somewhere behind the curtains before me, the winners were savoring the triumph of their careers—photographed, interviewed, congratulated—I could hear their laughter and merriment. My husband was there, part of the laughter and merriment. He had completely forgotten me.

Finally, George remembered. An usher came and led me backstage. Nearly everyone had gone.

That night I telephoned Mother. I said, "Yes, George won the award but this was one of the unhappiest times of my life." I thought: why does he share only his misery with me? Why can't he share his happiness as well?

At night, I would think: if I had a career . . .

WHEN it happened, it happened with unbelievable speed.

In the summer of 1951 George went to England—alone. I pleaded to go with him. "No, I can't take you, Cokiline, I'll be working on a film. Anyway, I'll be back in three months."

Before he left James and Pam Mason had us to dinner. Pam was exuberant. She had just been invited to appear on a TV panel show. After coffee, George said, "Let's see how good you are, Pam." He began asking her questions. James, who was always gallant to me, said, "Let Zsa Zsa try, too." So Pam and I took two chairs, and George fired questions at us. Pam, who has been on the British stage and has the self-assurance of a duchess, was brilliant. But with George playing quizmaster I was hopeless. I became flustered, then embarrassed, I couldn't think of answers. "Oh, she'd never do," my husband said. "She's just too dumb."

Those were almost his last words to me before he left. I still see myself running up the stairs to the window to wave goodbye to him, and how the tears rolled down my cheeks as I saw his car drive out of the courtyard.

George had left a little *Hausfrau* waving tearfully from a window.

Three months later, he came back to a celebrity. He walked off the plane to find my face smiling up at him from the cover of *Life* Magazine. He picked up a newspaper to find my bons mots quoted, to read, "Zsa Zsa (pronounced 'Wow!') Gabor is the hottest property in Hollywood." When he telephoned the house to learn why I hadn't met him at the airport, my butler answered, "I'm sorry, Miss Gabor is on the set at M-G-M, shooting—" When he called M-G-M, he was switched to my press agent, Russell Birdwell; and when finally he arrived home, proofs of my latest magazine layout covered the library table, the brass plate in the foyer was piled high with my telegrams.

What had happened?

Two days after George left, Tom Conway telephoned me. He was to appear on a new panel show, *Bachelor's Haven,* an advice-to-the-lovelorn program patterned after *Leave It to the Girls,* which had been highly successful in the East. "I think you'd be wonderful on it—all they do is read husband-wife letters and ask our advice," he explained. As a guest on the first show they wanted the wife of a celebrity and he had suggested Mrs. George Sanders. "But Tom—" George's last words still haunted me. "I don't know if I can do it."

"Nonsense!" said Tom. "All you have to be is yourself. Just chitchat, yak-yak the way you always do."

Mother had arrived to be my house guest. "Why not?" she said. "I always bring you luck. Try."

Tom drove me down to the CBS studio that night. The audience was already in their seats. We took our places at a table with the other panelists—Paul Coates, the Los Angeles *Mirror-News* columnist, and Kay Aldridge, wife of Arthur Cameron, an oil man.

Johnny Jacobs, the moderator, stopped as he began to introduce me. I had dressed carefully, wearing a stunning black off-the-shoulder Balenciaga dress and with it a large diamond bracelet, my diamond earrings, and my 20-carat solitaire. Johnny whistled. "Look at those diamonds!"

I held my hand out to the light. "Oh, these," I said disdainfully. "They're just my working diamonds."

The audience roared. From then on I could do no wrong.

What happened that first evening is still vague in my mind.

I have read many accounts of it, for those who saw it have never forgotten it. All I know is in that half-hour my career was handed me on a silver platter—as perhaps, subconsciously, I always knew it would. I remember Johnny reading a letter: "Dear Panel: I'm breaking my engagement to a very wealthy man. He gave me a beautiful home, a mink coat, diamonds, a stove, and an expensive car. What shall I do?"

I spoke up almost without thinking. "Give back the stove."

The audience burst into laughter—and I with them. Now that I heard what I said, I thought it funny, too.

A second letter: "My husband is a traveling salesman but I know he strays, even when he's home. How can I stop him?

Again I popped up: "Shoot him in the legs."

Even to this day I can't understand what was so funny about my reply. It was only common sense.

So the evening went on. I said whatever came into my head. Each time I smiled, each time I interrupted a commercial, each time I ad-libbed with someone in the audience—"Can you cook?" someone asked. "You betcha," I said. "When I was courting George Sanders I cooked three meals a day for him in his apartment until I catched him. Now I don't cook for him any more." I was being outrageous and loving it. Everything I said or did seemed to set the audience off again.

I was honestly surprised. I had always been saying this sort of thing: the exaggerated, the ridiculous, poking fun at myself. I dropped a "damn" and caught myself. I blushed at a *double-entendre* I hadn't intended, or perhaps had intended—I still don't understand why I was such a success that night or the many Monday nights thereafter. Even today I don't understand why people laugh at me on the Jack Paar show. They laugh at something I say—and until I say it, I don't know what I'm going to say. If you ask me to repeat an ad-lib line, I can't. I remember it only when I read it in the papers.

Next morning my telephone did not stop ringing. One of the first callers was Bundy Solt. "Zsa Zsa," he said in great excitement, "have you read the trades?"

"Trades?" I asked. "What are the trades?"

Bundy swore in Hungarian. "You dope," he said. "Wait—I'll read them to you." I had never heard of *Daily Variety* and *The Hollywood Reporter,* the show business publications everyone in the industry religiously reads every morning.

I listened, unbelieving.

Then Pam Mason was on the telephone. "Darling, you were terrific. You're a scream on television!"

Bill Brennan, producer of the show, was next. "We want to keep you on as a permanent panelist—you and Paul Coates," he said. "We can pay you the tremendous fee of thirty-six dollars an appearance—and if you're a good girl, a cup of coffee after the show. Will that be all right?"

Thirty-six dollars for a half-hour to "chitchat, yak-yak" as I had done as far back as I could remember—with the English girls in Switzerland, with Madame Inonu and Ataturk and Sir Percy and Karakhan and Conrad—I was being paid just to be myself. It seemed like thirty-six hundred dollars to me.

Now an avalanche of attention descended on me. Publicity led to publicity. At night clubs when I entered faces turned toward me. I heard, "Oh, Zsa Zsa, you were sensational last night!" *The Hollywood Reporter* had said, "the most beautiful girl ever to be seen on a television screen . . ." When I went shopping women stopped me in the street and spoke to me as though they'd known me all their lives. "Zsa Zsa, you're saying just what I've wanted to say to my husband for twenty years and never dared to." At the Mocambo I was dancing with Tom Conway when Mervyn LeRoy, the producer, tapped me on the shoulder. "I'm doing a new picture and there's a part— a cute French model—just right for you. Like to do it?" I thought he was pulling my leg. "No," said Mervyn, with his quick, warm smile. "I mean it. You're so right I won't even bother with a test." He described the role in the picture, an M-G-M musical, *Lovely To Look At.* My lines would be in French and each time I spoke, English subtitles would appear on the screen. "I'd adore it," I said. "If you think I can do it. When do we start?"

Mervyn laughed. "Come with your agent to my office at

noon tomorrow and we'll talk business." I'd completely forgotten that I would be paid for this, too.

Bill Shiffrin, George's agent, accompanied me next morning to the M-G-M offices. On the way he said, "How much salary should we ask?" George had been paid $250 a week in his first Hollywood film assignment. He added, "Why don't we ask an impossible figure—say, a thousand a week?" The sum simply did not register with me.

Twenty minutes later I floated out of Mervyn's office. Bill had asked for $1,000. Mervyn said, "O.K." I almost fainted. I was to call immediately upon Helen Vogeler, the dramatic coach who years before had helped me with my English. I rushed into her bungalow on the M-G-M lot. "Oh, dear Mrs. Vogeler," I burst out, "you can't imagine—I got the part of Mignon in *Lovely To Look At*." I hardly noticed a beautiful girl sitting in her anteroom.

Mrs. Vogeler stared at me. "Are you sure?"

"I just came from Mr. LeRoy himself—"

Then I saw the girl burst into tears and rush from the room. Someone had promised her the part; she had been studying for it for three months. It was my first experience with the Hollywood heartbreak I had read so much about.

I had appeared on *Bachelor's Haven* four times when Bill Brennan was on the phone almost stammering with excitement. "*Life* Magazine wants to do a story on you—on us— they're flying Philippe Halsman, the photographer, in from New York to do a cover on you!" He couldn't get over it. "We're just a small local program! . . ."

Mother said, "See, I always bring you luck." Then, "But why didn't you do all this sooner?"

Mr. Halsman arrived, a slender, intelligent European who had me pose endlessly for him, whenever I found time from my dancing lessons, my coaching lessons, studying my script, being interviewed. One morning just before I dashed off to M-G-M to discuss my costumes with Adrian, the designer, a smooth, cultured voice came over the telephone. "I don't know whether you know my name—I am Russell Birdwell." I had never heard the name. Later I found out that he was among Hollywood's most famous press agents. He had been living abroad and had just returned to reopen his Hollywood offices. He had been told I was to have a *Life* cover in a few weeks. "The whole country will be talking about you. You don't need me but I need you. I'd like to take you on as a client." I would have to pay him nothing, but if asked, was to say that he had helped arrange the publicity I was getting. I discussed it with Bill Shiffrin. "You don't need a press agent," he said. "Look at what you get without one. But I'd go with Birdwell. You're in the big leagues now."

Mr. Birdwell came to tea that afternoon—suave, handsome, persuasive. "I'm laying out a campaign for you," he said. "Our aim isn't to impress the whole country, as you're doing now. We want to impress the ten top picturemakers." He spoke intelligently and charmingly.

A new life opened for me. Russell began taking me to all the important openings, in baronial style with chauffeured limousine. At last I was able to use my magnificent clothes that had been hanging uselessly in my closets. Items began to appear in all the columns. I felt I was in good hands.

Two months had passed since George went to London.

I sat in Mervyn LeRoy's office as he picked up the phone and called Bert Allenberg, president of the William Morris Agency, largest talent agency in the country. "Our next star is with me," I heard him say. "I want you to handle her." Mr. Allenberg signed me to a contract. A press agent, a film agent —"You're going to need a business manager soon," said Mervyn, with a grin.

By the eleventh week my life had completely changed. Mother had left and by a stroke of unbelievably good luck a friend had sent me Mrs. Elizabeth Keleman, a widow, a former concert pianist in Hungary, who took over my child, my household, and me, and made possible the furious schedule I now found myself on. It was a schedule which hardly gave me time to do more than kiss Francie and play with her a few minutes before dinner. She was becoming a beautiful little girl, with Mother's enormous brown eyes and a marvelously sunny disposition, and I adored her. Thank God, I thought, that I have an Elizabeth to take care of my child. For now I was rising at 6 A.M. to dash down to M-G-M to be made up for *Lovely To Look At;* then there was shooting on the set from 9 A.M. to 5 P.M., and throughout the day, when they could be sandwiched in, appointments and fittings—with hairdressers, dressmakers, designers, dramatic coaches, reporters; calls from M-G-M, CBS, the William Morris Agency, Russell Birdwell; and in the evening, after a hurried bite with Elizabeth and Francie, there were openings to go to, fashion shows to visit, benefits to emcee, *Bachelor's Haven* and other shows, and autographs, autographs, autographs to sign—

In the midst of this, George, completely unsuspecting, came home.

19

"COKILINE, what you've done in three months!" George couldn't get over it. I had rushed back from the studio, still in my make-up, to greet him and proudly bring him up to date on everything that had happened to me. "Fantastic," he said. "Absolutely fantastic." He seemed genuinely excited by my success.

Almost his first act was to recommend me for Tallulah Bankhead's Sunday night radio program, *The Big Show*, in which the country's top stars—Jack Benny, Ethel Merman, Bob Hope, Jimmy Durante—were her guests. George had appeared on it twice, in New York and Paris. Now he had been told that one of the shows was to be done in Hollywood. "I'm going to get you on it," he said. He telephoned the writers and suggested they write a skit for us. I heard my husband say, "She'll be great—she's the hottest thing in town."

I went upstairs to unpack his luggage. On one of his handkerchiefs was a vivid imprint of lipstick. George came up as I was gazing at it. He grinned. "Oh, Cokiline, don't worry about that. It's Pamela Churchill. She wanted to make you jealous. I took her out in Paris and she did that so you could see it."

All at once, he did not hurt me with those words as he had in the past. I was becoming somebody in my own right—and I thought: Pamela Churchill is just Pamela Churchill, the former wife of the son of Winston Churchill. I felt stronger: George could still hurt me, but not as much, I told myself. The more I achieved on my own, the more immune I would be.

How wrong I was I learned when George, a few months

207

after his return, took me to a party given at Ciro's by Cobina Wright, the society columnist. Since we rarely went out, I knew this was something of an occasion. On the receiving line were Cobina, and a tall, slender woman I recognized as Doris Duke. Doris saw George. "Darling," she said fondly, kissing him on both cheeks, "didn't we have fun this afternoon?"

I stood there speechless. As long as I had known George, his face had lit up when Miss Duke's name was mentioned. He would joke, saying, "That's the woman I should have married." He would play with the idea of a rich wife. "You know, Cokiline, there's no greater aphrodisiac than money." It always upset me; I would grow angry and stalk off.

Now, as George and I moved to the buffet table, my mind was in a whirl. Someone said, "Your remark on *Bachelor's Haven* the other night—I've been quoting it all over the place!" Photographers trained their cameras on me, flash bulbs popped, and I turned in their direction, smiling brightly, but thinking frantically: when did he meet her? And if he met her, why didn't he tell me?

I said, when I could control my voice, "George, I didn't know you knew Doris Duke. When did you meet her?"

"Oh, didn't I tell you, darling?" Since he came back from London he had been taking voice instruction from a coach in Los Angeles. "Doris takes lessons there, too. I meet her every day. We had a drink together this afternoon."

I was like a woman possessed, standing there. I smiled and used small talk for people who came by, but I could only think: all this with Doris Duke! He knows her! And I'm at the studio all day . . .

I couldn't wait until we left the night club. We had come in my new car—a Cadillac that matched my hair, which I had bought out of my first month's salary saying to myself: I don't need Conrad or George to buy me what I want. George started the car and as we pulled into the street I began to hit and kick him. I pounded him with my fists, I kicked him in the leg so violently that he lost control of the car and we crashed into another car ahead of us. As a motorcycle policeman

208

roared up, George said to me, "What am I going to say? That my wife kicked me? That I'm drunk?"

I didn't care. "I hate you!" I cried. "I never want to see you again!" I was hysterical. I said to him all the stupid things a woman can say. I accused him of everything. He denied everything. "You're being ridiculous, Cokiline, utterly ridiculous."

I was being ridiculous but I couldn't help it. I was consumed with jealousy. I could compete with any woman on equal terms, I would match myself, beauty for beauty, sex appeal for sex appeal, against any woman, but I could not compete with the richest woman in the world.

For days I brooded. I could think of nothing else. This man I so desperately loved, this man I tried so desperately to make happy . . . Suddenly, as we were sitting on our terrace after dinner, I burst out, "All right, George. I'll get even with you. Wherever this Rubirosa is, I'm going to meet him."

I knew nothing about Porfirio Rubirosa. I had read about him in the tabloids, that he was the great lover of our time, that he had been Doris Duke's husband, that she still loved him deeply and had begged him in vain to remarry her. I said wildly, "I'm going to have an affair with Rubirosa."

I looked up at George as I said this, and his face dropped. For the first time I had gotten a reaction from him—an almost imperceptible look of dismay—at the mention of another man's name. He had never been jealous. He had paid no attention when anyone made a fuss over me, when I went out with other men, when I spoke admiringly of other men. He had given me a complex by his lack of jealousy. Rubirosa was just a name to me, a face, not too clear, that I had seen in the newspapers.

"You're a very silly girl," George said coldly. He rose and went into the house.

I tried to forget about Doris Duke. I never gave Porfirio Rubirosa another thought.

It was amazing now how the tables were turned. Now

George, who had no picture assignment, sat about the house waiting for me to return from the studios exhausted, complaining about my cameraman, the heat on the set, the director. Now George answered the telephone, took down messages, signed for my telegrams. Now when magazine photographers came, it was I who said, "George, I want you in the picture with me." He took it all with a kind of self-mocking, tongue-in-cheek amusement. Once, strolling down Hollywood Boulevard, we paused to look into a shopwindow. Half a dozen teen-agers descended on us, squealing. "Zsa Zsa!" Out came their autograph books. As I signed the last few, one girl turned to George. "You look awfully familiar," she said doubtfully. "Aren't you someone, too?"

George's lip curled. "Yes, my dear child," he said. "I am Mr. Gabor." He took my arm. "Come, Cokiline." I pretended I had heard nothing, but I felt for George. With his complex about the dead-end street of acting, how this must have cut him! On another occasion, at a party given by Humphrey Bogart and Lauren Bacall, we saw Ethel Barrymore across the room. She smiled at us. George began to preen; she rose to come toward us, we rose, too, and we met in the middle of the room. Miss Barrymore put her hand out to me and said in her magnificent voice, "Zsa Zsa, I want you to know that I'm one of your biggest fans. You can't get me out of the house on Monday nights." George, never at a loss, carried it off magnificently, appearing as pleased as if the compliment had been meant for him.

When the script for Tallulah's show arrived a few days later, perhaps I was in a bad mood, perhaps I didn't understand, but as I read it, I grew outraged. Tallulah's writers poked fun at me, they ridiculed our marriage. I read George's lines: "That was no lady, Tallulah, that was my wife"; and "We have been married two years and I haven't spoken to Zsa Zsa since she said yes." And such dialogue as:

Tallulah: "Does Zsa Zsa speak to you?"
Sanders: "Only in Hungarian."
Tallulah: "What does she say?"

Sanders: "I can only guess."

Tallulah: "Do you understand Hungarian?"

Sanders: "Not this one."

Tallulah: "Well, I don't see how you could possibly put up with that kind of a domestic setup."

Sanders: "Well, she's deliriously happy. After all, she can catch fleeting glimpses of me as I walk in the garden or dive into the pool and we do have a certain intimacy. We do share the top drawer of the dresser."

Reading these lines now, they sound quite silly to me. But I was deeply hurt then. I could poke fun at myself but I hated it when others poked fun at me. If Tallulah Bankhead and George had ribbed me before friends, I would have resented it; but to do it before an audience of millions—I was furious. And I did not understand Tallulah's sense of humor then. I felt she was treating me like "plain Mrs. George Sanders" too. Only a few nights before, I had come home late from the studio to find my house packed with people having a wonderful time—George had thrown a party for Tallulah's cast without telling me. I walked in, tired, and in no mood for a party. No one paid attention to me. George was playing chess with a pretty starlet and did not even rise to introduce me. I continued haughtily up the stairs to my room and closed the door. It had led to another quarrel.

Now when I complained about the dialogue, George pooh-poohed me. "That's the format of the show. Everyone tears everyone else apart—it's just a joke, my dear." I took the skit to Elsa Stanoff, my dramatic coach and adviser, and a European. "You can never say those lines," she exclaimed indignantly. "I simply don't understand Mr. Sanders' humor of insult."

The week of the broadcast George and I met at CBS for rehearsal. We sat on wooden stools still arguing while we waited for Tallulah. She arrived a half-hour late, wearing a nondescript sweater and slacks. This irritated me, too—I felt let down to see Tallulah Bankhead like that. A great star, I thought then, and still think, has an obligation never to de-

211

stroy the illusion of her beauty and glamour—she must always be seen in public as she is on the stage. I believe she owes it to her audience. "Hello, darlings," Tallulah cried gaily as she swept in. She saw George and hurried to him. "George, darling, I love you!" and to me, as she passed me by, "Darling, who are you?" without waiting for an answer.

We began reading our parts. George read, "Oh, yes, I have a wife, but she washes my socks, we never meet—"

I spoke up. "I don't want him to say that line."

Someone placated me. The reading continued. Now I had to read a line. "No," I said, "I won't say this. It insults both of us. It's got to be changed."

Tallulah withered me with a look. "Darling," she said icily, "nobody changes the lines here. This is a funny skit. It stays the way it is."

I said, "Then I am walking out." I put the script down.

Tallulah said, her voice rising, "Nobody walks out on Tallulah Bankhead."

I turned on her. "Well, I'm the first, then, and I'm sure there'll be many others." I marched off the stage. I heard George: "Zsa Zsa—" I had just reached my car and was getting haughtily into it when George grabbed my arm. His face was white.

"How can you do this to me—after I got you the job!"

"I don't care—I won't be ridiculed!"

He was hoarse with fury. "If you walk off now, I'm moving out of the house."

I said, "I won't say those lines," and got into my car and drove off to Mrs. Stanoff. I fought to control myself when I got there. "Yes, you did right," she said stoutly. "Stick to it."

At seven o'clock that night George and I were to go to a dinner party at the Jack Warners' honoring General de Gaulle's brother. I waited for George, but when he did not come home, I went alone, feeling heroic. I, who had just begun my career, had dared walk out on the great Tallulah. But at the Warners' my bravado left me and I blurted out everything that had happened. In the powder room Greer Garson and Rosalind Russell comforted me. "Don't worry, darling," Greer said, "George is just being temperamental, but he'll understand you're right when he has a chance to think it over." Rosalind was indignant. "Why should he say things like that? Why should he belittle you?"

I telephoned Elizabeth hopefully all through the evening, but George did not come home. I know where he is, I thought; he's back in his apartment again. But I was too proud to call him.

Next day on the set I showed an unconcerned face to everyone. *McCall's Magazine* had arranged to do a story about me and when shooting stopped, I began posing in my dressing room for the photographers and answered the questions of their reporter. He was asking, "Now, Zsa Zsa, what's the secret of keeping a man?" when someone interrupted us. There was a telephone call for me. I almost ran to the little telephone stand in the corner.

"Oh, Mrs. Sanders—" Elizabeth's voice trembled. "Mr. Sanders is upstairs packing his suits—"

"That's all right, Elizabeth," I said with a calm I did not feel. "He'll come back."

"But he's brought a truck and they're moving out the piano—"

I knew then that George meant it. I became frantic. "Don't let him!" I screamed over the wire, because I knew that as long as I had the piano, George would return.

"I can't stop him, Mrs. Sanders," Elizabeth wailed.

I hung up, helpless. I stood by the little telephone stand, a dozen stagehands around joking with me—and I did not know what to do with my tears. I returned to my dressing room, I was again the smiling Zsa Zsa, fencing with my interviewer, jesting about men, women, and diamonds.

My walkout made news. Within twenty-four hours it seemed the entire country was debating it. Dorothy Kilgallen, the columnist, nominated me "Woman of the Week" for refusing to treat the relationship of husband and wife in "comic-strip terms." The New York *Journal-American* announced a contest: $50 for the best letter on the question, "Was Zsa Zsa Right When She Resented Slur on Marriage?" Mother, Magda, Eva, George were interviewed. I said, "The script went too far. George doesn't want a glamorous wife—he wants a nurse to wait on him hand and foot." George announced, "I have been discarded like a squeezed lemon," which I thought quite witty until I discovered he had stolen it from Ferenc Molnár. Mother said, "That man is as cold as an icebox, but a Hungarian can always do something about a fellow like that." Magda said, "Zsa Zsa's absolutely right. The script was untrue and undignified. But they're very much in love and they'll get together again." Eva said, "I can understand George's point that an actor should speak his lines, but family instinct puts me on Zsa Zsa's side."

Everyone, even I, thought it screamingly funny—in public. But only in public.

I endured our separation for five days. At 2 A.M. of the sixth day, I could no longer fight it. I forgot my pride and telephoned George.

"What do you want?" came his gruff voice.

"When are you coming home?" I asked humbly.

"Never," he said.

"Oh, George, you can't be that mad—"

But he was. How dared I do what I had done? Tallulah had taken me only on his recommendation. It was an important program—it was a feather in my cap to be on it—and I had spoiled everything. As for the lines: I didn't understand them, they were tongue in cheek, I should not have been offended. I tried to explain to him that had I been an established actress, perhaps I wouldn't have minded. Everyone would assume that I was playing a part. But I had come on as his wife—"And Pam Mason is always pulling my leg that you treat me like a little dog and belittle me in public—"

George said something unprintable about Pam Mason.

214

We talked a little more. I was afraid he would hang up. "What are you doing?" I ventured.

"Lying here watching TV," he said. "There's an old movie on Channel Two."

I turned on Channel Two. "The Western?" I asked.

"Yes," said George.

So we remained for the next few minutes, George in his bed in his apartment, I in my bed in my house, watching the same program on television.

"George—" I began. I wanted so badly to be with him. "I miss you," I said. "I miss you terribly."

"You don't tell me," said George, as only he could say it.

"Yes, terribly, terribly."

There was a silence.

"You know what I miss, Cokiline," he said, in another tone of voice. "Mostly the sandwiches you make for me and the milk you bring me in the middle of the night."

I began to sniffle.

"Would you like to bring me a sandwich and a bottle of milk now?" said George. "I'm all out of milk. You can come here then and we can watch together."

"Oh, George!" I said. I dressed like mad and rushed down to the refrigerator and fixed a ham sandwich and wrapped it in wax paper and grabbed a bottle of milk and dashed into my car and drove the ten miles through the night to George's apartment.

He opened the door as if nothing had happened. I heard the crackling of gunshot from the television set. "Hello, my darling," he said, and I was in his arms.

Next day he moved back, bringing his two suits, his painting, and his ash tray. Once more the piano was in its accustomed place.

We sealed our reunion when I bought him an electric saw for Christmas.

215

20

NOW my marriage to George became a curious thing. There were two stars in the house. Our egos clashed at every turn. With the least argument George moved to his apartment, the press took over, there was bright talk of separation. "I'll take him back only if he gives up his apartment and approves my career," I would announce, through Russell Birdwell. From George, a few days later, a lofty bulletin: "Shall we say an armistice has been declared? Terms of surrender are being discussed." Then we reconciled, Louella Parsons reported we'd been seen dining together, and Hollywood went back to other matters. We were in love, but we tormented each other; when I pursued, he fled; when he pursued, I fled. We took turns visiting the same psychoanalyst—it would have been hilarious if it had not been so sad. But we both showed the same gaily indifferent face to the public.

If part of the problem was George's own indecision about himself, part of the problem was mine, too. Somewhere in me was a woman who wanted to be completely dominated by a man; but now there was also in me a restless, driving, ambitious woman who *had* to have a career.

And at last my career was coming at me—so swiftly that I hardly had time to realize what was happening to my private life. That year of 1952, in addition to weekly appearances on *Bachelor's Haven* and dozens of radio and TV engagements, I made five films. The day I finished *Lovely To Look At*, I began *We Are Not Married*, in which I played the gay young wife of Louis Calhern; then *The Story of Three Loves* with

Farley Granger; then *Lili,* in which I danced with Leslie Caron and Mel Ferrer. When I saw myself on the screen for the first time, I agreed with the critics. They said I was pretty and decorative, but as for my acting—well, I thought, I have just begun, how should I know how to act well when I have never been on a stage except for my brief Vienna experience? It took weeks for me to become accustomed to the camera, but with each film I gained more confidence. In *Lovely To Look At,* Adrian, the designer, let me choose my own costumes. The picture was in Technicolor; the other actresses— Kathryn Grayson, Ann Miller, Marge Champion—dressed in pinks, blues, reds, brilliant colors. I choose to appear only in black. No one had dared wear black in Technicolor: it created a sensation. The treatment the press gave me added to my confidence. In October 1951, I had been on the cover of *Life;* in the next months my photograph was on the cover of seven other major magazines, including *Look, Collier's,* Paris *Match,* and the London *Picture Post.*

It all led to my most important role until then—that of Jane Avril in *Moulin Rouge.* When I first read the script I thought: this was written for me. James Woolf, the English producer, in Hollywood, seeking an actress to play the beautiful dancer who lives only for love and the admiration of men, apparently thought so, too. "You're more like Jane Avril than anyone I can imagine," he said. I would have to sing, but they would be able to fix that. He had already signed José Ferrer to play the artist Henri Toulouse-Lautrec, and John Huston to direct the picture, which would be made in Paris and London.

Almost the day the script arrived, I began learning my lines. In Jane Avril I saw myself—or the self I wanted to be. The part was almost too perfect. One scene, so beautiful, yet so sad, haunted me. Toulouse-Lautrec is on his deathbed, and in a moving dream sequence imagines that all his favorite subjects—the beautiful women he painted—come alive to dance their farewell to him. I am the last to come dancing into his room. "Oh, Toulouse, I heard you are dying. I came to say goodbye. It was good to know you. I will see you soon, but

217

now I must run because I have the most beautiful man waiting for me at Maxim's." I blow him a kiss. "Goodbye, Toulouse,
goodbye"—and I dance out again. That was how Toulouse-
Lautrec died, that tragic, suffering man, seeing before his eyes
for the last time the gay, beautiful Jane Avril he always loved,
whom he knew when she was seventeen, to whom he could
say, "Look what you have achieved—all Paris is at your feet,
and you are only twenty-eight—"

I say, "Only twenty-five, my dear Toulouse. I shall never be
more than twenty-five."

It was full of such lovely, heartbreaking scenes, as if my
own heart were speaking the words.

And to be directed by John Huston, to act with José Ferrer,
to go to Paris and shoot scenes at Maxim's, the most famous
restaurant in the world with its crimson tapestried walls and
its memories of the handsome men and beautiful women—I
was beside myself. I kissed George goodbye—now I was going
away and he remained—and he said, "My dear, do you realize
that you will be in one of the most distinguished pictures of
the year?"

From the first John Huston, lean, leathery, and nervous as
a cat, had a paralyzing effect on me. He was the kind of dour,
listening man who makes me feel that he thinks everything I
say to him is a lie. I had no idea when I arrived in Paris that
John had turned me down for the part when my name was
first suggested. It was only Jimmy Woolf's insistence that kept
me in the picture—the only amateur in a cast of professionals.

John and I had a noon appointment for rehearsal before
shooting at Maxim's, and I came a little frightened of him,
but full of confidence. The Paris *Soir* had greeted me as *"Zsa
Zsa, la femme la plus chic du monde"*—Zsa Zsa, the most
fashionable woman in the world—but I needed all my assur-
ance that afternoon.

"Come upstairs," John said gruffly. I followed him to the
second floor into a huge banquet room, now deserted, filled
with rows of chairs turned upside down. John opened the

windows, letting in all the noise of Paris, and told me to take a seat against one wall. Then he walked across the room and sat down on the far side. "Now," he called to me, "let's see if you can project." He asked me to read a scene.

Why? I thought. *Moulin Rouge* was not a play. It wasn't necessary for my voice to be heard in the rear seats of a theater. In picture-making a microphone is always just over your head. Elsa Stanoff, my coach, had warned me, "Never speak loudly—the more conversational the better." But I tried to project now, to make John hear every word above the blare of taxi horns, the sound of lunch-hour traffic in the streets below. I did badly. I resented what I had to do. Why should a young actress playing Jane Avril, a frivolous little dancer, have to project and be Duse? Jimmy Woolf had hired me not as Duse but as Zsa Zsa—he wanted me to play myself.

Ever since the Theater an der Wien, this conflict has troubled me. Directors want me because I represent a definite personality—the Zsa Zsa I created—and then they insist on forcing the Stanislavsky method, or some other method, upon me to make me be Zsa Zsa. The result is that what is natural to me becomes contrived, and I feel ridiculous. When I am called upon in a film to say to a man, "I love you," I don't need anyone to tell me what to think, or how I must feel as I say the words. As a woman, I know. At the beginning John Huston's intense, precise directions tortured me. In the following days as the shooting began, we actually fought each other.

"Cut!" he would say. Again, "Cut! Why don't you do it my way!" Or, "Goddamit, she's dropping the ends of her sentences!"

Often there were spectators, members of the international set who had been allowed to come to watch John Huston make a picture, José Ferrer act, Zsa Zsa Gabor appear in her stunning, turn-of-the-century costumes. I realized that my fame was much greater than my acting ability at this time, but many of the people before whom John embarrassed me were my friends, whom I had met or entertained in my home. Now they saw John stop me, correct me, shout at me. "Zsa Zsa, if you go dead again on the end of a line, I'll shoot you, so help me!" I felt utterly humiliated before them.

I tried to explain to John. The Hungarian language is spoken with a singsong lilt; Hungarians are inclined to drop the last word of every sentence. "I understand," John said sourly. "Try it again."

The more he interrupted me, the more insecure I became. The set was unbearably hot. John had introduced a new technique in this Technicolor film; we were all to be photographed under blue lights and all about us were prop men with machines puffing blue smoke on us. He wanted everything to appear as Toulouse-Lautrec saw the world about him, in shadows of blue and green—the colors that haunt his paintings and express the sadness of his spirit. This was a mark of John's genius, but it added to the strain.

José Ferrer helped me through the ordeal. When we sat rehearsing lines at a table and John Huston turned savagely on me, Joe would grip my hand and whisper. "Don't worry —you'll be fine." I got into the habit of watching Joe's face each time I shot a scene. John Huston would be sitting behind the camera, looking unhappy, sipping tomato juice and vodka, seemingly hostile to the entire world, but I kept my eyes on Joe. If he smiled I knew I had done well; if he shook his head I knew it could be better and I would ask John, "Can we reshoot that?"

In London, later in the picture, Constance Collier, the great actress, took me under her wing. She was coaching Katherine Hepburn in a play, *The Millionairess*, and Jimmy Woolf suggested that she coach me, too. I wanted desperately to be perfect in my part; to make doubly sure, every day I telephoned Elsa Stanoff in Hollywood and talked over my lines with her. The result was that I now had three experts—John, Constance, and Elsa—giving me their interpretation of my role, and I was in a state of absolute confusion. None the less, somehow I managed. My high moment came in the famous stair scene, when I appear dancing down the stairs at Maxim's, singing "The Song of Moulin Rouge." Though there were many stars in the film, in this scene I felt myself the star of them all. *I* sang the song, *I* danced the dances *I* had improvised, the delight in being young and beautiful and adored by all the world was *my* delight—I was Zsa Zsa living a dream, I was Jane Avril come to live again in a world of beauty and bittersweet love—it is impossible to express how I felt. When John said quietly, "Cut—that's it," there was a moment of silence until everyone came back to reality, and then even the stagehands burst into applause. It turned out to be one of the great scenes in the film. Even today, when I enter a night club anywhere in the world, the orchestra will break into "The Song of Moulin Rouge," as I make my way to the table.

It wasn't all work. On July 14, Bastille Day, when millions of Parisians pour into the streets to celebrate a kind of Fourth of July holiday marking the fall of the Bastille, and the skies are brilliant with fireworks, John Huston said, "We'll take a holiday, too." The entire cast of *Moulin Rouge* dined at the Tour d'Argent, a famous restaurant on the Seine overlooking Notre Dame Cathedral. I found myself seated next to a jaunty, dark-eyed man with an extraordinarily winning smile—Prince Aly Khan, whose marriage to Rita Hayworth was coming to an end. "You're one of the few women in America I've longed to meet," said His Highness. And then, his eyes twinkling, "Do you know, you look as though you're made of sugar and spice." I did, too. I was all in pink; my hair silver blonde with an enormous chignon, a pink accordion pleated taffeta gown with an accordion pleated coat to match, by Madame Schiaparelli, pink shoes, pink gloves, and my diamonds to make me sparkle. When the dinner was over, somehow everyone else vanished and Aly and I found ourselves laughing and pushing our way through the crowded, lantern-lit streets with the rest of celebrating Paris. Later we made a round of little cellar night clubs, each one darker and more fascinating than the other. It was dawn when Aly brought me, flushed, tired, gayer than I had been for a long time, to my hotel.

"When will I see you again?" he asked. Only after our

company had gone to London, I told him. I had been in London a few days when Aly called me from Paris. "I'm coming over tomorrow night. Will you dine with me?"

Next morning dozens of roses were delivered to my room. At 2 P.M. there was a telephone call from Aly's French secretary in Paris. "Madame, the Prince has just taken the airplane. He wishes you to know that he will be in London in a few hours and you may expect him at 7:30 o'clock."

An hour later the telephone rang again. It was the London airport. A man's voice said, "His Highness, the Prince Aly Khan, has just arrived. He wishes you to know that he will be very happy to fetch you at 7:30 P.M. He will be in black tie."

An hour later, again, the telephone. This time it was Aly's English secretary at the Ritz Hotel in London. "Madame, His Highness has arrived at the hotel. He is taking his bath and he wants you to know that he will be there at 7:30."

A few minutes later, more flowers.

At 7:30 I was ready—and waiting. At 8:00 I was still waiting. At 8:30 Aly was at my door. "My darling, forgive me for being late—" He kissed my hand and we went out.

He was the most charming, debonair, thoughtful companion any woman could wish for. He had the gift of making me feel from the moment I met him that I had known him all my life. He danced cheek to cheek but somehow I sensed that while our cheeks touched, his eyes were sweeping the room, alert for a new face, a new adventure.

He invited me as a house guest to his villa, romantically named "Château de l'Horizon" in Cannes. I could not accept. Would I allow him, then, to take me to Ascot, where one of his horses was running? I agreed. All that stands out in my mind of that afternoon is our five o'clock tea. As we had our tea on the terrace, every few minutes he was called to the telephone by women calling from various parts of the world— and each received a sweet charming invitation to the Château de l'Horizon.

Then there was the evening Count John de Benden took me to dinner at Les Ambassadeurs, a favorite night club of

Americans in London. Not far away sat Honeychile Wilder, the Princess Hohenloe, with Ayisa, the Maharani of Jaipur. Seated at their table was a man who seemed carved into impassivity in contrast to the two women chatting together so busily. John saw my glance. He bent toward me and whispered, "That's that absurd Rubirosa guy."

I heard myself saying, almost shocked, "*That* man?" Was this the man whose name I had whipped George with?

As I stared Rubirosa rose and vanished into another room. I had caught only a glimpse of him, and I was not impressed. I turned to John. "Not my type at all," I said. This was no tall, blue-eyed prince, no Ataturk or Hilton or Sanders. Rather, what I had seen of him reminded me of Burhan Belge, and I had no wish to be reminded of Burhan.

We opened our menus and ordered.

Twice the name of Rubirosa had been brought to my consciousness and twice I had let it fade away.

I had been back in Hollywood only a short time when George, who had been wandering about the house like a disembodied spirit brooding over his inactivity, received a cable from Roberto Rossellini, the great Italian director. Would he come to Rome to co-star with Ingrid Bergman in Rossellini's new film, *A Voyage?* George was like a new man. We both admired Rossellini—we had seen his *Open City* and *Paisan*— and George instantly wired back a delighted acceptance.

I didn't want to be separated again from my husband. "Take me with you," I begged him. "Please, George."

"No," said George firmly. He was like himself again—even more so. "No, my dear, you'll spoil my fun."

Very well, I told myself bitterly. Thank God for a career! I threw myself into work. I appeared on the Bob Hope, Bing Crosby, Frank Sinatra, Red Skelton shows. I signed a contract to make a nation-wide personal appearance tour promoting *Moulin Rouge* after its New York première early in 1953. I signed for my first night-club appearance, at the Flamingo in Las Vegas, to begin immediately after my tour ended. I would appear as a Professor of Love, gorgeously gowned and jeweled, and deliver a monologue based on my *Bachelor's Haven* character. I had never been a night-club entertainer but I was ready to attempt anything. Hadn't I been nominated for the Emmy—equivalent to the Oscar—as the Outstanding Female TV Personality of the Year? Five thousand dollars a week for my tour, $7,500 a week in Las Vegas—that would help take the sting from George's words, "You'll spoil my fun."

In the last week of 1952 we flew to New York together, George to go on to Rome, I to remain for the *Moulin Rouge* opening. In my suite at the Plaza I pleaded with him. "Darling, at least stay over New Year's Eve with me—there'll be parties—"

George refused. He loathed New Year's Eve parties. But he had an idea. He picked up the telephone and rang Jerry Ohrbach, a most attractive man. "Jerry, old boy," I heard him say, "why don't you take out my wife New Year's Eve? I'll be leaving for Rome that night—"

Jerry would be happy to.

I said, when he hung up, "That's sweet of you, George." I could play it his way, too.

"Now, Cokiline," said my husband chidingly. "You know I wouldn't dream of letting you be alone New Year's Eve."

At 7 o'clock New Year's Eve I drove George to Idlewild Airport to make his 10 o'clock plane to Rome. I kissed him goodbye and drove back to my hotel. Jerry's corsage had already arrived. He was to pick me up at 10:30.

At 10 o'clock George telephone. "Cokiline, we're snowed in. Nothing's taking off for hours. What shall I do?"

I dropped all pretense. "Darling, come home."

Jerry took it gracefully when I telephoned my apologies, explaining that George was coming back and I would spend New Year's Eve with my husband.

George arrived and went to bed and promptly fell asleep. Not even the loud bells and whistles at midnight awakened him. I opened a bottle of champagne and sat before the TV set, sipping the champagne and watching the gay crowds in

Times Square welcome 1953. Most of the night I was up, answering the calls from the airline every few hours giving the latest take-off time for George's plane. At 9 A.M., bleary-eyed, I drove my husband through the snowy streets to Idlewild again and put him on his plane.

Then, utterly exhausted, I drove back to the Plaza. I walked unseeingly into the elevator and stood there half-asleep. The door closed and the elevator rose.

"Good morning, Madame," said a man's quiet voice. "What are you doing here in New York?"

I turned. In the elevator, standing a few feet from me, was Porfirio Rubirosa.

21

I STARED at Mr. Rubirosa. As the elevator continued to rise, he repeated his question. "Madame, what are you doing in New York?" His voice was low-pitched, gentle, his English beautifully modulated with a faint French accent.

I found my own voice. "I am here to open my picture—*Moulin Rouge*—"

The elevator stopped, people entered. Mr. Rubirosa found himself a step nearer me. He said, in faultless French, "A pleasant coincidence, is it not? I am here with my President, General Trujillo." He smiled, darkly handsome. "It would be an honor if you would join us for a drink, at your pleasure—"

I began, "I really don't know—" I was flustered to come upon Mr. Rubirosa so unexpectedly, but I was also so tired that my mind refused to function. Before I could think what else to say, we were at my floor, the tenth floor, the door slid open and I stepped out automatically. Mr. Rubirosa bowed formally, his eyes followed me, the door closed and the elevator continued on its way.

I should have said something, I thought. I should not have been so distant. I walked into my room like someone drugged, almost fell into bed, and was asleep instantly.

When I woke it was late afternoon. Everywhere I looked, I saw red roses. They had arrived in such quantity that the maid had borrowed half a dozen vases from other suites. Whoever had ordered the flowers had obviously selected each one with care; I had never seen such long-stemmed, dark red roses in my life. The engraved card read *Don Porfirio Rubirosa* and below it *Minister Plenipotentiary The Dominican Republic.* He had written in ink, "For a most beautiful lady," and signed it, "Rubi." Later, as I sat under my dryer with curlers in my hair, preparing for a party at Mother's that evening, the telephone rang. "May I come over for a drink?" It was Rubirosa.

"Oh, no, no, no," I said hastily. "It's impossible." I had already decided I would have a drink with him but I could never let him see me with curlers in my hair. "Perhaps later?" he asked. His voice was low, of such timbre that even over the telephone it seemed to me he was whispering in my ear.

Perhaps later, I said. I thanked him for his roses. "You chose them so beautifully," I said. We chatted for a little while. He remembered having seen me at Les Ambassadeurs—I had no idea he had noticed me—but it was his custom when in the company of women never to indicate that he even knew of the existence of any other woman. He said, "This is a world of strange coincidences. Would you believe it, we have adjoining suites. You have only to open your door, and I mine—"

Had Mr. Rubirosa been sufficiently impressed to move into the suite next to mine? "If you will call me tomorrow, Monsieur le Ministre," I said with dignity.

"A bientôt, Madame," he said, and hung up.

The morning of the *Moulin Rouge* première I climbed a white ladder at Fiftieth Street and Broadway and while the cameras turned, I replaced the street sign with one reading "Rue de Montmartre" in honor of our opening at the nearby Capitol Theatre. I heard nothing from Mr. Rubirosa who had told me he would be busy with his President.

That evening I was struggling to get into a black broadtail dress lent me by Maximilian, the furrier, which I was to wear at the première. If it was one of the most elegant costumes in the world, it was also one of the most complicated, with a

227

zipper in the back which I could not close. I rang for a maid; there was none to be had. I stood, fuming. Harold Mirisch, associate producer of the film, was to meet me in the lobby in fifteen minutes.

Just then the telephone rang. It was Mr. Rubirosa. I had an inspiration. "Will you take that drink now?" I asked him. I went on hurriedly, "I hope you won't think I'm silly, but I can't zip up my dress and there's no maid. If you will be good enough to zip it up, I will unlock my door, you unlock yours and you may come in."

A moment later Mr. Rubirosa stepped through the connecting doors. He zipped up my dress deftly, and then, as I turned around to thank him, we stood for a moment, smiling almost sheepishly at each other. It was a ridiculous, French-bedroom-farce situation, and without saying a word, we both knew it—Zsa Zsa Gabor and Porfirio Rubirosa in this parody of a comedy. He drew back. "I will help you on with your coat, Madame," he said very formally. He helped me with the coat—white mink lined with matching black broadtail—opened the door, and escorted me to the lobby and the waiting Mr. Mirisch. Perhaps we would meet after the theater.

The next four hours passed in a whirl. Walter Winchell presided at the ceremonies outside the Capitol—proceeds of the première were to go to the Damon Runyon Fund—and he introduced me to the crowd behind police lines; klieg lights played on us, there were cheers and applause as one celebrity after another arrived—and Mr. Mirisch and I went inside.

Moulin Rouge began, and I watched myself. How bitterly I had fought with John Huston, how I had struggled with my part, how terrified I had been through all the shooting—now I was repaid. The evening was a triumph. At my staircase scene the audience broke into applause, and when the lights went on, I heard voices: "Zsa Zsa! We want Zsa Zsa!" Mr. Mirisch, beaming, nudged me. I was in a daze. I thought: if only George were here to share my triumph! To see these distinguished men and women applaud as I slowly rise and bow.

As I sank into my seat again, my mind flashed back to an afternoon just after George had signed for *All About Eve*. I had asked him to help me get a tiny part in it, little more than a walk-on in the last minutes of the film. "It's such a small bit, George, I'm sure I could do it, and after all I was on the stage in Vienna—"

George had looked at me. "Cokiline, acting isn't for you. Please don't be silly."

Whatever I had done in this film, I had held my own with the finest professional actors of America and Europe. Why couldn't George have been here?

Mr. Mirisch took me to the door of my room and kissed me on the cheek. "You should be very happy, my dear," he said. But the moment I entered my room, it struck me again: I was alone. The maid had put a telegram against the dressing-table mirror. I read it:

YOU AND TECHNICOLOR SAVED OUR PICTURE. CONGRATULATIONS! JOHN HUSTON.

I sat, holding the telegram.

The telephone rang. Mr. Rubirosa was in the Persian Room downstairs with Prince Bernadotte and a party of friends. Would I join them?

I remember chatting with the Prince, whom George and I had known in Paris. The others at the table I cannot recall. But sitting there, I had a chance to observe Mr. Rubirosa closely and unhurriedly for the first time. John de Benden had said, "that absurd Rubirosa guy." I thought: he doesn't seem absurd to me. He is so solemn. Almost tortured. His hair was black, brushed neatly in a part to one side, his eyebrows were heavy and black, almost glowering over somber dark eyes, and on either side of his mouth deep furrows formed, like parentheses; a man whose lips were compressed, a man, I thought, who always has himself under control. He sat almost as if by himself, remote, detached, ordering champagne and sending it back with a curt "C'est bouchonné"—it tastes of the cork. He drank steadily, quietly, responding to others' questions with little more than a monosyllable. At one point, with a murmured "Pardonnez-moi," he rose and walked to the bar. He moved with a kind of catlike grace, balanced, as though on his toes, as a bullfighter moves, or an athlete. Somewhere I had read that he was a ranking polo player, that he rode horses and raced sports cars with the same iron-nerved skill. When he came back, he took the chair next to me. He filled my glass. "You must drink," he said. "It is your night." I drank, and felt warmed. He began to talk. He spoke about his President. Until he first mentioned the name, I had never heard of General Trujillo. He spoke of his country, the Dominican Republic. It was equally vague to me. Through the haze of champagne I saw him, a dark man with glowing eyes, watching me, enveloping me in a gaze of such naked intensity that everyone else at the table seemed to melt away and there were only the two of us. I thought uneasily, fighting for my own calm: this is a primitive; this man does not toy with a woman. He is all purpose. He plays for keeps.

Then the evening was over. Everyone rose. Mr. Rubirosa escorted me up the elevator and accompanied me to my door. I heard him say, "May I come in for a brandy?"

I did not answer.

Mr. Rubirosa bent his dark eyes on me. He moved closer but he did not touch me. There was no question of it; a terrific magnetism emanated from this man, silent, restrained, who came from a country and a place I had never heard of, for all I knew a mysterious island somewhere in the South Seas.

He waited.

And I was drunk that moment—drunk with power, drunk with achievement, drunk with yearning for George. I was in a daze—so overexcited, so overhappy, so overemotional, so overmiserable because George was not there for my moment of triumph, because George had said, "No, don't come to Rome, you'll spoil my fun," because here was Rubirosa, the most pursued of men, the only man whose name could make

George grow pale—because I was overexcited and overmiserable and overlonely and overeverything, I said yes.

So it all began.

George was psychic.

How else do you explain the fact that next morning there was a cable, which had been sent the night before, at the very hour Rubi escorted me to my door. It read:

AM IN LONDON I MISS YOU TERRIBLY I LOVE YOU I LOVE YOU

GEORGE

Book 3

22

SOMETIMES in the fantastic year or so that followed, I said to myself: I am not Zsa Zsa, I am a character in a play by Pirandello, or Molnár, or a heartless Noel Coward. For on the one hand there was my husband, indifferent, supercilious, mocking, hurting me far more than I allowed anyone to know. And on the other there was Rubi, who, I discovered, was the world's most jealous man, who wanted to know my every thought, who watched me as though I might be stolen from him at any moment, who resented it even if he had to let me out of his sight while I went to the powder room. Such intense concentration by a man upon a woman I had never known before. After George's "I-can-take-you-or-leave-you" treatment, there were times when I thought: Rubi has been sent me as a gift from heaven to make me feel a woman again. But I was in a ridiculous position. I found myself rushing from George to Rubi—tears in my eyes because I was leaving my husband; then, a few weeks later, rushing from Rubi back to George— tears in my eyes because I was leaving Rubi. Like a shuttle-cock I flew back and forth trying all the while to understand what was happening to me, and how this would all end . . .

If George was not psychic, I have no other way to account for what occurred in the seventy-two hours or so after I first met Rubi. Next day Rubi left with President Trujillo for Florida and I went on to Philadelphia, the first city on my tour. There I received a second cable, this from Bill Shiffrin, George's agent in Hollywood.

IMPORTANT YOU GO SOONEST ROME GEORGE UNHAPPY NEEDS YOU DESPERATELY.

It was followed by a telephone call from Bill. "You simply must go to him," he said. "I don't know what's happening—you must go!"

How could I cancel my tour? Plans had been made for my appearance in ten other cities, this was a responsibility I had to meet. That night, when I returned to my hotel from the Philadelphia opening, George himself was on the trans-Atlantic telephone. "Cokiline"—his voice trembled—"you must come here. I'm going mad with this picture, with Rossellini, with everything. Please!"

I canceled my tour with much difficulty and flew to Rome, where a nervous, distraught George awaited me at the airport. If you look at the photograph of my arrival, in the Italian newspapers, you can see George kissing me on my cheek but I am looking away, smiling. I had to look away because I dared not meet his eyes, and I smiled because the camera was on me and I could not do otherwise.

Four days later I flew back to Las Vegas, appeared in my two-week night-club act, and immediately flew back to Italy to comfort George again. He could hardly find words to explain his difficulties. Most of them stemmed from the film, which Rossellini was shooting in Naples. The man might be a genius but he used no script, he improvised as he went along, and never to know what scene was to be shot next, or even what the scene was about; it drove George out of his mind. Rossellini was unpredictable in other ways, too. He would stop shooting abruptly to go skin-diving in the Bay of Naples, or, if the urge came upon him, dropped everything, leaped into his Ferrari racing car, and raced the Naples-Rome express to Rome, 150 miles away, leaving everyone—George, Ingrid, the rest of the cast, the stagehands—staring after him. "I tried to get out of my contract," George said, "but Rossellini said he raised much of the money on the strength of my being in the picture." He shook his head wretchedly. "Don't leave me, Cokiline."

236

"Oh darling," I cried in an agony of remorse, "of course I won't leave you." I dared not tell George that I had met Rubirosa, but my mind was full of him. When we had parted in New York, Rubi had said, "You'll hear from me, mon amour." He meant it. From whatever city his diplomatic duties took him—Palm Beach, Washington, Buenos Aires, his home in Paris—his telephone calls, cables, and flowers followed me to New York, to Rome, to Las Vegas. On my third night in Las Vegas he had rung me up from Paris. "Why must you be so far away?" he said. He had two days of leisure; he had decided to fly from Paris to Las Vegas to spend one evening with me, then fly back to Paris the next morning. I was overwhelmed. He lives up to his reputation, I thought. I heard myself saying, almost primly, "I will be here."

Midafternoon of the next day he was on the phone from Mexico City. He had just arrived and was about to change to a Las Vegas plane. I said, sounding a little annoyed, "You're late." There was a moment's silence. "Don't you want me any more?" he asked. I could not help it; I had to play with him. He had made himself vulnerable by going to such lengths, by revealing how badly he wanted me. "I'm not sure," I said.

When he arrived, he said, "That you should tell this to me when I have already come halfway across the world to see you for one night!"

Now, in Italy with my husband who needed me, I promised myself to forget Rubi. My place was with George. On the set in Naples, George introduced me to a little, balding man with a protruding stomach. I couldn't believe this was Roberto Rossellini. I couldn't imagine the passionate love affair the entire world had read about between this unimpressive, nervous man and the great Ingrid Bergman, the Swedish Brunhilde of our time, so healthy, so bursting with life. . . . Yet, when he suddenly smiled and his dark eyes—George later called them "hot eyes"—turned on me, I said to myself, "Well . . . but this is a man."

Until Rubi, I could not understand the attraction of such a man for women. Until Rubi, a man to attract me had to be tall, blond, blue-eyed, an arrogant and lordly man. But now I was beginning to understand that a man's magnetism for a woman had nothing to do with his size or shape, the color of his eyes, his hair, his appearance. I had wanted only heroes until now. Perhaps, I thought, I am growing up. I am no longer drawn only to figures out of fairy tales and story-books.

Next day we went up to the tiny town of Ravello, where Rossellini wanted to shoot several scenes. There we met Jennifer Jones, Humphrey Bogart, Gina Lollobrigida, and John Huston, making *Beat the Devil*. George and I were having tea with them on the terrace of our hotel when a tall woman in a sweater and gray slacks strode up to our table, her hand out-stretched. "I want to meet George's wife," she said. It was Ingrid Bergman.

Perhaps I was too sensitive but I resented Ingrid calling me "George's wife." I had *Moulin Rouge* behind me, I was embarked on a career, I was Zsa Zsa Gabor—not simply George's wife. So I said, as we shook hands, "And I also want to meet Rossellini's wife."

Whether this meant anything to her, I don't know. A moment later she was gone. I had the impression—I could have been wrong—that it came to her that she did not wish to appear as she appeared then, completely without make-up, in a shapeless sweater and slacks. I admired greatly Jennifer Jones in her lovely tailored little black slacks and white blouses, looking always as though she stepped out of *Harper's Bazaar*. Ingrid—so it seemed to me—was too big, too solid a woman to dress as she had.

As I watched the shooting of the picture later, I had to admit her greatness as a human being. One scene George and Ingrid had to do over and over. It was taken in the center of a street. Suddenly Rossellini lost his temper. He rushed from behind his camera and began to scream at her in Italian. He was like a man gone berserk. Hundreds of people had gathered to watch, all of us were there—and Ingrid stood and took it. I said to myself: if any man would shout at me like that!

Ingrid looked down, her eyes averted, and after a minute or two walked away.

By lunchtime everyone had forgotten it, and Rossellini and Ingrid were chatting together as though nothing had happened. Would we like to see the house they had taken, Ingrid asked us? They drove us over the beautiful Amalfi Drive to a typical Italian villa. "Come," said Rossellini, "we show you our children." Suddenly the villa, which had seemed so impersonal, became a warm Italian household. There was a fat Italian nursemaid with the two most beautiful twin girls I had ever seen. "They're like Botticelli angels!" I exclaimed. Rossellini grabbed them up, hugging and kissing them. There was the smell of milk and wash in the air, the whole villa was warm, beautiful, and I thought: my God, if I could have children like that with this wonderfully warm man. I watched Rossellini, black-eyed, shining, and I saw him for the impulsive, recklessly emotional man he is. All at once I could understand why Ingrid Bergman could have defied the world for him and with him.

George took it all in—the delighted father, the beaming mother, the heartbreakingly beautiful little girls. "Roberto, old boy," he said a little impatiently, "weren't you saying something about showing me your new Ferrari?"

Little by little, my husband was becoming himself. I began to realize it when we took a walk with Humphrey Bogart. I was wearing high-heeled shoes and began stumbling on a stretch of cobblestoned street.

"This girl needs sandals," said Bogey. "Why don't you get her a pair?"

"I can't afford it," said George.

"You stingy bastard," said Bogey, much like Stewart Granger at the M-G-M commissary. "I'll buy them for her." And he took me into a shop and bought me a pair of espadrilles.

If I had any doubt about George's recuperation, it was resolved one morning when our breakfast tray was brought to

239

us in our hotel room. Next to the coffeepot lay a telegram addressed to me. I reached for it; George snatched it. "There should be no secrets between husbands and wives," he said, opening it with great deliberation. It was from Paris and read:

NO WORD FROM YOU MISS YOU AND LOVE YOU MUCH WIRE ME 46 RUE DE BELLECHASSE RUBI.

I said desperately, "George, pay no attention to it—it doesn't mean anything—I'm all finished with him—he's been wiring me for days and I haven't replied—"

George tossed the wire to me. "Cokiline, what a conquest!" He spoke like an indulgent father. "The great Rubirosa! He's in love with you. Now, that's really an achievement!"

He had known all along that I had met Rubi. "You forget the public prints, my dear." Hollywood gossip columns had reported that Rubi and I were seen dining together in Las Vegas.

"But George, it's all over. I'm finished with him."

"Oh, no," said George. He poured himself coffee. "That wouldn't be courteous, Cokiline. You must answer his wire."

"No, no, no!"

"Then I will," said my husband. On the back of Rubi's telegram he wrote: MON CHERI I LOVE YOU TOO AND CANNOT WAIT TO SEE YOU AGAIN. He signed it "Zsa Zsa." He rang for a boy. "I'm sending it off," he said, taunting me, testing me.

"If you wish," I said coldly, thinking: what does he prove? What does he do to himself? What is he trying to do to me?

He sent it off to Rubi in Paris. I was too proud to stop him. He should not have sent that wire.

I had meant it when I said I was finished with Rubi. I was not yet deeply involved with this strange, violent man who was to affect me like a kind of hashish from which I fought again and again to free myself. I needed George to help keep me away from Rubi; and George, for whatever complex, self-punishing, self-mocking reasons, was throwing me into Rubi's arms.

It is my fate, I thought.

Many times before, echoing my Turkish friends, I had said this, trying to understand cause and effect in my life. I had said it when Burhan took me to Karpiç's restaurant the very night Ataturk came to dine; when Conrad Hilton sat down in the chair next to me at Ciro's; when I walked into Serge Semenenko's cocktail party to see George Sanders seated half-way across the room. Now I said it again. For only a few days after Rubi's wire, a French producer telephoned me. Fernandel, the great French comedian, wanted me as his leading lady in a film to start shooting almost immediately—in Paris!

The call came as a group of us sat on the terrace in Ravello where I had first met Ingrid Bergman. When I told George about the offer, it was impossible for me to read his face. But I heard him say, "Don't take it, my dear. Stay here with me."

John Huston turned on him. "But this is a terrific break for her," he exclaimed. "You're not going to stop her, are you?"

Suddenly I was sick of being toyed with.

"No," I said. "He won't stop me."

When I landed at Orly Field, Paris, a week later, Rubi was there to meet me.

Now I began to learn more about this man. I lived at the Plaza Athénée; each day I worked on the Fernandel film; evenings I saw Rubi. When I arrived he had driven me to my hotel and then waited for me, for I was to dine with him that night at his home.

His car took us over the Seine to the Left Bank and the Rue de Bellechasse, a narrow street in the Faubourg St.-Germain. No. 46 was a seventeenth-century, three-story house hiding behind an enormous white wall; at first glance, it looked like a small fortress. We stood before the enormous black iron gate; Rubi pressed a button; I heard the bell clang somewhere deep in the recesses of the house. The huge door opened and a smiling man with a wooden leg stumped out. "This is Jean, my concierge," said Rubi. I met his valet, Victor, a huge Russian whom Rubi had found in the Argentine when he had been Ambassador there. These two men, smiling and bowing at me, seemed ready to cut off their hands had Rubi asked it. I met Marie and Maria, his two Spanish maids, black-eyed and curtsying, in little black silk dresses and white aprons with white lace caps on their heads.

Surely, I thought, no girl dreaming a romantic dream could have asked for more. Everything was type-cast to perfection: the one-legged concierge, the giant valet, the maids, and now the interior of this house in which lived the man who entertained some of the most beautiful women in the world. Within, all was perfect and in exquisite taste: the paintings, the Aubusson rugs, the furnishings, polished and gleaming, even the scents I loved: leather, tobacco, sandlewood. Rubi showed me his house. He took me through his kitchen and I met his Spanish chef; then, to his dining room with apple-green and gold paneling identical to that at Versailles, and wall cabinets holding his collection of china and porcelain. We mounted to the upper floors. On the third floor was a gymnasium complete with boxing ring, rubbing table, and a steam bath. "I work out every day," Rubi said. "Victor here is a formidable sparring partner." He led me into another room. It displayed saddles and riding equipment of every kind, and to my surprise, bullfighting costumes and paraphernalia. I said, "Rubi, you collect porcelain and you fight bulls—" He nodded, smiling. "Each in its own time," he said. On the walls were photographs of his favorite polo ponies, the standard of his team which had won the world's championship in Deauville the year before, and his helmets, including a red one he always wore on the field for some reason I could never understand. And everywhere in the house—in the bathrooms, the library, the kitchen, the concierge's rooms, the maids' rooms—trophies, trophies, trophies, the gold and silver loving cups awarded him in polo, or for racing his Ferraris and Mercedes Benzes on courses in Europe and South America.

We dined alone on food which tasted vaguely familiar. We had had our coffee and were sipping a sweet, intoxicating liqueur when suddenly I realized why the dishes had seemed familiar. They reminded me of Hungarian food—the same

242

thick hearty soup, the strong spiced meat. "No," said Rubi, "everything you have had tonight was Dominican. I thought you might enjoy something different." I said something to the effect, how strange that his country's food should be so much like my own. "Can anyone imagine two worlds so far apart being so close together—the Dominican and the Hungarian?"

Rubi smiled. "I do not find that so difficult to imagine," he said. I began to blush. I consider myself a sophisticated woman—yet I blushed as if I had never even shaken hands with a man. Rubi, watching me, saw it. "That is your charm," he said, in French. "Women to whom love is all are forever innocent."

He rose, lazily, and came around the table toward me. I could not help it. I found myself rising to meet him.

How do you explain Rubi, I thought. What is his appeal? I thought: he is everything a woman can want in a man—if she does not think, if she asks herself no questions of today or tomorrow. He is all male. Whether he talks with you, dances with you, walks with you, you know he is a man, thinking only of you and always of you as a woman to be taken and possessed and kept away from all other men because, being so feminine and desirable, you are their natural prey. He pays you the strange compliment of being female, first, and a person, second. I know that American women, with their ideas of equality, think this an insult, yet American women too find Rubi irresistible. He knows what goes on in your mind every moment—he has the instinct of a wild animal to sense your every mood. He can read it by the way you turn a doorknob before you enter, by the subtlest intonation of your voice. He is completely, blindly, recklessly possessive. You feel this man will tear down walls, smash through mountains, overturn worlds to reach you. He is wild, impatient—like Father, a violent man—but he will give you his heart. When he wants you —and he wants you all the time—it is with a single-mindedness that gives you no time to think, to protest, to assert yourself.

243

He draws from you, in spite of yourself, what is primitive in you, like himself.

Yet, I thought, if he is a primitive, he is in another way as civilized as the most civilized Frenchman. Look, I thought, how he lives—in utmost elegance, choosing his food, his clothes, his sports, his pastimes, with the grace of a grand seignior . . .

In evenings to come, I was to meet in Rubi's home the ex-King and Queen of Yugoslavia, Baron Elie Rothschild, the Maharajah of Jaipur, French, British, Italian, and American international society. I thought, how different from what I had known in Hollywood. Here were not the people who make movies but the people about whom movies are made. And Rubi moved among them, immaculate, perfection in dress and person, looking more like a movie star than any star could hope.

I discovered that though he was always surrounded by a court of beautiful women, whom he attracted like honey and who spoiled him dreadfully, he was a man's man too. All day at his house he had his friends; when he bathed, dressed, breakfasted, it was in the company of men—his fellow polo players, sportsmen from other lands, assorted guests to whom it was always open house at 46 Rue de Bellechasse. With them Rubi talked, laughed, sparred, or, playing his guitar, joined them in cowboy songs of the Argentine pampas.

For two insane months—the time it took to shoot the Fernandel picture—I lived Rubi's life. During the day I worked on the set; Rubi would call to take me to late dinner. He had been playing polo, or lunching at the Ritz, or attending to his duties—I never quite understood what they were—as Dominican Chargé d'Affaires in Paris. Our evenings were spent in night clubs. Here, in the Paris night clubs, Rubi was king. The French admired him, for he was a romantic in their great tradition. Often after the club closed, he hired the entire orchestra to trail behind us, playing soft music as we walked through the Paris streets. He was known everywhere; when we entered, we were bowed in and led ceremoniously to the best table. I began to learn of Rubi's unbelievable jealousy. Father was a jealous man, but he was jealous of his wife. Rubi was jealous of me, whom he had not known long, with such a passion, such a darkness, such a violence that I was terrified. I dared not look at another man, above all, smile at another man. I had to refuse every request to dance. Rubi held my hand in his so that I could not even leave his side. If I spoke on the telephone to an agent or a fellow actor and said, "Darling, of course—" Rubi's face became black. "Why do you call him 'darling'?" It was no use explaining that in Hollywood everyone called everyone "darling."

All evening I sat at Rubi's side. He sat, drinking steadily, listening to the music, hour after hour. Sometimes, in night clubs with Latin American bands, he took his place behind the bongo drums, and began to play them. Sitting there, pounding the drums, he himself became like a bongo player, dark and mysterious. His black eyebrows slanted up like a devil's as he sat there pounding the drums, keeping his eyes fixed on me. Sometimes I thought he must eat exotic herbs brought by the bongo players from worlds unknown to me. . . . Or that the drinks he poured for me were love potions. . . . He had such power over me that I had no will of my own. Once a Paris newspaper printed a photograph of us, Rubi looking at me and I gazing back at him. The caption read, "The beautiful Zsa Zsa bewitched by M. Rubirosa as a snake by a snake charmer." It was true.

The night went on. Rubi drank. I said, "Please, let's go—take me home—I must get up early to work." Rubi did not listen.

The first time this happened and 2 A.M. arrived and still Rubi would not leave, I left him in the night club. I rose as if to go to the powder room, and escaped. At 4 A.M. he rang me. "Why did you leave?" It was an insult to him. One did not leave one's escort. "Why did you leave?" And then, "I wait for you." He hung up.

Like a sleepwalker I rose. I remember myself not once but many times putting on a black skirt and a huge black wool

245

sweater so that no one would recognize me, and slipping out the side entrance of my elegant hotel, and into a cab and saying to the driver, "46 Rue de Bellechasse"—glamorous Zsa Zsa Gabor going like a schoolgirl over the Seine to the Left Bank and an assignation. How many times after a quarrel with him in a night club did I drive over the Seine in the night in a taxi, dying to see him, knowing it was wrong! It was wrong! I loved George; he was my life, my husband, however he treated me. But I could not help myself. How many times in my black sweater and skirt I stood before that house just before dawn, and touched the bell . . . knowing how loudly it rang inside, that it was heard everywhere, that neighbors' windows lit up, and faces stared out to see who stands at Rubirosa's gate. I would avert my face and wait.

And Rubi always received me as he should. First Jean, the concierge, in his tasseled nightcap, limping to open the gate, his face beaming as he bowed me in, playing his role with delight; then Rubi standing inside the door of his house like a guilty little boy. Now he was not the mysterious, threatening man: he was as adorable as a little boy. He felt as guilty as I: we were two partners in guilt, and when we met, we met like giggling children. We went into the kitchen and cooked our barbarian food—Dominican, Hungarian, South Seas, whatever —and devoured it as though we had never eaten, and then we passed through the halls, through the dining room, up the stairs, past the rooms with their leathery, smoky, wonderful fragrance, and into his suite . . .

I loved Rubi, I did not love him. It was George I loved, Rubi I wanted. I thought, George is difficult, complicated. He is like Hungary compared to America. With George it was quarrel and conflict of egos but when we were happy we were completely happy and completely satisfied. Not for a moment was I ashamed of him. I was proud of this man who was my husband. But he was like Hungary: in my happiness always there was a challenge and a problem—what will happen tomorrow? Will the Russians come in? The Germans? What will happen? This was George.

With Rubi—all was against my better judgment. Had I not worked for a career? How desperately I wanted a career! Now in Paris I had my opportunity, appearing in a film with the great Fernandel. I knew that if I remained up all night, if I arrived on the set in the morning unprepared—sleepless, red-eyed, exhausted—I could not do justice to my part.

For two months, three months, Rubi was a sickness to me. The film was finished, we went to Rome, Deauville, Cannes. In Cannes we attended a party in André Dubonnet's dream-like villa overlooking the Mediterranean. Everyone was dancing on the terrace under gaily colored lanterns. When we appeared, I in an enormous white Dior gown, Rubi in a black tuxedo with his dark sun tan, everyone, it seemed to me, stopped dancing to turn and stare at us. Here was French society, Geneviève Fath, Commander Paul Louis-Villieur, Suzy Voltaire; British society, Lord and Lady Beatty, Lady Sylvia Ashley Gable, Lord Porchy Carnarvon; American society, Bill and Barbara Paley, Anne Woodbury, Lorelle Hearst—friends who not long before had seen me arrive at parties on the arm of my husband. Now I entered on the arm of Rubirosa. . . . Though I lived in my Paris hotel and Rubi in his house, we were always together. I was already compromised, though until now it had been only a whisper. Now, for the first time, we arrived together openly at a function . . .

Each day I said to myself, well, one more day, then I leave and go back to my life, to George, where I belong. On the trans-Atlantic telephone Mother was furious. "This is madness! It will never work out. Never!" But even Mother was powerless against Rubi's voodoo.

Then, finally, I broke away. Rubi helped me when he said, "You must divorce and marry me." This terrified me. Now I *had* to go home. Rubi took me to the plane. "My darling, my love, you must make up your mind. Arrange it in America and come back to me."

In New York George waited for me at the airport. "Coki-line, you have made me the laughingstock of the world, but I forgive you. Oh, Cokiline, how I have missed you!"

Then the cables, the telephone calls from Rubi. Had I decided? Would I divorce George? When would I come back to Paris?

Sometimes I ignored his cables. Sometimes I replied—always evasively. It drove Rubi wild . . .

July 9, from Rubirosa to Miss Gabor, Plaza Hotel, New York: MY LOVE WHY DO YOU NOT RESPOND TO MY CABLE?

July 10, from Rubirosa to Miss Gabor, Plaza Hotel, New York: WHAT A TRIP MY POOR DARLING I MISS YOU COME BACK HOME VERY SOON

July 12, from Rubirosa to Miss Gabor, Plaza Hotel, New York: I LOVE YOU DARLING I WAIT IF YOU DO THING I ASKED

July 14, from Rubirosa to Miss Gabor, Plaza Hotel, New York: SO HAPPY TO HEAR YOUR VOICE MY DARLING COME BACK VERY SOON TO DECIDE OUR WAY

July 15, from Rubirosa to Miss Gabor, Plaza Hotel, New York: RECEIVED YOUR LETTER I LOVE YOU AND WAIT FOR YOU COME DARLING WRITE ME MORE

July 16, from Rubirosa to Miss Gabor, Plaza Hotel, New York: YOU ARE MY ONLY LOVE AND FOREVER IS IT THE SAME FOR YOU?

July 19, from Rubirosa to Miss Gabor, Plaza Hotel, New York: COME SOON I LOVE YOU MY CHERIE

July 21, from Rubirosa to Miss Gabor, Plaza Hotel, New York: I AWAIT YOU CABLE ME ARRIVAL TIME I LOVE YOU

July 25, from Rubirosa to Miss Gabor, Bellagio Place, Bel Air, California: WHAT HAPPENED I HOPE EVERYTHING IS ALL RIGHT I LOVE YOU CABLE ME

July 27, from Rubirosa to Miss Gabor, Bellagio Place, Bel Air, California: DARLING YOU SAY YOU HOPE OR YOU SAY YOU TRY BUT YOU NEVER SAY YOU WILL

July 29, from Rubirosa to Miss Gabor, Bellagio Place, Bel Air, California: I HOPE ITS GOOD NEWS YOU SEND ME TOMORROW MY DARLING CHERIE

August 1, from Rubirosa to Miss Gabor, Bellagio Place, Bel Air, California: I LOVE YOU DARLING BUT AFTER READING YOUR

CABLE I SEE THAT YOU ARE NOT WILLING TO SEPARATE AND COME
HERE SO BE FRANK AND DECIDE ONCE AND FOR ALL

How could I decide?

I stayed with George. In the autumn of 1953 I had to go to
New York for a television show. Rubi flew in from Paris
almost immediately. The next day it was in the columns.

Thirty-six hours later George dropped a bombshell. He
filed for a divorce.

23

I REFUSED to believe it. I never wanted to divorce George; I wanted desperately to change him, for George, made over, would have been all I could ask. But to divorce him was unthinkable, even though I had threatened to do it time and again. He was part of my life—like my child, my father, my family. I thought: it will always be George and me, teasing each other, tormenting each other, but in the end clinging to each other.

Jerry Geisler, my attorney, warned me. "You must file a countersuit—you have no other recourse." I followed his advice but still I could not believe it. Even George's complaint sounded tongue in cheek; he had been subjected to "inhuman treatment" by me; his marriage "has left me in a rundown condition—" It was unreal. Separation, divorce, these were simply the odd, temporary aspects of our marriage.

So matters stood late in 1953 when an offer came from the Last Frontier Hotel in Las Vegas. They had been struck by an inspiration. Would I join my sisters in a night-club act—for the first time anywhere, Magda, Zsa Zsa, and Eva Gabor on one stage together.

My first reaction was no. Although Magda had appeared in the theater, she had no experience in night clubs. Eva had no need of me to help draw an audience; and as for myself, I had had my own show in Vegas, and I had no need of Eva to help draw an audience.

"But it will be such an easy act," my agent pointed out. We

were to satirize ourselves, and men, and love. We were to appear on stage dressed in identical gowns of different colors —Magda, all red sequins, Eva white, I black—each of us behind a pink, heart-shaped reading stand, and alternately read from witty scripts prepared for us by Hollywood's top writers.

For a week our telephone calls—Magda's, Eva's, Mother's, and mine—crisscrossed each other from one coast to the other. At least, said Mother, it was a relief to talk about something other than Mr. Rubirosa, who was now bombarding me with cables from Deauville, where he had gone for the polo season with a promise to visit me as soon as he could. We finally agreed that we did not wish to do the show. We demanded impossible fees—including separate suites and separate entourages, complete to our own maids, hairdressers, make-up people, and press representatives.

To our astonishment, the Last Frontier acquiesced. We would open the day after Christmas.

I plunged into rehearsals. Mother arrived as my house guest and to help supervise my wardrobe. In the midst of rehearsals, Rubi arrived. Then, a few days before Christmas, Magda and Eva. On Christmas Eve, the night before we were to leave for Las Vegas, I invited them all to dinner—Mother, Magda, Eva, Rubi. I thought: this is the first Christmas George and I have not been together. The tree in the living room glittered with decorations, little Francie played among the presents—including a set of records I had bought for George, hoping he would drop in. I felt sad; Rubi, too, seemed strangely preoccupied. He had bought Francie an elaborate electric train for Christmas, but even her delight—she had run to him and kissed him with an ecstatic, "Oh, Uncle Rubi!"—did not shake him out of his mood.

Later when we were alone, he told me. He had seen Barbara Hutton in Deauville. He had met her at the Casino, they had gone out together. He said, "She wants to marry me, but I love only you." Yet if I did not marry him, he would marry her. I could not believe it. What an impossible situation I had

251

gotten myself into! Here I was, more and more deeply involved with Rubi, and now when I had compromised myself before all the world, and had done everything to lose George, I find I am trapped, I cannot really get away from Rubi, and he tells me he will marry Barbara Hutton unless I marry him. I was not prepared to marry Rubi.

We talked endlessly. He unburdened himself as he had never before—

Suddenly there was a crash of shattering glass, a sound of heavy objects falling, and then men's voices, muffled, cursing, coming from the direction of the French windows. I had left my packed suitcases there. Someone had broken through the window and fallen over them. There stood George Sanders. He had broken into my room from the terrace roof. With him were three men.

On the edge of hysteria, I stammered, "How dare you—this is my house—" But George paid no attention to me. Instead he walked to my desk, picked up a portrait of him I had there, and deliberately tore it into shreds. Somehow, in some way, in the confusion Rubi vanished.

And George—I had not seen my husband in months. He had grown a beard for a new film—ironically enough it was *Knights of the Round Table*—he wore a blue turtleneck sweater I had bought him in Naples, and faded blue jeans, and he looked beautiful—a big, bronzed, bearded, blue-eyed man, so much more beautiful, I thought, than Rubi could ever be.

When I was able to speak I said, "Oh, George, why did you have to do this?" Why should he deliberately make this scandal which all Hollywood would know about in a few hours. To obtain evidence so he could name Rubi as co-respondent if I asked for alimony? No woman with alimony in mind would have traveled everywhere so openly with Rubi.

"I had to, Cokiline," George said, not unkindly. He sat heavily at my desk, quite winded. "Darling," I heard myself say. "What is the matter with you? Why are you out of breath?"

"My dear," he said, "I'm an old man—I have no business climbing ladders." He rose, and without further word, opened the door and went down the stairs. I watched him go. He had entered like a thief; he was leaving like the master of the house. I called after him, remembering, "George, I have your Christmas present under the tree."

George turned at the bottom of the stairs. "And this visit, Cokiline, is my Christmas present to you."

I cried bitterly, bitterly. Rubi said, "You don't know it, but you're still in love with him. You're not crying because he saw us together. You are crying like a little idiot because you love that man."

In this mood I flew to Las Vegas Christmas Day, the day of our dress rehearsal. Rubi followed me in the next plane. I thought: surely he doesn't plan to marry Barbara, otherwise he would not dare come after me to a place like Las Vegas which exists in a fishbowl of publicity. Everyone else had already arrived, including Russell Birdwell, who was handling my press relations. Rubi was dour and silent, calling me on the telephone at intervals of a few hours to ask, "Are you going to marry me?" Each time I said, "I am going mad with rehearsal, I haven't been able to sleep, I am upset about George—please, please, don't ask me questions."

At 2 A.M. after the last rehearsal—it had been arduous and upsetting, for when I am with my sisters, each of us has her own will—Rubi came to my suite. As we sat there the telephone rang. It was Igor Cassini, who writes the Cholly Knickerbocker society column in the Hearst newspapers, calling from New York. "Zsa Zsa, I'm trying to reach Rubi. Have you any idea where he is?"

Rubi put his finger to his lips.

"No, Ghi-Ghi, not the least idea," I said.

"We know he's in Vegas—"

"Then he's probably gambling," I said. "Try him in one of the gambling rooms."

There was a brief silence. Then: "Is it true that Rubi is going to marry Barbara Hutton? Have you any comment?"

"I don't know anything about it," I snapped, and hung up. He *had* planned to marry Barbara. It was true.

I rose, and very *grande dame,* walked to the door, I flung it open. "Now, Rubi," I said, "you get out of this room and as long as I live I never want to see you again."

"No," said Rubi. "Say you'll marry me—or I go back to New York and marry Barbara."

"No," I said. "Get out."

He walked to the door, black and silent. He stood in the doorway, glowering at me. "Just tell me one thing—why don't you marry me?"

I knew I had lost George, I was enraged at Rubi, enraged at myself. I almost shrieked, "Because I love George, I've always loved him, and I'll always love him! Now get out of here and marry that woman!" I rushed at him and pushed him, hard.

He struck me. I fell sharply against the bathroom door, which was ajar, hitting it with my forehead. For a moment I was dazed. Then Rubi was holding me in a grip of steel and pressing a silver dollar against my forehead above my right eye. "Are you mad?" I screamed. I pulled away from him and ran to the mirror. Above my right eye was an ominous swelling. My God, I thought—and I must open tonight!

I turned on Rubi and began beating him with my fists. "Get out!" I screamed. "Get out!" I pushed him through the door and slammed it. The next few minutes were utter confusion. Suddenly Mother, Magda, Eva were in the room, each more outraged than the other. Russell Birdwell appeared. A physician, Dr. Edgar Compton, gave me a sedative and applied ice packs. There was no question of it: by nightfall, when we opened, I would have a black-and-blue eye. I dozed off.

Hours later I woke, still under the influence of the sedative, and rang room service for breakfast. I was still groggy as I opened the door to the waiter's knock—and standing there, carrying the tray high in one hand, was Rubi, on his face the same sheepish expression I remembered when he stood waiting for me in the night at 46 Rue de Bellechasse. "Mon amour," he said pleadingly, still balancing the tray. "Oh, Rubi," I said weakly, and let him in.

He sat beside my bed and spoke comfortingly to me. "My love, ma cherie—" He was all remorse. He had tried again and again to telephone me but they would not put him through. He had gotten drunk, wandered across the street to the Sahara to see Marlene Dietrich's show, then to the Sands to see Lena Horne's, and then he had gambled. Thousands of dollars. He had no idea how much he had lost. I listened to him, half-hearing his words, worrying about my eye, about my lines for the show, worrying about Rubi. Would he really marry Barbara?

He bent over and kissed me. "Darling—I love you," he said, and left. I dozed off. When I woke again with a violent headache, my room was full of red roses. Rubi had sent them from the airport before taking a plane to New York—and Barbara. With his flowers was his card, and written on it: à bientôt.

I sat at my dressing-room table staring in the mirror. My right eye was black. Marlene Dietrich came in, very chic in white leather slacks. Eva had told her what had happened.

"I've brought you some panstick to cover that eye," she said. She examined it, then sat down on the bed. "Darling," she said, "he's a beast. But he must love you very much to strike you like that."

Russell Birdwell said, "Either we try to hide what happened, or we tell the press the truth." His advice was to tell all: they knew about it anyway. And he had a wonderful idea: I must wear a black eye-patch over my injured eye.

I was shocked. "Oh, no!" Eye-patches were for pirates and Hathaway shirt advertisements. How could I wear an eye-patch?

"I'll have you know that one of the most famous beauties in British history wore an eye-patch," my press agent retorted. He stalked out.

255

Mother and I tried to talk about other things. "Oh, my God," she said, sighing, "I must say, you are the strongest woman—any other woman would have collapsed—she'd call off her opening night after what you've gone through this week." Then she sighed. "Thank God, Zsa Zsa, I only have one of you."

Birdwell brought me the eye-patch. "Try it," he said. "I'll have photographs taken—they'll go out all over the world. After these heartaches you ought to have some good publicity." He knew how hurt and humiliated I was, and he knew, too, that I would do almost anything rather than show it. "Make a lark of the whole thing."

I tried it as a lark. I posed with the eye-patch at a press conference that afternoon, a few hours before our opening. Yes, I said, as the photographers' bulbs flashed, Rubi had struck me because I refused to marry him. I never wanted to see him again.

"What about Miss Hutton?"

Even had I wished to be charitable to Miss Hutton, I could not. "I wish her all the luck in the world—she'll need it. She's a very brave woman if she marries Rubi." I couldn't help adding, "On the other hand, for a rich woman he's the very best pastime she could have."

Birdwell was right when he said the photograph would go out all over the world. It appeared everywhere. The black eye-patch became an international cause célèbre. When Marlene appeared on stage one night, all her chorus girls wore a black patch. When I flew to New York some days later, I was greeted at the airport by over twenty newspapermen, each wearing a black eye-patch. New York shops blossomed out with jeweled eye-patches, at charity balls the hostesses appeared with black eye-patches—it had become the rage.

Despite everything, our opening night had turned out to be a hilarious success. It seemed all Hollywood came to Vegas to see us. Most of the time I hadn't the slightest idea what I was doing or saying. I had sufficient presence of mind at the last minute to throw away the patch and appear on stage with

256

Marlene's make-up and dark glasses hiding the bruise. Standing before our pink, heart-shaped stands, Magda, Eva, and I read our lines. At one point I turned two pages of my script, but kept on reading blithely. Eva brought me up short. "Zsa Zsa, you skipped a page." "Did I?" I asked, giggling idiotically. Nothing made any sense to me, anyway. Eva, suffering like Sarah Bernhardt, later accused me of clowning. Perhaps that is as good a word as any. By this time everything seemed half musical comedy, half nightmare.

In my bed next morning when I opened the Las Vegas newspapers to read reviews of our show, the headline on page one ran: BARBARA HUTTON MARRIES RUBIROSA. Then, every day stories, more stories, interviews, more interviews. In the end the eye-patch photograph boomeranged on me. A newspaper reversed the print so that I now appeared to wear the patch over my left eye. Suddenly everyone said I never had had a black eye, that I was guilty of a publicity stunt in the worst possible taste. Suddenly everyone was on the side of Barbara and her millions, Rubi became a heroic figure because he had married her, and I was the woman scorned. It got so that I dreaded to open a newspaper.

Then toward the end of our engagement in Las Vegas, one morning the newspaper came up and Marilyn Monroe's face was on page one. She had married Joe DiMaggio. Until she reads this she will never know how grateful I was to her that she married Joe DiMaggio that day and took me and the dreadful stories off the front pages.

"Mr. Bill Perkins is on the line," the operator said.

I was in my Plaza Hotel suite. We had ended our Las Vegas engagement the night before and I had flown to New York to emcee a fashion show. "I don't know any Bill Perkins," I told the operator.

She came back a moment later. "He says he was referred to you by a Mr. Bellechasse."

Oh God, I thought. "Put him on."

I heard Rubi's familiar voice. "Ma cherie—"

257

"Rubi, how dare you—where are you? Where is Barbara?"

"Cherie, I die to see you. I'm across the street at the Pierre. I'm coming over this minute."

"No, no, no!" I pleaded with him. "Are you insane? You can't be seen here, you've just married, this is Conrad Hilton's hotel—" I stammered, I stuttered. "You can't make such a scandal—"

I finally convinced him. "So be it," he said sullenly. "Then I go with Barbara to Palm Beach. Goodbye!"

But from Palm Beach, from the Maharajah of Baroda's magnificent home which Mr. and Mrs. Rubirosa had taken at $10,000 a month for their honeymoon, Mr. Perkins called me four and five times a day. He called all hours of the night. His flowers were in my suite, his name was on the telephone slips piling up in my box, his messages were relayed to me by headwaiters when I arrived at "21," the Stork Club, the Colony Restaurant. At the end of the month I flew to Hollywood to prepare for a new Paramount film, *Three Ring Circus*, with Jerry Lewis and Dean Martin.

And Mr. Perkins' calls followed me.

24

THE French have a word, *soulagement*—relief. A strange *soulagement* had come upon me when Rubi married Barbara Hutton. At the time I had said outrageous, scornful things about her to cover my own hurt. "I love you," Rubi had told me, "but I marry her." Now that was over. I thought: he is gone, the temptation is taken away, I can be myself again. I can work again: work is the best therapy, work makes me happy.

On an April day in 1954—it would have been our fifth wedding anniversary—I left the set of *Three Ring Circus* long enough to testify in my divorce suit against George. I said George was a born bachelor, he had never wanted to be married, and now I was giving him back his freedom. In spite of myself I cried on the stand. It was the first time I had ever shown my true feelings in public. But a few moments later I was again Zsa Zsa. "Now George and I will be better friends than ever," I told the reporters. "He always said we'd be happier as lovers than as husband and wife."

I pretended gaiety when I returned to the set and to everyone's bantering— "Well, you're free again, you lucky girl." Grace Kelly, who was making *The Country Wife* with Bing Crosby on an adjoining set, came to my rescue. She said to the crowd around me, "Why don't you stop teasing her? She's much unhappier than you think. Can't you just let her be?" I have always been grateful to Grace for her friendship that terrible day.

I tried to forget everything. Who cared? Before I left for Phoenix where we were to do a month's outside shots for the picture, I threw an enormous costume ball, inviting my guests to "come as your favorite character." That night in my home there were three Rubirosas, two Howard Hughes, two Dwight D. Eisenhowers. Marion Davies came as General Douglas MacArthur, James Mason as Superman, his wife Pam as Zsa Zsa Gabor, in a bright red nightgown, a gold wig, and diamonds to her elbows. I came as Jane Avril. It was a successful party; I remember myself floating from one table to another in my lovely Schiaparelli dress, dancing until morning—gay, wild, happy. Time and again my partner was Franchot Tone. I thought as I danced with Franchot, the world doesn't consist only of George Sanders and Porfirio Rubirosa.

And Rubi telephoned—telephoned.

When I arrived in Phoenix, his calls became more insistent. He had now been married nearly two months. "I must see you," he said, over the phone from Palm Beach. "I can't stand it."

"It's impossible, Rubi. You are mad to telephone me from the house—"

"I am coming to Phoenix. I will fly to you."

"You can't," I cried. "You mustn't."

"My darling, my love, I must see you!"

"Please, Rubi, don't come. I have a contract which says I can't have another scandal." It was true. Every Hollywood contract has a clause permitting the producer to cancel it at any bad publicity.

"Zsa Zsa, I must come. I can't live without you—it is life or death for me!"

I replied, "Don't come, don't come—" He hung up.

In desperation I turned to a friend, Mary Lou Hosford, who was later to become Mrs. Cornelius Vanderbilt Whitney. Mary Lou, whose husband was in the East, was a pretty blonde who adored film people. She was building a beautiful home in Scottsdale, a suburb of Phoenix; meanwhile she lived at the Jokake Inn, my hotel, a lovely rambling Spanish-style hacienda. I took her into my confidence. Rubi—Mr. Perkins—was coming to Phoenix. He must be incognito and he must be hidden. Mary Lou promptly reserved a guest room for Mr. Perkins.

Mr. Perkins arrived. He came in the night, in his private plane, from Palm Beach. He came to stay forty-eight hours.

And somehow it was all as it had been before.

The evening of the second day, as it grew dark, Rubi and I ventured out together. Mary Lou drove us to the house she was building; on the way we bought a barbecued chicken, a huge loaf of rye bread, crisp green peppers, and a bottle of heavy red wine, and when we came there we dined, the three of us, in her roofless, unfinished kitchen, under the open sky. There was not even a corkscrew. Rubi, with one blow, smashed the neck of the bottle against a rock: the red wine frothed out; we drank it from the bottle, laughing, like gypsies, letting it trickle down our chins. We tore the chicken apart with our hands and ate greedily with our fingers, and as I ate I watched Rubi out of the corner of my eye, attacking his chicken leg with such zest, such lusty appetite, and I thought: this is my man after all—this is a man!

Then we drove back to the Jokake Inn.

When it grows dark in Phoenix in the spring the dusk is pink dark, luscious, rose-colored; the sun sets late in that high, dry altitude, the air is clear as a lens, incredibly beautiful clouds hang low in the sky, and the distant mountains that surround the city float rose-red and purple, breath-taking to see. How right this setting, how perfect this pink-dark, luscious dusk, I thought, for two people who have been together so much and have not seen each other for so long, who shared such a tense, emotional ordeal—this man had not only struck her, the press had not only made fools of them both, but he had climaxed it by marrying another woman in a klieg-light of world attention, a woman of fabulous name and fabulous wealth . . . Now he was back. He had to come back. Not even one of the richest women in the world could hold him, because he wanted nothing else, he wanted only one thing—me. He had come back after the insults, after the stories accusing me of using him and myself only for publicity—after all this, he had come back to me.

Now, in one stroke, everything was wiped out—the insults, the scorn, the humiliation—because he was here, with me.

How shall I describe this night? The pink light from the sky, the towering mountains guarding us, the gay, blonde American woman so thrilled to be part of this exciting, conspiratorial love affair, jumping up and down almost like a little girl to bring us wine and food . . .

We parked behind the inn and then Mary Lou and I, laughing and chattering, walked on ahead in the darkness, Rubi behind us, quiet, somber, and as we walked down a dimly lit path between rich, luxuriant shrubbery on either side, suddenly a thin little stuttering newspaperman in shell-rim spectacles and a Brooks Brothers suit popped up out of the shadows and planted himself in front of me:

"Miss Gabor, is it true that Mr. Ru-Ru-Rubirosa is here?"

I stared at him, stunned. Had it been an important newspaper personality such as Walter Winchell, I might have fainted. But because it was not, and because I was strong, because Rubi had made me strong with wine, I said icily, "How dare you! Mr. Rubirosa is happily married to Miss Barbara Hutton!" and walked on. I said it loudly so that Rubi, two steps behind me, would hear.

And Rubi, just behind me, heard; he vanished into the bushes. Like a panther, he disappeared.

The reporter stepped aside; Mary Lou and I swept haughtily down the walk to my bungalow and then, like two schoolgirls, we collapsed, half hysterical with laughter, on the bed. "What now?" I gasped. The thought of Rubi, with all his continental dignity and savoir-faire, crouching in the shrubbery . . .

I telephoned the manager. No sooner had I begun to talk than he said, "Don't say another word—I'm coming over." A moment later he was in the room. "The switchboard is jammed with calls, reporters are listening in on your wire, there's a hundred photographers swarming about the place—" Had we heard the fantastic rumor? That Mr. Rubirosa had left Barbara Hutton in the middle of their honeymoon, taken the $200,000 plane she bought him as a wedding present, and flown to Arizona to see me?

"It's true," I said. "He's here."

The manager stared at me. "Oh, no!" And then: "Where is he now?"

I said, trying to keep a straight face, "Hiding in the bushes."

The manager turned to Mary Lou. "Mrs. Hosford, if you could put him in your bungalow for a little while—" He knew of a house in the mountains where he could conceal Rubi until morning, the owner was out of town. Mary Lou followed directions. She came upon Rubi, cursing behind an oleander bush, and smuggled him into her bungalow.

Minutes later Mary Lou, Arthur Wilde, a young Paramount press representative, and I pushed our way through the crowd of reporters gathered before my bungalow to Arthur's car. Arthur had advised us, "All we can do is try to lose them." We drove to downtown Phoenix followed by three automobiles of reporters. With the coast clear, the hotel manager quietly backed his sedan to Mary Lou's door, a fuming Rubi slipped inside and was driven to the house in the mountains outside Phoenix.

Meanwhile, Arthur, Mary Lou, and I played our game of fox and hounds. We stopped at the Biltmore Hotel for a drink. The reporters camped outside. After an hour we moved to the Arizona Club—our press escort followed us. I wanted desperately to see Rubi, but there was nothing I could do. The reporters clung to us. For the next three hours—we had left the inn at 9 P.M., and it was now midnight—we went from night club to night club trailed by our entourage. Not until 2 A.M. did we manage to lose them.

Then we roared up the mountain to where Rubi waited. We found him alone in the empty house seated at a circular bar, a glass in his hand, brooding. He turned on me as we walked in. His hair was tousled, his eyes black. "Where were you?"

Oh Rubi, I thought. When Rubi was drunk he was a planet in an orbit of his own, a belligerent, dangerous, reckless man. I had seen him so in Deauville. If his team lost at polo, he invariably made for the bar. "One for the road!" he would growl. He tossed down glass after glass, growing more angry, more belligerent until he had to be forcibly escorted outside, or until he passed out and had to be taken home to be undressed and put to bed by Victor, his valet. I could imagine what had gone through Rubi's mind, sitting here, drinking, in this deserted house. That—! She doesn't come to me because all she thinks about is her career, what Paramount will say, what the press will say—she thinks nothing of me . . .

"Rubi—" I began.

"I know why you took so long," he growled. He pointed a long finger at Arthur. "You're in love with that man—" He looked ready to leap on Arthur.

Poor Arthur took a step back. He was here for one reason: only to protect Paramount and Hal Wallis. His hands were full with Jerry Lewis and Dean Martin, who were already quarreling. He had his troubles, too, with Joanne Dru and me, for we were co-starred and there was no love between us.

I thought: how will I get near him? How can I talk to him? He must leave in a few hours . . . "Rubi," I said, "please give me a drink." He poured a huge Scotch for me and we sat down against each other, like two wild animals who are going to destroy one another. We sat there, glaring, as if to see who would strike first.

From a great distance I heard Arthur's voice: "Well . . . I think I'll take Mary Lou home—"

Then we were alone, at last.

At 6 A.M. Rubi telephoned his pilot to come for him. As we drove through the dawn to the airport, he clung to my hand as if he were a drowning man and my hand alone kept him above water. We parted before we reached the airport, lest someone see us.

His plane took off into the rising sun, and I thought: now

264

I must face everything alone—the producer, the director, the press. At 7 A.M. I must look beautiful as well. In *Three Ring Circus* I played a temperamental trapeze artist: I wore black tights, long black stockings, high wooden shoes. I was always ill-at-ease in this costume: I have too voluptuous a figure for such attire, especially to go about before scores of men—the cast, the extras, the stagehands—and all whistling at me. This day I did not want another man even to look at me.

I reached the set and then the telephones began ringing.

"Darling—" It was Louella Parsons from Los Angeles. "Is it true, Zsa Zsa? Did Rubi come there to see you?"

"Of course not, Louella," I said. "It's so silly. He's on his honeymoon in Palm Beach."

"When did you hear from him last?"

"Darling, not since that dreadful time in Las Vegas—"

I heard Louella sigh. "Zsa Zsa, why do you lie to me?"

Then Harrison Carroll, and Cholly Knickerbocker, and the New York papers, the Chicago papers, the London papers, the Paris papers . . .

Then Hedda Hopper, whom I love. "Zsa Zsa, you know I'm your friend. You can tell me the truth. Is it true that Rubi was up there with you?"

I could not lie to Hedda. "Please, Hedda—" I was silent. "Was he there, or not?" I still could not speak. "All right, all right, my dear, you don't need to answer."

Jerry Lewis arrived, full of bounce. He kissed me on the cheek and leaped up on a box and grabbed a microphone. He clapped his hands for attention. "Good morning, everybody!" he shouted. And, unexpectedly, "And Rubirosa, good morning to you *wherever* you are!"

Everyone roared, and I sat in my chair in my black tights and high wooden shoes and everyone stared at me. I thought: Jerry makes of him the silly Latin-American lover they like to make of Rubirosa, but he is not that to me, he is like a sensitive wild animal—lost as I am lost in a world of pretense.

Rubi flew back to Palm Beach and to Barbara, and when

265

the press asked him where he had been, he said he had flown to his ranch in the Dominican Republic. No one believed him. It was the end of their marriage.

A week later he and Barbara separated. They had been married seventy-two days.

25

IN PARIS in the spring Rubi and I announced our engagement.

Now—perhaps it would take a psychologist to explain—I was madly in love with him. I could not be without him. Perhaps because we had both gone through so much together. Perhaps because we were both defying the world, against our own best interests. Perhaps because he had gone to another woman —and unable to fight his desire, had come back to me.

We announced our engagement after the great press chase: across the United States from Los Angeles to New York, across the Atlantic from New York to Paris, through Paris from Orly Field to 46 Rue de Bellechasse—all in an attempt to surprise Rubi and me together. For Barbara had returned alone, to New York, from Palm Beach saying, "Call me plain Miss Hutton, please"; Rubi had vanished; and the moment shooting ended on *Three Ring Circus,* I was nowhere to be found.

The fact was that Rubi lived for a week in Eva's apartment in New York, while Eva visited Mother. The press followed me on my daily calls to Eva, tipped their hats as I entered her apartment, waited for me to emerge, then followed me wherever I went, hoping that I would lead them to Rubi.

We flew to Paris separately, Rubi in his plane, I by commercial plane that was greeted at Orly Field by the press of the world—French, British, German, American, Italian, even Chinese, asking, "Where is Mr. Rubirosa? Are you meeting him?" I denied everything. Rubi had said, "I will await you in my house," but it was impossible to shake the reporters and photographers who followed me from the airport. I went to a little hotel on the Left Bank and telephoned Jean, Rubi's concierge. "Madame, Mr. Rubirosa has not yet arrived—his plane has been held up by snow in Alaska—but I will arrange all."

That night, disguised in a black wig, I slipped into the house on Rue de Bellechasse with the help of Pierre and Ingrid Smadja, Pierre, a dark, handsome Algerian, Ingrid, a tall, slim, pale Norwegian, both warm friends of Rubi's and mine. Rubi arrived early next morning followed by half a dozen cars of newspaper people. No one knew where I was, but they suspected. The press rented the upper floors of a building across the street and there, day and night, they kept watch with telescopic lenses trained on every window, every door of Rubi's house. Bulletins appeared in the Paris newspapers: "Eight P.M.—a light went on in the kitchen . . . 10 P.M.—a light in the bedroom . . ." Pierre and Ingrid brought the newspapers to us and we read them gleefully. We played games with the press: we turned lights on and off all through the house at all hours and the French, who love their boudoir intrigue, were utterly entranced. "Ah, that Rubi—*il est formidable!*"

Once our engagement was announced, we appeared in public together. Our friends seemed delighted by the news. Everywhere it was Rubi and Zsa Zsa. "But of course," they said. "But of course." We were both impressed to learn that in London even Dame Edith Sitwell, the poet, was concerned about us. "When do you think Rubirosa and Zsa Zsa will marry?" she asked a British interviewer. Then she said, "He sounds like a charming man. Pity he doesn't read more." Rubi was annoyed. "How does she know how much I read?" It was true. Rubi read a great deal of history, and especially everything he could find on Napoleon, who was one of his heroes.

Wherever we went we were entertained as though we were visiting royalty. At a party given by Mrs. Terry Nichols, now Baroness Ponts, my attention was caught by a group of people. A heavy-set, bearded man was sitting on a sofa, surrounded by women. I was presented to him: it was ex-King Farouk of

Egypt. He smiled and said, "I'm delighted to meet you, Miss Gabor." And then, to my astonishment, "How are your mother and your sisters?"

I said, "Your Royal Highness, how do you know about them?"

"Just what I read in the newspapers. And what I read"—his eyes twinkled—"is not so good."

I retorted, almost without thinking, "Your Royal Highness, you have not such a good press, either."

Farouk burst into roars of laughter. "You know, I'm going to like you," he said.

Rubi and I were dinner guests of Geneviève Fath, Jacques Fath's widow. "Darling," said Geneviève, herself a skilled couturière, "We're going to make you your wedding gown." I remember the moment she said it. Rubi and I were sitting together, holding hands, the table gleamed with a cream-colored satin tablecloth and silver cutlery and red roses, and I was thinking how beautiful Geneviève was in her low-cut dress. I echoed, "Wedding gown?"

Suddenly I woke up. I thought: am I going to marry him?

Geneviève said affectionately, "Yes, we'll make you a lovely wedding gown. You're going to marry soon—"

"Oh, I don't know, our divorces aren't final yet—" I said. It was true. It would be at least a year for both Rubi and me. We went on to talk of other things, but the words "wedding gown" disturbed me. I pushed them aside. I was happy with Rubi, I did not want to think of the future. Perhaps I preferred not to admit the truth, that I loved Rubi but did not approve of him. If sometimes I thought he should have been born in another century, a Spanish prince, temperamental and moody, surrounded by courtiers entertaining him and beautiful women dying for his glance, at other times I resented the fact that he lived a life without purpose. I could not forgive him that he did not work. I worked hard: I might admire princes, but the men I married had been self-made men. One of our most violent quarrels came when Rubi said, "Give up your career—I will not have a wife who works." I had exclaimed, "Rubi, look—I am working and I will keep on. I will never give it up." I was proud of what I had achieved. All my life a husband had supported me and I had always felt indebted. Now with my films, my night-club and TV performances, I had a new-found freedom; I was on my own; I could pay my own bills. I could do anything I wanted to—I was *me*. I would never give up my career.

I said to Rubi, "How can I respect you when you don't work the whole day?"

"Work?" Rubi had retorted angrily. "I have no time for work." His diplomatic duties took him a few hours each day; that was enough. He had explained long ago that he had a generous income from fishing interests in French Equatorial Africa and from a cocoa farm in the Dominican Republic. I knew that he never seemed to want for money. He had given me magnificent gifts on our engagement: a bracelet studded with rubies and diamonds, a gold powder box with rubies and matching lipstick and cigarette case, and a white mink coat. When we went out in the evening in Paris, or London, or Cannes, or Madrid, always with a party of guests—for Rubi had friends all over the world—though they included fabulously wealthy men, Italian princes, Indian maharajahs, South American millionaires, Rubi always insisted on being the host. I remembered, too, that his string of polo ponies, everyone in Paris said, surpassed Prince Philip's . . . "No," said Rubi. "Why should I work?"

I was not happy when he said this.

Now, at the film festival in Cannes and later in Madrid, I tried not to think of marriage. Rubi was a perfect escort, but as usual his jealousy suffocated me—it made life almost impossible. He never let me out of his sight. He took me to the hairdresser's and waited for me. He took me to style shows and sat with me. He took me shopping and as I tried on dresses by the hour, he waited in an anteroom. In Madrid, when I began *Glittering Death*, he took me to the set and stayed there throughout the shooting. I had many love scenes, and Rubi, sitting off-stage watching, seethed. Each time my leading man,

French star Daniel Gelen, gazed ardently at me, Rubi squirmed; when we held hands, Rubi all but growled; when I had to whisper, "I love you," Rubi nearly exploded. He jumped from his chair and paced up and down, furious. The director was outraged. "Madame, if he continues to make these disturbances—" When Daniel took me in his arms and kissed me, Rubi had to be barred from the set. He spent most of his time drinking apéritifs at a sidewalk café across the street from the studio, waiting for me to emerge.

I tried to explain to him. When actors play love scenes love is the remotest thing from their minds. They are too busy remembering lines, instructions, techniques—"If you were an actor, you'd understand"— Suddenly it came to me. I wanted Rubi to work. Why couldn't he be an actor? All he need do is play himself. Surely audiences would respond to his masculine charm, to that special quality he possessed, so much like a dark, silent Latin-American Clark Gable. Why not?

Within the hour I had Bundy Solt on the telephone in Hollywood. He had just finished writing a screen story for Paramount. Would he be interested in turning out an original script for us?

"What an idea!" Bundy exclaimed. "I start it next week!"

It was to be called "Western Affair," starring Zsa Zsa Gabor and Porfirio Rubirosa. Bundy enthusiastically outlined the story to us a month later in Hollywood. He had conceived a hilarious take-off on all Westerns. Our picture began with Buffalo Bill's triumphant tour of Europe in the 1880's when he and his cowboys were received by the crowned heads of the Continent. Among his men was handsome, dashing Dusty who fell in love with a French countess. To their marriage was born little Françoise. She grows up in a French château and we see her at ten in the formal gardens of her estate, twirling a lariat and showing her skill with a six-shooter. For though her maternal grandfather was Napoleon's aide, her pride is her Western grandfather. She rides like a Westerner, wears cowboy chaps, and can outshoot anyone in France.

Years later word comes that her father has died in far-off America, leaving his entire fortune to her. She arrives blithely in California, thinking herself an heiress, only to find her inheritance consists of a broken-down saloon in Deadwood Gulch. The owner of the popular saloon in town is a handsome Spaniard, Don Castillo—none other than Rubi. The story of "Western Affair" was the story of their feud and what happens when the two bitter rivals fall in love. As Françoise I had to sing and dance in my own club, I had to outvamp the dancing girls in Don Castillo's saloon and outtrick Don Castillo himself. Everyone agreed that we had a charming, amusing picture that could start Rubi on a new career.

I had never seen him so enthusiastic. Somewhere in him was a man who desperately wanted to achieve something for himself. He gave up everything—even passing up the polo season in Deauville, which he had not missed in years. For the next five months he was a changed man. He no longer went night-clubbing; he rose early each morning for his acting lessons with Michael Chekov, Hollywood's finest dramatic coach; he spent hours each afternoon watching Western films. When he visited me we walked about twirling guns and practicing our Western drawl. On my tape recorder, which George once used to capture his voice singing "Some Enchanted Evening," Rubi and I now recorded our dialogue. As Don Castillo Rubi sat strumming his guitar and rehearsing the Spanish love songs he was to serenade me with. When I had time from my work—I was busy with TV performances ranging from *Matinee Theatre* to the Bob Hope, Milton Berle, and Red Skelton shows—we swam, boated, rode. Rubi bought me an electric organ and we took lessons on it. Each day we shopped at the Farmers' Market for the Spanish meats and vegetables he loved. He taught me to make a Dominican rice and bean dish which usually takes twenty-four hours to prepare. I came home triumphantly one day with a canned bean and bacon soup and a box of minute rice—and made him the same dish in ten minutes. He couldn't get over it. Friends whom I invited—the Gary Coopers, the Humphrey Bogarts, the James

Masons—met a Rubi they would never have believed existed: a man so simple, so childlike, so engaging, that they were enchanted. To see Rubi and Gary Cooper meet in the center of the room—Rubi, his hand extended, saying, "Howdy, pardner," and Gary, clasping his hand in a mighty grip with "Why you ol' ornery buzzard!"—was enough to make us all double up with laughter. With Francie, Rubi was perfect: he bought a pair of peashooters and the two of them dashed about the house trying to ambush each other; he taught her archery and set up a target range for her at the swimming pool; he took her riding—Rubi sat a horse like no other man in the world—and showed her the fine points of horsemanship. I found this Rubi adorable.

But "Western Affair" was not to be. Republic Pictures was ready to produce it, we had selected our costumes, Rubi could whip out a pistol with the speed of Billy the Kid, when the U.S. Immigration Service announced it had turned down Rubi's application for a work permit. Since he had not been a professional actor in his own country, he could not be allowed to work here as one.

It was a tremendous blow to Rubi, to his hopes, and to his pride. He went on a drinking spree—again he was up all hours in the night clubs, bitter and belligerent. "Your country!" he cried. How the American press had hounded him ever since he knew me! Now the Government itself chose to insult him by refusing such a small courtesy. As he became more vituperative, I became more chauvinistic. How dare he attack my country! We fought, and Rubi packed his bags; we made up, and we flew back to Paris. I went back with my fiancé to his house, to his old life—with his South American friends—every night a bistro, a club, one night drunk, the next sober, one night I adored him, the next I left him . . .

26

IN ANY relationship between a man and a woman, one is always more in love than the other. One suffers more than the other—and I like to suffer, because it makes love even more exciting. I like the game of love. To be sure, the moment you think of it as a game, it no longer is one. It is a game, wonderfully intriguing only if you love being in love, if you cannot wait to send little telegrams, to receive notes, to sit by the telephone waiting for a call—when all this happens, then it is something strangely and beautifully exciting.

Now, with Rubi, the telegrams, the trans-Atlantic calls, the pledges of love, the meetings every few months, this game continued for a long time. During this period I lived as a bachelor girl in Hollywood. I concentrated on my daughter and on my career. I appeared in the next two years in nearly fifty television shows, I made six films in three countries, and I could write Mother that my face had now been on the cover of thirty-two European magazines. It was the first extended period of time since my fifteenth birthday that I had not been married. Ironic though it may seem, when I did not see Rubi on his visits to the United States or on mine abroad, now and then I saw George. George had been right. Our divorce had made us good friends. There was a part of my heart that would always belong to him.

These were fantastic days. I remember Rubi taking me to a plane in Paris; George waiting for me at the airport when I arrived next morning; and Conrad Hilton taking me to lunch that afternoon. I prided myself that I remained on good terms with my ex-husbands. Even Burhan at long intervals through the years sent me a greeting; he was now a member of the Turkish senate.

But it was George in whom, as always, I could confide. When I complained of Rubi, his temper and jealousy, the scenes he made, George said, almost paternally, "You see, Cokiline, you're only getting back the treatment you gave me. Now you know how it feels." And when I lamented Rubi's way of life, George was magnanimity itself. "Now, he's not such a bad fellow," he would say. "Don't be so hard on him."

And my ex-husband sat at my piano and sang the songs he sang when he courted me.

Rubi and I had found each other in an elevator at the Plaza.

On the playing fields of Deauville we began to lose each other.

It was August, the heart of the polo season, when all international society gravitates to this little French town. Just before Rubi went on the field for the first chukker of a match, we were introduced to a handsome peacock of a man—six feet four, blond, blue-eyed, with a tiny red British mustache and a world of charm. His name was Derek Goodman.

I had heard of him: heir to a fabulous South African gold-mining fortune, one of the world's highest ranking polo players, a sportsman at home on three continents. Moments later Derek and I, watching the game, had the kind of conversation one has while sitting in a box watching polo in August in Deauville.

Said Derek, "Have you any idea, Miss Gabor, why I am here?"

I said, "No, but I overheard you inviting Rubi and his team to play your team in South Africa."

Derek said, "Oh, that's just part of my Machiavellian plot. Do you remember the fellow who kissed you at the cricket match in London last year?"

I had been there with Rubi. The judges asked me to present the silver cup to the winning English team. The captain stood at my side as I made my little speech of congratulation: then, as he accepted the cup, he unexpectedly took me in his arms and kissed me ardently. I pulled back, laughing, the crowd burst into applause.

"Yes, yes," I said, "wasn't he the most beautiful man!"

Derek smiled. "He is." Then he added, "He told me he thought you were one of the most beautiful women he had ever kissed, and said I must meet you. That's why I'm here."

"Really? I'm so flattered. You must give me his name if he admires me so much."

He gave me the name. "Now, don't you fall for him," he said. "He's married to one of my best friends and I won't have you break up their marriage."

I laughed. "I? Rubi's fiancé—I'm not interested in other men."

We talked in this fashion—for no one is so ill-bred as to speak seriously in Deauville—and he said, "They told me all about you in London—you're the woman I want to marry."

I laughed and flirted with him, because I saw Rubi playing, and though Rubi was intent on his game, galloping furiously across the field this way and that, it seemed to me that he still kept his eyes on me, piercing me through, watching me flirt. I turned my head away so that Rubi could not see my face: still I felt his presence.

When Rubi's team lost he stalked into the bar. "One for the road," he ordered. All evening, he drank; later, Rubi, Derek, and I were dinner guests of Baron Elie Rothschild. Rubi saw that Derek had eyes only for me. He drank still more. At one point he said suddenly, "I'm going to gamble in the casino." He rose, pushed by me roughly, and left. We followed half an hour later to find him sitting at the *chemin de fer* table over which hung the ominous sign, "No limit." André, the owner of the Deauville Casino, hurried up to me. "Please, Miss Gabor, take Mr. Rubirosa away. He has lost over twenty thousand dollars already."

When I tried, Rubi shook me off. "No. Go away with your lover!"

I knew better than to reason with him. I moved to a nearby table with Derek and we played there, laughing and chatting with the Maharajah of Cooch Behar. Everyone saw me standing with Derek, this handsome man, and Rubi, sitting alone at another table ten feet away. I was conscious that Derek and I looked well together. My gown was a striking, dark, embroidered Pierre Balmain so new that no one even in Deauville had seen anything like it, and Derek was breath-taking, with his blond coloring and blue eyes, in a dark red velvet tuxedo.

After a little while he suggested that we go to Casanova's, Deauville's top night club. I tried to persuade Rubi to join us but he said gruffly, "I will come later." So, for the first time, I dared to leave Rubi and go with another man to a night club. I thought: if I can do this, the voodoo is beginning to wear off. We entered to find Elie Rothschild, Pamela Churchill, Henri, Count de Montbrisson, and his lovely wife, Simone, at one table; at another, Aly Khan and his beautiful Bettina, the French mannequin; and at a third, Danny Kaye and his wife, Sylvia.

All eyes turned as we walked in. Deauville is like a small village, save that in season the villagers are people who live in the headlines of the world. Everyone knows everyone else; and everyone knew that Rubi never so much as allowed me to nod at another man.

Aly said, across the tables, smiling, "Darling, you look ravishing, can we dance later?" He had never dared to say that to me when I was with Rubi; it was an unwritten law between these two men that if one is with a girl he loves, the other does not speak to her. A moment later, I heard, "My sweet Hungarian—" Charming, gay Danny Kaye kissed me on the cheek.

At this moment Rubi entered with three men, and paying no attention to me, sat down on the opposite side of the room. I rose and joined them, Derek following me. Rubi continued to ignore us both. I turned to Derek. "Talk to me," I said, and Derek, suave, super-British, enjoying this intrigue, talked to me of inconsequential things.

Next morning a dour Rubi left for Paris to pick up $30,000 in cash to pay his gambling debt. He would return the next day. Did I wish to come with him? "No," I dared say. "I'm tired. I'll wait here for you."

Derek and I went riding that morning. Seeing him in his riding habit and jodhpurs, I thought: how beautifully he rides a horse. Until this moment, in my eyes only Rubi sat a horse beautifully. In the evening Derek took me to dinner. To my surprise, he came with a lovely brunette girl, with a face like a Madonna. "This is Martha," he said, and explained privately to me that she had flown in from Johannesburg to see him. Suddenly, because a beautiful woman pursued him, he became more interesting to me. I cannot help it—I find myself judging men by the women who find them attractive.

In the restaurant with three women sat Aly Khan—dozing. I smiled. Aly never has time to sleep, so he must catch it when he can. A moment later he awoke; he smiled at me; his eyes fell on Martha—he gave her one of his long, searching looks. Now I had even more respect for Derek. If a girl so beautiful as to take Aly's eye can fly all the way from Johannesburg to see Derek . . .

When the evening was over I realized I had not even missed Rubi. Until now I could not imagine being anywhere in Europe without him. When he returned from Paris next morning carrying the francs in a brown paper bag, I was almost curt. "Why must you lose so much money! You could have bought a castle in Spain with it!"

"You can only think of castles," Rubi retorted icily. "I lost the money, I can pay it, so what business is it of yours?"

Within the week I returned to the United States to do a Bob Hope show. Rubi followed a few weeks later. I called for him at the airport. The reporters asked, "Mr. Rubirosa, why have you come to America?"

278

"To marry Miss Gabor," said Rubi. "Our divorces are now final."

I heard myself say, "No, I cannot marry yet."

Rubi flushed. "Mr. Rubirosa," the reporter asked, "when will you two get married?"

Rubi said gallantly, "As soon as she says yes."

I could not say yes.

Marry me, said Rubi. Give up your career. We will live in Paris and follow the sun. I will give Francie the biggest debut, she will be raised beautifully, I will find a wonderful husband for her—I will marry her off to a duke or a prince. I will be a good father to her and a good husband to you. Marry me, mon amour!

I could not say yes.

In the months that followed—in Germany where I made a film, in Hollywood where I appeared steadily on TV, in Las Vegas where I appeared in my night-club act—I still could not say yes. When I accepted a TV dramatic show, *Autumn Fever* with George Sanders, Rubi was furious. When, a few months later, I began a film with George, *Death of a Scoundrel*, in which we had many love scenes, Rubi, beside himself, flew to Palm Beach and his beloved polo. Again his telephone calls, "My darling, my fiancée, when do you come to me?" I said tomorrow, tomorrow, tomorrow.

The fact was that I did not want to give up my career and I was frightened to get married again. Then at a party I met Hal Hayes, an architect and contractor, who, when he was not creating entire cities, lived in the reflection of glamorous women. There are many men like Hal in Hollywood: handsome, wealthy, perennial bachelors, who wear beautiful women on their arms as they might wear carnations in their lapels as decorative ornaments to show off. When I met Hal he had been escorting Kay Spreckels, Susan Hayward, and Ann Miller about Hollywood; slender, quiet-spoken, in his late forties, Hal had flown with Barbara Hutton to Honolulu immediately after her divorce from Rubi. I thought: how small the world is! Or

279

is there some kind of ironic pattern in my life? After the *Sturm und Drang* of Rubi, it was relaxing to dine with Hal, to know he was always there, controlled and unpossessive, to take me to openings and parties. He was sweet to me and to Francie. Marion Davies, an old friend of his, had just taken over the Desert Inn in Palm Springs. He was inviting some friends down there. "Why don't you join us?" he said.

I did so, and Rubi, in Palm Beach, read about it. He telephoned me, violent. "I ask you to come here—instead you go there—I am flying back home. Goodbye!"

It was the beginning of the end.

I had one more encounter with Rubi.

My sister Magda was to be married in New York. Hal accompanied me there, and being a man of direct action, when the press questioned him he said, "Miss Zsa Zsa Gabor and I are engaged." I dared not issue a public denial—I had had enough publicity of this kind.

But the news brought an enraged Rubi flying into New York from the Dominican Republic. I remember sitting in my Plaza suite while Rubi, white with anger, paced back and forth. I began to cry. Rubi said, "I am very sorry for you."

"Why?" I sobbed.

"Because a woman is not her best when she cries. And furthermore, after a few minutes she looks like hell."

I cried the more.

He said, "And I am sorriest of all for you because you're marrying that man."

"I'm not," I said, "I'm not."

"Never in my life was I so hurt, so insulted, as when I read that you're engaged to another man!"

He stood by the fireplace, looking down at me, handsome in a gray suit, but suddenly seeming so much older. "You don't know how I loved you," he said sadly. "You'll never know."

I understood Rubi so well. It had been perfect casting, Rubi and I. It seemed to me that every shopgirl, every romantic reader of the newspapers—yes, even Dame Edith Sitwell— wanted Rubi and Zsa Zsa to marry.

I understood, it seemed right, us two.
We had had a great love, Rubi and I.

Back in Hollywood, that summer of 1956, I began to run.
I accepted every job, every offer. I knew what was happening
to others—Grace Kelly had married Prince Rainier, Tyrone
Power had married, Porfirio Rubirosa had been taking out Ava
Gardner and now was seen with Odile Rodin, a nineteen-year-
old French model—but I tried to run so fast I would be
touched by nothing. Yet I was grateful for all the silly, wonderful, flattering things that happened to lift my *amour
propre*. In New York I went to see *My Fair Lady* in its third
week; I caused a commotion because at intermission many of
the audience followed me and would not return to their seats
until I did so. I flew to Kansas City as Queen of the International Exposition of Beauty, and was paid outrageously well
for simply making an appearance. I flew to South Africa with
Pat O'Brien and a group of Hollywood entertainers to do a
series of benefit shows for the Cerebral Palsy Fund. Flying
high over the plains of darkest Nigeria, a radio message came
up to us from a lonely weather station below.

"Is that the plane carrying Miss Zsa Zsa Gabor?"

"Yes."

"Then we order you to land at once. The natives are
restless."

We stopped for an hour, at 8 A.M., at Lisbon; over one thousand persons were waiting, many since dawn. It was fantastic,
and became more so when we landed at Johannesburg. I was
welcomed like a reigning queen. Seated high in the back of
the lead touring car, I was driven down Eloff Street while
thousands lined the streets, applauding: I was given the Royal
Suite in the Carleton Hotel. The crowds jammed the square
below, shouting and cheering, "Zsa Zsa! Zsa Zsa!" and refused
to leave until I came out on the balcony and bowed to them.
Derek Goodman was on hand to introduce me to his family,
to drive me to Kruger National Park, and show me South
Africa. Then I was off to Paris and dinner with Aly Khan, his

father, the Aga Khan, his stepmother, the Begum; then to London and the Palladium, where I was Mistress of Ceremonies for Sir Laurence Olivier's great annual actors' benefit, *Night of 100 Stars;* then, with hardly time to catch my breath, back to the United States for a night-club engagement at *El Rancho Vegas.*

On a chill October afternoon I returned home to Bel Air with Helen Greco Jones, a dear friend. I had asked her to stay overnight because I felt very lonely. I had been thinking of Rubi. All my running had left me emotionally right where I was before. I had only exhausted myself. The constant scripts to memorize, the hours rehearsing, the time spent at the beauty parlor, the endless traveling, the endless packing and unpacking, the ordeal of appearing constantly smiling in front of photographers, gay and witty in front of reporters, dazzling in front of audiences . . . "Oh, Helen," I said, "this career is such hard work, it is such a lonely life, maybe I should have married Rubi, maybe he was right all along." I thought: where will I find a man who loves me as much as Rubi? And what man is perfect? Why do I ask so much of life?

As we prepared for bed, Elizabeth came with a message. "Paris is calling."

I leaped up. "You see," I cried delightedly to Helen. "He's thinking of me, too."

It was Rubi. We talked, and I said after a little while, "I hear you're going around with a beautiful girl."

"Yes," said Rubi. And then, "As a matter of fact, my darling, we are getting married tomorrow. That's why I called you—I wanted you to hear it first from me, not to read it in the newspapers." And he added, "Odile is giving up her career for me—she loves me very much."

I was too choked up to say more than, "Well, darling, I wish you all happiness," and I had to hang up.

Next day it was in all the newspapers.

"Mother," Francie said, "is it true that Uncle Rubi got married?"

"Yes, darling."

"But I thought he loved only us."

In my night-club acts I have a brief skit in which I appear as a Professor of Love. I thought: Francie, if you only knew how little your mother knows about it!

George comforted me. "Now, Cokiline . . . now, Cokiline . . ."

When our film, *Death of a Scoundrel*, had its première at the Hollywood Paramount less than a month later, George and I made our first public appearance together since our divorce.

We read the reviews together. The *Hollywood Reporter* found me "excellent"; *Variety* "very good"; the *Los Angeles Examiner*, "Zsa Zsa is not only good, but wonderful—a personality grown to the status of actress!"

Said George, "Well, what are you bawling about? Isn't that what you wanted?"

27

I WAS now a one-woman business called Zsa Zsa Gabor, earning more than $200,000 a year. If I made a great deal of money, I spent a great deal. Elegance and fame are never cheap. For me everything had to be in high style and the latest fashion—I had to wear what was to be worn before anyone else knew it existed. People expected it of me. Had I tried to do with anything less, I would not have been Zsa Zsa.

As a result, in my closets in my Bel Air home was a personal wardrobe perhaps equal to that of any woman in the world: more than two hundred evening gowns, the latest Traina-Norells, Balmains, Diors, Howard Greers, Givenchys, Balenciagas; a hundred cocktail dresses, a score of tailored suits, cases full of blouses, a white mink coat, a beige mink coat, a sable stole, a black mink stole, a light mink stole, a leopard coat, a leopard stole, a beaver coat, a blue fox, a white fox, a black fox, sequined coats, embroidered coats, gold brocaded coats, hundreds of hats, gloves, shoes, scarves. One maid was kept busy through the week simply maintaining my wardrobe, pressing and altering, and weeding out frocks no longer in style which were sent to various charities.

Next to my bed were three telephones. They began ringing as soon as I finished my morning coffee. The calls came from London, Paris, Chicago, New York; from my agents, my business manager, my press representative, my lawyer, and my accountant; from promoters, producers, directors, writers. Would I do a night-club performance in Rio de Janeiro? What did I think of an American theatrical tour—thirty nights in thirty different cities? Was I interested in a one-day visit to Montreal on behalf of the Canadian Fur Industry Exposition, my fee to be the $12,000 mink coat I modeled? Would I consider giving my name to *Zsa Zsa Cosmetic Products?* Or *Zsa Zsa Fashion Creations?* Or *Zsa Zsa Jewelry?* Was I interested in a television series, "Life With Zsa Zsa"? A radio series, "This Is Zsa Zsa"? A guest shot on *What's My Line,* the *Dinah Shore* show, the *Arthur Murray Party?* A dramatic role on *Playhouse 90? Climax? Lux Theatre?* Appear as homecoming queen at UCLA? Present an Oscar at the annual Academy Awards Dinner? Accept a plaque from *Filmland* Magazine as "The Most Exciting Actress of the Year"? from the Foreign Press Association as "The Most Glamorous Actress of the Year"? A Citation of Merit from the Muscular Dystrophy Association, a Distinguished Service Award from the United Cerebral Palsy Association, a Certificate of Commendation from the National Guard? Endorse this wine, pose with this political candidate, accept an Honorary Colonelcy from Texas, Arkansas, and the American Legion? Appear at the Americans For a Free Hungary Rally? Go on a coast-to-coast promotion for my thirteenth film, *Girl in the Kremlin,* fly to Germany to do my fourteenth film, *Bal des Nations,* to England for my fifteenth film, *The Man Who Would Not Talk?*

Hour after hour it went on. My agents and managers advised me, of course, but in the end I had to make the final decisions.

Next to my bedroom was the suite that had been George's. Now it was the headquarters of my secretary. On her desk was an enormous white leather-bound book; in it were most of the names, addresses, and private telephone numbers of every important celebrity in international society—the men and women one sees in the chic night clubs and restaurants of the world. My secretary helped me oversee my household staff—it had now grown to housekeeper, butler, cook, maid, governess, gardener, and dear Elizabeth, a second mother—and assisted me in my parties, perhaps a dozen a year. Like my clothes, my parties had to be more original than anyone

285

else's, and it was gratifying to find them covered by correspondents of French and British newspapers as well as American.

Another room had been turned into an enormous office complete with typewriters, dictating machine, a small post office—requests for my photograph came from all parts of the world and hundreds were mailed out each month—files, records, scrapbooks. Each morning there came a large manila envelope of newspaper clippings about myself, sent to me by my press representative, which had been cut from the world's newspapers. On the walls of this room were framed the magazine covers on which my face had appeared; they now included every major picture magazine published in England, France, Germany, Austria, Italy, Turkey, Sweden, South Africa, Brazil, Argentina, and the United States.

I could wander through my enormous house, beholden to no man, kept by no man, supported by no man; through my great stainless steel kitchen which could serve fifty people; through my salon, my green room, my red room, admiring my paintings, my sculpture, my antiques; I could stroll through my gardens and pick a rose that had been named for me; I could sit on my terrace, swim in my pool, ride my horses, drive in my Cadillac and Thunderbird . . .

I could do all these things. I was Zsa Zsa, Incorporated.

In the last days of summer the letter arrived. I stared at the familiar handwriting. "My darling, for the sake of our wonderful memories—I cannot think of them for they still make me sad—I ask a favor. My President's son and my dearest friend, Ramfis Trujillo, is studying in Kansas. He thinks of visiting Hollywood presently—he would be so happy to meet American film stars. Please, when he comes, introduce him to the movie society . . ."

It was from Rubi, in Paris.

I remembered Rafael Trujillo, Jr. When Rubi and I first knew each other, Rubi had asked me to inscribe one of my photographs for Ramfis. Rubi had sent it off himself from

Paris, saying, "He will be very happy—he is so impressed by film stars." A year later I had met Ramfis in New York. Rubi had brought him to my suite—a slender, dark, handsome young man in his middle twenties, the son of Generalissimo Rafael Trujillo. Ramfis admired Rubi tremendously; his half sister, Flor d'Oro Trujillo, had been Rubi's first wife, and the two men had remained friends ever since. I had also been introduced to Rubi's nephew, Gilberto Rubirosa, who was Ramfis' aide. We had gone to dinner at the Colony Restaurant —Rubi and I, Ramfis, and my sister, Eva. Both Eva and I had been impressed by this young man—nervous, impatient, carrying himself with such dignity. I could understand why his friends called him "Ramfis" after the powerful high priest in the opera *Aïda*.

A few days after I received Rubi's letter, Gilberto arrived in Hollywood to give me the details. Ramfis was studying at the Army General Staff College in Fort Leavenworth, Kansas. Though he had been trained in military science since childhood and now, at twenty-nine, held the rank of General in the Dominican Air Force, he had come to study in this country, rather than England or France, because the Generalissimo admired the United States, Gilberto explained to me. And he added, "He's so bored in Kansas—may I call him now and put you on the phone to him? He'd love to talk with you." A moment later I was giggling and joking with Ramfis. "I die here," Ramfis confessed. "I don't know a soul, I am like a fish out of water, I can hardly wait until I come there." He expected to take a sick leave within a few months. "Will I meet all your friends? All the stars?"

"Of course you will," I said.

"I have a terrible crush on Kim Novak," he said. "Will I meet her?"

"I love her—she's one of my best friends," I told him. "Of course, you'll meet her—I'll introduce you to everyone."

And Bob Mitchum? Gary Cooper? Clark Gable?

I thought: Rubi is right. He sounds as star-struck as though he lived in Kansas.

Now Ramfis and I were on the telephone three or four times a week—simply to talk. It was obvious that he was homesick; he needed desperately to talk to someone who was not Kansas, who was not Midwest America, someone who knew Rubi, and Paris, the international set, who knew his language. It became a fantastic telephone friendship. He called to ask about the weather in Los Angeles, to report on his studies, to tell me that he had received one of the highest IQ ratings in the school, to remark that he was sure he had done badly on another test—"but it is a subject about which I have already forgotten more than they teach." I became his confidante, his sister, his contact in America with the world he missed.

One day Gilberto called from Kansas. "Where will you be on Christmas?" he asked. "Ramfis has a little surprise for you."

"Oh, how nice!" I said. I would be in New York working on a film, *Country Music Holiday*.

"I see," said Gilberto mysteriously. "Thank you." He hung up.

On December 5 I was rehearsing for the George Gobel show at NBC in Burbank when a man approached me, "Miss Gabor, there is something for you outside—please come with me." There next to the curb, was a little red Mercedes Benz roadster. To make certain I would get it before leaving for New York, Ramfis had had it flown from Kansas.

He was on the phone an hour later. "Do you like it?" he asked, like a little boy who wants to share my enjoyment. I thought: if he were here, he would be standing by, watching me when I first saw it, as I stood by when I bought Francie a pony—to see the expression on her face. "Oh, Ramfis," I said, "it is such a beautiful gift—you shouldn't have. How can I thank you!"

"Your friendship is thanks enough," he said.

"But Ramfis—" I began to protest.

"Please," he said. There was the slightest rebuke in his voice. "If you wish really to thank me, don't ever mention it again."

The order of events from then on is as clear in my mind

as if I had set them down. I appeared on the George Gobel show, I put my Mercedes Benz in my garage to take its place beside my other cars, and flew to New York. In the four weeks it took me to shoot my film, Ramfis and Gilberto must have been on the telephone to me two dozen times. They were like schoolboys on a holiday who don't know what to do with themselves.

The picture finished, Earl Blackwell, head of Celebrity Service, invited me and Millie Considine, writer Bob Considine's wife and herself a columnist, to Palm Beach for the opening of Frank Hale's new playhouse, and a fortnight of parties, charity balls for the Heart Fund, and polo games. It was the height of the winter season. Mrs. Horace Dodge 2nd and I presented the Dodge Trophy to the winning team; one day I sold tickets for the Heart Fund Ball and it was amusing to see the dowagers crowd about me and examine me through their lorgnettes.

Again, Ramfis. He was in New Orleans for the Mardi Gras. His yacht, the *Angelita*, was in port there. "Why don't you come down here as my guest?" Ramfis asked me over the telephone. "I have the Consul General of the Dominican Republic and his wife aboard, and several other friends—you'll be well chaperoned—come and stay on the yacht as my guest."

I went to New Orleans, arriving at night. At the airport Gilberto and two other aides waited to whisk me in an enormous black limousine through the city to the dark, black docks. It was like a murder mystery—squads of police on guard, secret-service agents in the shadows, and there, looming like a great trans-Atlantic liner, the magnificent *Angelita*. It was the largest yacht in the world; it had belonged to Mrs. Joseph E. Davies, wife of the former ambassador to Russia. I saw dark sailors in white uniforms peering out; I heard, floating across the water to me, the soft Caribbean music of the orchestra aboard . . .

I was escorted aboard the yacht. I was all in white, white wool dress, white hat, white fur coat. I descended the stairs and was ushered into the salon. I saw a table set with gleam-

ing silver, with caviar and champagne, and about it seated six
or seven Spanish men and three or four lovely Spanish women.
And the young man with whom I had been on the telephone
for three months—whose face I could hardly remember—rose
and said, "Zsa Zsa, I'm so happy you are here."

He seated me, pressed champagne and refreshments on me,
and he began to talk—about his country, his people—and Rubi.

I was fascinated by him. He was so dignified, and everything about him contributed to this atmosphere: the yacht,
the entourage, the stewards noiselessly serving us, the people
about him so hushed, listening to him with such attention.
When he took a cigarette, three men leaped up with a light.
When he rose, a half-dozen men pulled out his chair.

He said, "Why don't you change and we'll go out and see
New Orleans—Bourbon Street . . ."

I went down to my suite. It was his mother's, a palatial
dream of a suite, furnished in Louis Quinze, an enormous gold
bed on an Aubusson rug, the bathroom in pink marble with
gold taps, every appointment in absolute luxury.

We went out that evening: Ramfis; Gilberto; Victor Sued,
another aide; the Consul General and his wife; and two Dominican girls who were dates of the two men. When Ramfis
and I walked, no one walked before us: the entourage followed us as courtiers in a royal party.

We went to the Roosevelt Hotel Blue Room and watched
the show. In the powder room, a woman followed me. "I'm
such a fan of yours," she said. She carried a small camera.
"May I have a snap of you?" I posed for her.

It was nearly daylight when we returned to the yacht.
Ramfis said, "Tomorrow we are having the Mayor and his
wife for lunch. Can you be ready at one thirty o'clock?"

When I went to sleep that dawn in that golden bed, next
to me a golden telephone with which I could dial London,
Paris, Buenos Aires, any capital of the world, I was not only
impressed but I wondered what should it be like to live in
Ramfis' world. Not as a princess of today, but of medieval
times, for this boat, this entourage, this man was not of the

twentieth century, but of centuries before. Ramfis and his yacht, his way of life, the land he came from were left over from that time. Somehow these people—Ramfis, Rubi, and I—we belonged to that century.

I walked into the dining room of the *Angelita* at 1:30 P.M. It was set as perfectly as an Embassy party in Ankara. I found Mayor Chet Morrison of New Orleans and his wife, Corinne, a handsome, delightful couple. The Mayor said, with a smile, "Have you seen this?"

He had brought along a newspaper. On page one was the picture of me the woman had snapped in the powder room and over it a headline: ZSA ZSA IS HERE; BUT WHERE? IS SHE VISITING ON THE TRUJILLO YACHT?

I laughed. "Scandal—they love to make scandal wherever I go." But inwardly I was furious. How dare they insinuate harm where there was no harm!

Mayor Morrison laughed, too. "Don't let it annoy you," he said. "Will you accompany us back to City Hall? I want to present you with the keys to the city and name you an honorary citizen of New Orleans."

That night the Hermes Carnival Ball, climax of the Mardi Gras, was to be held in all its pomp and ceremony, presided over by the King and Queen of the Mardi Gras and their court. The Mayor turned to Ramfis. "General, could I persuade you and Miss Gabor to attend the ball as my guests?"

He added, "You would need only wear white tie or your uniform."

Ramfis demurred. "I don't have my uniform here. It is in Kansas."

"Then we'll rent you a white tie," said the Mayor.

"Rent me a white tie?" Ramfis laughed. "Gilberto, call up Kansas. Charter a plane and have them fly my uniform to me."

But all planes were grounded by weather in the west, and in the end Ramfis' aides supplied him with evening clothes and white gloves, and we went to the ball. At the height of the ceremonies there was a blare of trumpets, the spotlight played on the Queen, and a delegation of three courtiers advanced to her throne and presented her with a bouquet of flowers.

The applause had hardly ended when there was another blare of trumpets. To my surprise, the spotlight suddenly fell on me. From the curtains a second delegation of three men—Mayor Morrison, Ramfis, and the Grand Marshal—appeared, bearing an enormous bouquet of orchids which they brought, with great ceremony, to me. I was wearing a flaming red hour-glass dress: I rose in that brilliant light and bowed.

Tradition was broken again a moment later. In the Grand March closing the ball, only the King, Queen, and court proceed once around the great hall. But as the Marshal passed my box, he extended his hand, drew me to his side, and for the first time in Mardi Gras history, a commoner walked, smiling and bowing, side by side with the Queen of the Mardi Gras.

Next afternoon, Corinne, the Mayor's wife, took me to the races at the Fair Grounds to preside at a "Zsa Zsa Handicap."

And that night I left for California.

"It's a mistake to get involved with anyone named Trujillo," my friends warned me. "You are the only one who can be hurt."

I said, "He is Rubi's friend. So long as I do nothing wrong I don't care. I am not political. I judge people as they are."

How could one get angry, how could one turn on Ramfis? He had gone back to school and once more was on the telephone every few days. He could not wait for his sick leave—he was to undergo an operation to correct a sinus condition in a Los Angeles hospital—and he looked forward to his visit eagerly.

One night when he called I said, "Do you know who is dining with us tomorrow night? My sister Eva and Kim Novak."

Ramfis said, "If I come, am I invited to dinner?"

Next evening he was there. He had chartered a plane and flown from Kansas with his aide, Gilberto; his guitar player;

and his German shepherd dog. We ate and laughed and chatted while Ramfis' guitar player played his soft, sweet music. From the moment Kim and Ramfis met, they talked only to each other. There was no doubt of it; Ramfis was tremendously taken by Kim. When he left to fly back to Kansas, Kim told me, "He's the most attractive man I've met in years."

Now Ramfis moved to Hollywood for three months, renting a house in Holmsley Hills, near Bel Air. First came four aides; then four servants; then his cook; then his guitar player, his doctor, his dog. For the next weeks my staff had no time for me—only for Ramfis. My business manager opened charge accounts for him, my secretary sent flowers, telegrams, presents to the people he named, my cook made Hungarian food for him.

When we went out together—Ramfis and Kim, Gilberto and I—it was like a family, for Gilberto was like Rubi's brother, and Ramfis had been Rubi's brother-in-law. Sometimes it was George and I, Ramfis and Kim. When Kim became busy with night shooting of her film, *Bell, Book and Candle,* Ramfis took me out. As yet he was unknown in Hollywood. He escorted me to the Academy Awards Dinner and Louella Parsons described him vaguely as "a cousin of the President of the Dominican Republic." It seemed to me that Ramfis and Kim were very much in love. It was quite possible that they would marry. Ramfis had told me he was being divorced. Had they married, to my mind it would have been comparable to Grace Kelly's marriage to Prince Rainier.

In the midst of this ferment, Francie's eleventh birthday arrived. Each March 10 I have given Francie a party, and each party has been different. Now I racked my brains. Each year the children all but tore my house apart. It would look like a shambles after thirty youngsters had finished with it. I was struck with a marvelous idea. If all of Francie's little friends came as grown-ups—the girls in long evening gowns and long white gloves which they could not remove all evening, the boys in tuxedo and black tie—they would be little ladies and gentlemen, on perfect behavior. My house would emerge unscathed.

The party was amazingly successful. From Conrad came a lovely gold and pearl necklace. Ramfis sent Francie a white-and-pink bouffant ball gown he ordered for her in New Orleans, fragile, lacy, beautiful. A week before I stopped in Magnin's to buy her a pair of white gloves. The manager of the children's department literally fell on my neck. "Oh, Miss Gabor, you should see the excitement—every mother is rushing here with her little daughter for ball gowns." And the children came dressed to perfection. Franchot Tone's two boys, Jeff and Pat; Tracy Wynn, Keenan Wynn's son; Van Johnson brought his daughter Schuyler; Dick Powell brought his Pamela; Deborah Kerr's adorable little redheaded Melanie came up to me and smoothed out her dress with, "This is Mama's dress. Isn't it funny—it's too short on her and too long on me."

Francie received her guests as though it were her own debutant ball. My butler served ginger ale and grenadine cocktails on a tray, as he would serve grown-ups. Then everyone carefully sat down to a dinner of fried chicken and mashed potatoes, after which they danced to an orchestra until ten o'clock. There were many surprises. Eddie Fisher entertained—everyone teased him, demanding Pat Boone song hits. Then Pat Boone himself, in New York, telephoned Francie to sing "Happy Birthday" to her over the long-distance wire. Finally Johnny Mathis sang—to the accompaniment of Grandmama Jolie.

All was decorum, every child was propriety itself—until the evening grew late. Then suddenly all the little ladies and gentlemen became babies again. One started to cry; another didn't want to go home; a third was tired. At the height of the party they had been having the time of their lives; but toward the end the boys took off their black ties, the little girls took off their shoes, and they started to fight. It became a children's party again and ended as all children's parties end

—with annoyed parents tugging at twisting, squirming, tear-stained youngsters who didn't want to leave.

But for my sweet daughter it was the night of nights, and for me, her proud mother, it was a wonderful evening. A week later Francie could rush home with the March 31 issue of *Life* Magazine, which had done a "Life Goes to a Party" on *her* party—with three pages of photographs of Miss Francesca Hilton and her guests.

Perhaps it was the success of this party; perhaps it was always in the back of my mind as part of my promise to Rubi —"introduce Ramfis to the movie society," he had written—the idea came to me to give an enormous party for Ramfis and invite everyone he wanted to meet.

What made it even more timely was the arrival in Hollywood of another friend of Rubi's and mine—Jorge Guinle, whose family owns the famous Copacabana Hotel in Rio. I told Ramfis about my idea. "How nice of you, Zsa Zsa," he said. And since I was so thoughtful, he would make me a little present—he would fly Rubi and his wife from Paris to the party. I wasn't sure what kind of present Mrs. Rubirosa was to me, but to see Rubi again . . .

So it was done. I remember how I dictated last-minute instructions from my reahearsal room at CBS, for I was then doing a Little Red Riding Hood skit on Jack Benny's *Shower of Stars.*

I had one hundred and ten guests—Hollywood itself. When I give a party it is an incredible ordeal for me. Every flower must be in place, an ash tray cannot be awry, house, food, help, decorations, program, music—all must be perfection. When my guests arrived they found my garden, the trees, the shrubbery, the swimming pool, the lawn, completely encased in cellophane. Cellophane tents had been set up; red table-cloths were on every table, silver candelabra with white candles and red roses—the color scheme was that of the Hungarian flag, red, white, and green. Red and white balloons floated everywhere; a dance floor had been placed over the tiled floor of my library; two orchestras played; my dining room had been turned into an enormous bar; the terrace was a dream of red, white, and green. Each waiter wore a distinctive jacket of another color; all the wine stewards were dressed in red jackets—even the food had been chosen for color as well as to delight the palate.

Mother and Eva had flown in from New York and we received together. And now my guests began to arrive. The Jimmy Stewarts; the Robert Taylors; the David Selzniks; the Robert Mitchums; the Kirk Douglases; the James Masons; the Charles Vidors; the Van Johnsons; Louella Parsons, Beatrice Lillie, Rhonda Fleming, Ginger Rogers, Shirley MacLaine and Jeanne Crain, Maureen O'Hara and Kathryn Grayson, Ann Miller, Spike Jones and his wife; George Sanders: "Dearest Cokiline, this is a party to end all parties"; Jorge Guinle and his friend, Count Francisco "Baby" Pignatari; Ramfis and Kim.

And Porfirio Rubirosa and his wife, Odile.

They walked in, Rubi darkly handsome as always, and Odile, a very pretty girl. In a fury of excitement I took them about introducing them. Suddenly I found myself next to George. He rose.

Automatically I said, "Mr. George Sanders—Mr. Porfirio Rubirosa," and only after I spoke it flashed through my mind: Oh, my God, they have never met before. They shook hands, each with a frozen smile on his face, they stood pumping each other's hand for the longest time as if they were unable to let go, as if an electric shock had glued their hands together. Oh, my God, I thought again, what a situation! George must have thought so too, for in his left hand he held a goblet of champagne which he spilled all over me.

As it turned out, I hardly had a chance to talk with Rubi. Odile confided in me. What could she do about Rubi's nightclubbing? "He stays up all night in the clubs, he doesn't come home until dawn—" I said, yes. There was nothing to do. That was Rubi.

And my guest of honor? Ramfis was enjoying himself as I had never seen him before. This man, who appeared so bored, so impatient, bowed to and treated like royalty in New

Orleans, was absolutely delighted here. Everywhere about him were the Hollywood stars he admired. For him to meet Bob Mitchum, whose devil-may-care attitude toward the world fascinated him, to discuss horses with Jimmy Stewart, to trade ship experiences with Kirk Douglas—this evening was a memorable one for him. I had hired a photographer to take candid shots throughout the evening. Ramfis, like a little boy, ordered a dozen prints of every snap taken. Jorge Guinle, Brazil's most famous host, and "Baby" Pignatari, whose lavish parties were the talk of South America—they were in their element, too.

And I? As hostess I was everywhere. Not a petal of a flower drooped that I was not there instantly, literally willing it back to health; not a false note was sounded by the orchestra that I did not hear it, not a guest was left alone for a moment that I was not at her side, bringing her into the gaiety again . . . I discovered something about myself. As long as Rubi and George were there, I was tremendously excited. But when Rubi left, the intrigue was gone. George and Rubi together in one room made that room interesting, exciting; but when one left, the other became boring to me. I thought, a little sadly: they both belong in my past.

By 4 A.M. the house was empty, the lawn deserted, the last balloon bobbing against the cellophane ceiling. Mother, Eva, and I all agreed it had been a gay, a charming, a wonderful party. The affair had been catered for me by the Escoffier Room of the Beverly Hilton, one of the great restaurants of the world. They had outdone themselves to make my party for Ramfis Trujillo a conversation piece for days. It had cost me roughly $100 a person—over $10,000—but I had had a beautiful, beautiful party.

Two days later I was called by my furrier. Would I drop in at my earliest convenience? A chinchilla coat had been ordered for me. Would I please choose the style I preferred?

"Ordered for me?" I gasped. "Who ordered it?"

It was Gilberto who explained. "Ramfis had such a perfect

time—you have made his visit here so enjoyable in every way —he wants to show his gratitude."

How could I have known what furies would be set loose by Ramfis' princely generosity!

How could Ramfis have known!

28

YOU must see me on a stifling hot day in Washington, D.C., rehearsing my act for my opening at the new Café de Paris, a night club on the outskirts of the city. Rehearsing was an ordeal; backstage was tiny, the room in which we worked was hardly larger than a child's room. Then, as it always seems to happen—these moments of crisis—the telephone rang.

It was the United Press.

"Is it true, Miss Gabor, that General Trujillo gave you a Mercedes Benz roadster?"

For a moment I was taken aback. Then I said, "Yes, of course it's true. Why?" That had been in December, six months ago. Why the sudden interest now?

The reporter ignored my question. "And is it true that Miss Kim Novak got a Mercedes from the General, too?"

I said, annoyed, "I don't know anything about that." It was the truth. Only later did I learn that a week before Ramfis had bought Kim a Mercedes, in Los Angeles—and had bought himself one, too.

But that night there were headlines: KIM NOVAK AND ZSA ZSA GABOR RECEIVE GIFT AUTOS FROM TRUJILLO.

I stared at the words. Scandal, scandal, scandal! Whenever my career seemed to be moving beautifully—I was to receive $1,000 a night for my Washington engagement, then go on to Atlantic City, and Chicago, and New York, to appear on the Jack Paar show, which had already brought me thousands of letters—every time things appeared to look up, something unexpected and dreadful like this had to happen! Frantically I tried to reach Ramfis. I found him in Santa Monica Hospital in Los Angeles. He had just undergone his sinus operation and was too ill to speak. But Gilberto came on the telephone.

"My God, Zsa Zsa, the press is driving us mad! How did all this start? Why are they so excited?"

Twenty-four hours later, another reporter was questioning me:

"Is it true that General Trujillo also gave you a chinchilla coat?"

Now I was furious. "Yes. Yes, it's true. But why do you ask?"

"Would you mind telling us why he gave it to you? It's an awfully expensive gift."

I said, "I don't know that it's any business of yours, but he gave it to me because I worked so hard to make his visit here pleasant, and because I gave a terrific party for him and he's not the kind of a man who says thank you with a bouquet of flowers!"

I hung up.

And there were more headlines and more stories.

It had to be explained to me. Ramfis was very much in the news because the United States had recently given the Dominican Republic $1,300,000 in foreign aid over the protests of certain congressmen, and now they charged that Ramfis used this money for his living expenses and to pay for the gifts he showered on his friends. I read Victor Sued's statement to the press: "The General is known to be one of the wealthiest young men in the world and he has always believed that any man, wealthy or not, should have the right to spend his money as he sees fit. It's ridiculous to believe there's any connection between the money he spends on his personal life and any funds given to his country."

If I thought this ended it, I was wrong.

"Miss Gabor," said the reporter, "what do you think about Representative Hays' saying that you are the most expensive courtesan since Madame Pompadour?"

300

I couldn't believe my ears. "Who said that?" I demanded, as I stood by the wall telephone outside my tiny dressing room at the Café de Paris.

He said, "Representative Wayne Hays of Ohio." And he quoted Mr. Hays' remark in the Congress of the United States: "If he (young Trujillo) continues fooling around with Zsa Zsa Gabor, who is apparently the most expensive courtesan since Madame de Pompadour, then the old man will have to raise the ante."

I managed to say, "No comment," and hung up.

My God, I thought. It can't be true. It's a joke. Someone is pulling my leg. Me, a courtesan? They should see me now—in this blouse and skirt and flat shoes, my face streaked, hot, perspired, working like a day-worker in this steam bath of a rehearsal hall, worried about my lines, upset over our skits, troubled about our sets, costumes, props, so exhausted at the end of the day that I go to a Nedick's for a supper of hamburger and orange juice—how am I a courtesan? Representative Hays should see me now—some courtesan! If I were a courtesan, if I were a Madame Pompadour, I would live in a villa on the Riviera and my greatest toil would be to entertain royalty . . . Courtesan! I grew more and more furious. I have done nothing wrong, I work to earn my living, I deprive no one, I hurt no one . . . how dare he!

I did not know what to do. I called a friend, a New York newspaperman. On his advice I said to the press, "If Mr. Hays comes from behind his Congressional wall of immunity and repeats that statement, I will sue him for slander."

Representative Hays did not accept my invitation.

My self-respect was somewhat soothed by the reception given me when I opened at the Café de Paris. It seemed most of Washington had made the long drive to this tiny night club to applaud me. In the audience were Pearl Mesta, Gwen Cafritz, the French, English, Italian ambassadors and their wives. Later, backstage, a Who's Who of the Capital crowded to greet me. On the days of the blackest headlines I was guest at a luncheon given by Mrs. George W. Malone, wife of the

Senator from Nevada. Congressman after congressman came up to me later to kiss my hand, and their wives consoled me and told me to ignore the insult. I was feted and complimented. I thought, as all this was going on: this is an American comedy. Or perhaps an American tragicomedy. I was not sure.

Thinking over what had happened, I thought: thank God for television. Thank God for the Jack Paar show, the panel shows, all the other shows on which I can appear. For I can always go before the public and they can see, I hope, that I am not that wicked woman the press writes about. Perhaps I am sometimes thoughtless, but despite all the headlines about me, I have never done anything really wrong.

I was on the *December Bride* show with Spring Byington in Hollywood when Louella Parsons called me. "Darling, did you hear that George Sanders is engaged to Benita Colman— Ronald's widow?"

"No," I said. No. It can't be. "I don't believe it."

"I just talked to him in Spain and they are absolutely madly in love. He is so excited and so happy."

I would not believe it. I cabled him, "Georgie, it can't be true, is it true?"

His reply came, "Unbelievable as it sounds, Cokiline, it is true."

A letter came from him:

Dearest Cokiline:

Don't be unhappy. I am really much too old for you. You need someone closer to your own age, someone who can respond to your admirable effervescence, someone who can identify himself with your goals, someone who has a little more vitality.

I shall always love you, and yield to no one in my admiration for your many qualities.

A big kiss for Francesca, a hug for you.

George

302

A few weeks later, he wrote me from Madrid. Tyrone Power had died of a heart attack while working with George in the picture, *Solomon and Sheba.* George had delivered the eulogy at the funeral; he enclosed a printed copy of the eulogy.

George's letter read:

Dearest Cokiline:

I know that you are a friend of Tyrone Power, consequently I am sending you the enclosed card in compliance with the desires of his widow.

I hope you are well and happy and that Christmas will bring you good cheer and prepare you for the prosperity which I am sure will be yours in the coming years.

For myself, I am now quite confident that I have made the right decision to settle down permanently in Europe. I have, as you know, been dickering with this idea for the past ten years. It was an ambivalence I found hard to resolve. I am "au fond" a European, not an American. After 22 years of residence in America I find that I have not changed. In spite of my efforts to absorb the American cultural value system, in spite of my unbounded admiration for the accomplishments of the American people, in my thoughts and my heart I dwell upon this side of the Atlantic.

When I am in America I always have the feeling that I am looking across the Atlantic from the wrong side. When I am in Europe, my orientation is readjusted.

My constant references to my wistful desire for a fisherman's cottage on the Costa Brava were the imaginary pregnancies of my deep desire to live among my own people.

Benita's experiences parallel mine. After 22 years of uninterrupted residence in America, she remains incontrovertibly English. I find that we think alike on all subjects. Our values are the same. I think we have a good chance to be happy together.

I hope you have the good fortune to find someone that suits you equally well.

Love,
George

He had written it on the stationery of the Castellan Hilton

Hotel in Madrid. And at the bottom of each page, the words seemed to merge as my eyes smarted: "A Hilton Hotel" . . . "A Hilton Hotel" . . .

How strange, strange this life of mine!

. . . PARIS, 1960—and my birthday. I sit in my flower-covered emerald green suite in the Hotel Lancaster, waiting to be called for by my friends. Alexander Hill, my gallant new beau from New York, is giving me a birthday party at Maxim's tonight. My maid is still unpacking, my secretary is opening my birthday telegrams, and Mr. Magoo, my adorable Yorkshire terrier—last in the succession of dogs I have loved, Lady and Mishka and Ranger and Harvey and Josephine and Suzy —Mr. Magoo, ears up, tail high, his long silky hair trailing to the ground, trots like a little Chinese lion to my chair and leaps into my lap. I read again Francie's letter, which had been awaiting me, written from her boarding school in the Ojai Valley, two hours from Bel Air. I read the scrawled, little-girl script:

Dear Mummy:
    I just hope you have a wonderful, wonderful birthday. Have you had a nice time so far? Are all the noisy motorcycles still running? Did you buy me some chestnuts? Were you able to telephone Granddaddy? Gosh, but it's been raining here a lot. Such silly weather—some days it's perfect and the next it's raining something awful. Mummy, the weather does such goofy things to me. When it rains, I could just sing. Isn't that funny? I don't mind it at all, I just love it. Do you know what I mean? I want to tell you about Pal. He is just wonderful. I'm sorry about the bad showing he made when you were here. Now he's fine and not spooky any more though you ought to hear me when I have to clean out his stall. Couldn't you

305

send me clothes that aren't so fancy, like cotton, maybe? I'll
say happy birthday again now and close.

Love you, love you,
Francesca

P.S. Please send new cowboy outfit and chaps.
P.P.S. How old are you anyway, Mummy? All the girls'
mothers are dying to know. Still 21? It can't be!

I put the letter down, thinking: cotton clothes! My little
tomboy! But tomboys change. She only has to ask her mother,
who at this moment is trying to make up her mind what dress
to wear. What *shall* I wear—tonight, at Maxim's? How shall I
dress Zsa Zsa? Shall I choose a dream of a gown made for me
in New York, a beautiful, eggshell-pink chiffon with ostrich
feathers tinted to match? Or will it be my sexy, sequined,
tight-fitting, low-cut dress made for me in Hollywood? Or my
exquisite tulle and silver hand-embroidered Christian Dior
which doesn't show off my figure? New York, pretty; Hollywood, sexy; Paris, chic . . . Tonight, I decide, I must be
pretty.

I put on my pink chiffon, and with it my diamonds. My
diamond bracelet, my diamond ring, my diamond necklace,
my diamond earrings. I look at myself in the mirror and think
madly, extravagantly, because this is my mood in this city on
this night: if I had to go in a cart to the guillotine, though
they stripped me to the skin I would still have worn my
earrings.

Every moment more telegrams arrive, and flowers, and
champagne. Then, at the door, are my old friends, Ingrid and
Pierre; then Alex. They burst into the room with kisses and
greetings, carrying lilacs, violets, and mimosa—it is Happy
Birthday, Happy Birthday!

We go, laughing, downstairs and outside, to pile into a
little French car and go to Maxim's. From her high, little red-
velvet cubicle, Paulette, the wardrobe attendant, greets me
with a smile: "It has been a long time, Mademoiselle Gabor!"
and then, as she stretches forth her hand to take my new

mink, the skins carefully selected to match the color of my hair, "Eh, quelles merveilles de vison!" We enter the dining room. Roger, the headwaiter, approaches to bow us into this room which is like a pink cloud, where the very air is pink, and as we follow him to our table, arranged with roses and lilacs and bottles of champagne, the orchestra breaks into "The Song of Moulin Rouge."

I hear, as I take my seat, "Zsa Zsa! Darling!" I turn. "What are you doing in Paris now?" It is Anatole Litvak sitting at a nearby table with Billy Wilder. I say gaily, very *grande dame,* "I wanted my birthday at Maxim's," and the two men laugh. On the banquette beside me Ingrid, tall, slim, pale, takes her place and opposite her Pierre, with Alex. Pierre and Alex talk about the Algerian situation.

Ingrid says to me, "Zsa Zsa, Rubi is in Teheran with Odile. You know, he sold his house—" Ingrid tells me this, Ingrid with whom Rubi and I had such good times in Rue de Bellechasse.

What a pity for the house, I say to myself, and then, aloud, "But you don't understand, Ingrid. I'm not interested in him any more."

I dance with Alex and as we turn, I see, unbelievably, Rubi. He is in a camel's-hair sports coat at the entrance of the room, peering in to see who is there. His eyes fall on Pierre and Ingrid—a moment later, with Odile at his side, he comes to the table and sits down.

Dancing with Alex, I say, "Rubi's just arrived—I thought he was in Teheran—he's at our table."

Alex says, "Why not? I want to meet him."

We return to our table, Rubi rises and kisses my hand. "You get more beautiful every year," he says. We talk. "Rubi," I ask, "how is your life?"

He smiles. "I do not complain. All I need is four polo ponies —four." He repeats the figure.

A glass of vodka is placed before me. I drink. I say, "Rubi, if my new television series is a big success, you'll have ten." Rubi smiles. "No, *four.*"

I say, "No, *ten.*" I drink more vodka.

I hear Odile say in my ear, "You know, Zsa Zsa, I love him. I love him. But then I have always liked older men." I look suddenly at Rubi. He has not changed a day since I first met him. Rubi? An older man?

I drink more vodka. To our table they come now—Simone, Countess de Montbrisson, Guy and Mimi, the Count and Countess d'Arcangues, kissing me and wishing me happy birthday, Geneviève Fath and her Prince Jimmy . . . And all at once I am back with my old friends, in Maxim's.

I turn to Alex. "Let's dance!"

He takes me to the center of the floor. I whirl in his arms, the wine-colored damask walls spin faster and faster. The music increases in tempo; it grows gayer, wilder, at my birthday party. Is it the vodka, the music, the dancing, the excitement? I do not know. The strangest spell, the strangest sense of unreality comes upon me. I think: was it here I danced in *Moulin Rouge* as Jane Avril? Was it all fantasy then, a dream and an enchantment? Is it all fantasy now, fantasy and dream and sorcery?

Jane Avril, Sari Gabor, Zsa Zsa—

Who knows, in this life of ours, what is really true and what is enchanting make-believe?

ABOUT THE AUTHOR

Gerold Frank, who is generally recognized to have introduced a new literary genre with bio-autobiographies of glamorous women, was born in Cleveland, Ohio, August 2, 1907. He prepared for a writing career by taking a B.A. and then an M.A. in English Literature, for which he wrote a thesis on E. E. Cummings and T. S. Eliot. In 1933 he joined the staff of *The Cleveland News* and began contributing to *The New Yorker, The Nation, Harper's,* and other magazines. In 1937 he moved to New York and embarked on a career as a foreign and war correspondent, which took him to Europe and the Middle East for considerable periods of time. From 1952 to 1957 he was senior editor of *Coronet*. His first book was published in 1943; in the next ten years he wrote eight others. Many of them were best-sellers, but as ghost writer Mr. Frank received no public credit. The appearance in 1954 of *I'll Cry Tomorrow,* the Lillian Roth story, and the revelation that he was a co-author, suddenly acquainted readers with his extraordinary role in the literary world. Since then Mr. Frank emerged fully to the public eye with the best-sellers *Too Much, Too Soon,* the Diana Barrymore story, in 1957; *Beloved Infidel,* the Sheilah Graham-F. Scott Fitzgerald story, in 1958; and now *Zsa Zsa Gabor*. Mr. Frank's hobbies are swimming, chess, travel, and reading. He is married to the girl he first wrote poetry to during their undergraduate days at Ohio State University, and he is the father of two children, Amy and John.

This book was set in

Caledonia and Mistral types by

Brown Brothers Linotypers.

It was printed and bound at

the press of The World Publishing Company.

It was designed by Larry Kamp.